Inside Web Dynpro for Java

 PRESS

SAP PRESS and SAP Technical Support Guides are issued by
Bernhard Hochlehnert, SAP AG

SAP PRESS is a joint initiative of SAP and Galileo Press. The know-how offe-
red by SAP specialists combined with the expertise of the publishing house
Galileo Press offers the reader expert books in the field. SAP PRESS features
first-hand information and expert advice, and provides useful skills for professional decision-making.

SAP PRESS offers a variety of books on technical and business related topics
for the SAP user. For further information, please visit our website:
www.sap-press.com.

Liane Will
SAP APO System Administration
Principles for effective APO System Management
2003, 240 pp., ISBN 1-59229-012-4

A. Rickayzen, J. Dart, C. Brennecke, M. Schneider
Practical Workflow for SAP
2002, 504 pp., ISBN 1-59229-006-X

Frédéric Heinemann, Christian Rau
Web Programming with the SAP Web Application Server
The complete guide for ABAP and web developers
2003, 528 pp., ISBN 1-59229-013-2

Horst Keller, Joachim Jacobitz
ABAP Objects. The Official Reference
2003, 1094 pp., 2 Volumes and CD Set
ISBN 1-59229-011-6

Helmut Stefani
Archiving Your SAP Data
A comprehensive guide to plan and execute archiving projects
2003, 360 pp., ISBN 1-59229-008-6

Chris Whealy

Inside
Web Dynpro for Java

Editor Florian Zimniak
Copy Editor Nancy Etscovitz, UCG, Inc.,
Boston, MA
Cover Design Silke Braun

ISBN 1-59229-038-8

Out of intense complexities,
intense simplicities emerge.

Sir Winston Churchill

The voice of ignorance speaks loud and long,
But the words of the wise are quiet and few.

Ancient Proverb

Contents

4 Web Dynpro naming placeholders   49

5 Naming conventions   53

6 The context   61

9　The Common Model Interface　189

10　The Adaptive RFC layer　193

11 Web Dynpro phase model 257

12 Class and Interface Reference 263

Preface

Target audience

This book has been written for those people who have:

▶ Java programming experience
▶ Attended the standard SAP training course(s) for Web Dynpro for Java programming

This book is not a tutorial of "how to" style exercises and answers, but rather it discusses the design and coding principles required for the development of successful Web Dynpro applications. The focus of this book is the core of Web Dynpro technology.

Certain Web Dynpro related subjects are not covered in this edition because they are not fundamental to your understanding of the subject. This book is designed to lay a foundation upon which other publications can then build.

Knowledge of SAP's ABAP programming language would be beneficial (particularly when reading Chapter 10), but is not essential.

Author's Apology

Having been a technical SAP consultant since 1993, and a professional software developer since 1986, I have learned[1] that forming a rigid set of *rules* about how problems should be solved has a fundamental weakness. That is, the rules formed for solving problem A often cannot be applied to solving problem B, even though problems A and B are similar.

Instead, I have found that many diverse and seemingly unrelated problems can be solved using a common set of problem-solving *principles*. The problem-solving process then starts with an analysis of the particular situation to identify which of these principles are applicable.

This process of problem-solving is much like the process of abstraction that takes place during the design of an object-oriented program—that of condensing a problem down to its most fundamental, often abstract, elements—and I have spent much of my professional career developing these principles.

---

1   By attending the school of hard knocks!

In writing this book, I do not wish to lay down an inflexible set of rules to which all developers should conform. Instead, I aim to equip the reader with an understanding of the fundamental principles that must be understood in order to build powerful and efficient Web Dynpro applications.

Since Web Dynpro is a programming toolset, it is not immune from abuse; in the areas in which problems could arise, it may appear that I am laboring the point. If I have described the same concept in several different ways, it is because I am stressing its importance. I trust that this approach will serve to communicate the necessary understanding to all readers, and not be too tedious for those people who "always grasp things the first time."

As with any set of tools, the results obtained from the use of Web Dynpro are determined by the skill of the operator, not the brand name on the handle! Therefore, to achieve the best results from the Web Dynpro toolset, each developer must have a thorough grasp of the principles that underpin its design and operation.

I leave it to each developer to apply these principles to his or her own specific situation. Using this approach, no two solutions will ever be the same, yet all will be derived from a common set of fundamental principles.

It is these principles that I aim to communicate in this book.

Note to readers with ABAP development experience
For those experienced with classical SAP software design, the design concepts used by Web Dynpro represent an entirely new way of thinking, the mastery of which will require a significant shift in your thinking. For this category of reader,[2] it is even more important that these principles are fully grasped and understood.

Please allow this book to alter and expand your thinking, and guide you through the mental transition that is required to move from classical R/3 design to Web Dynpro design. Failure to realize that such a transition is required will cause you to become frustrated by the fact that Web Dynpro does not meet your established expectations. This, in turn, can lead to all sorts of erroneous conclusions about the quality of the product!

---

2 In which I include myself.

Conventions

Use of terminology

Certain words such as "component," "element," "context," and "interface" have specific meanings within the Web Dynpro context (sic!). Therefore, to avoid ambiguity, such words will be used only when their Web Dynpro meaning is intended.

Screenshots

For the sake of brevity, various graphical figures in this book have been cropped or resized. Therefore, when you look at the corresponding screen in your installation of the SAP NetWeaver Development Studio (NWDS), it may be larger than the image displayed in this book.

Errata

For those readers with access to SAP's Online Support System (OSS), please check note number 699531 for any corrections to errors or omissions discovered after publication.

For readers who do not have access to the OSS system, please check the SAP PRESS Web sites *www.sap-press.com* and *www.sap-press.de* for corrections, omissions, or additional content that may be delivered after the publication of this book.

Acknowledgements

The author would like to thank everyone on the SAP Web Dynpro development team for their enthusiastic help and support while this document was being written. They all managed to find a few spare clock cycles in their very busy schedules to proofread and correct the many iterations through which this document passed before finally ending up on the printed page.

These are Björn Goerke, Stephan Ritter, Johannes Knöppler, Markus Cherdron, Jens Ittel, Uwe Reeder, Harry Hawk, Thomas Chadzelek, Bertram Ganz, Arnold Klingert, Joseph Brown, Stephan Dahl, Werner Bächle, Harry Hawk, Malte Wedel, Timo Lakner, Jörg Singler, Thorsten Dencker, Stefan Beck, Reiner Hammerich, Armin Reichert and Harry Hawk.

I would also like to thank Simon Harbour, Karl Kessler, Masoud Agha-davoodi Jolfaei, Markus Tolksdorf, Peter Tillert, Carsten Brandt, Marco Ertel, Karin Schattka, and Peter Barker for their input and support during the writing of this book.

Chris Whealy,
November 2004

1 Introduction

1.1 What is Web Dynpro?

From a technological point of view, SAP's Web Dynpro for Java is a revolutionary step in the development of form-based user interfaces. It is completely unlike any design paradigm ever used by SAP before, and represents a quantum leap in the development of Web-based, Enterprise Resource Planning (ERP) applications.

1.2 What is the design philosophy behind Web Dynpro?

All Web Dynpro applications are built using declarative programming techniques based on the Model View Controller (MVC) design paradigm. That is, at design time, you specify what user interface elements you want to have on the client, and where those elements will get their data from. All the code to create the user interface is then generated automatically by the NWDS. This relieves you from the repetitive task of writing the actual form-based interface and then making it interactive with some scripting language such as JavaScript. The only manual coding required is that necessary to interact with the back-end business system, and to prepare the information for presentation.

There is no particular requirement to have an SAP system as your back-end business system.

1.3 Improving the user's experience

SAP's Web Dynpro technology provides a development and runtime environment for form-based applications. The most common example of this is a browser-based interface implemented in HTML and JavaScript, but this is only one example of the type of interface that can be built using Web Dynpro. Any HTML, XML, or WML-enabled device can potentially act as a front end for Web Dynpro applications (see *http://service. sap.com/mobileui* for more details).

Within the scope of browser-based application development, SAP's Web Dynpro allows the developer to build applications with user interfaces that are easily adaptable, and provides a design paradigm that is cost-effective, responsive, and maintainable.

Web Dynpro is a completely new development toolset whose main features include the following:

▶ Abstract modeling

▶ Personalization and customization

▶ Separation of presentation layers and business logic

▶ Generic services

▶ Portability

1.4 Building a high-fidelity Web user interface

The main aims of Web Dynpro are twofold:

▶ As far as possible, to avoid having to code the user interface (UI) layer

▶ To allow the business application to exist in a form that is independent from both the back-end business platform and front-end presentation layer

Web Dynpro delivers a declarative metamodel to develop user interfaces; this has the direct consequence that less programming code needs to be written.

If a standard browser[1] is used as the client layer, then Web Dynpro uses JavaScript to achieve a flicker-free, interactive presentation.

1.5 How is Web Dynpro different from other Web development tools?

Many differences could be mentioned here, but from a developer's point of view, the most fundamental difference is this: In other Web development tools (e.g., Java Server Pages), the unit of development is the Web page, and your application consists of a set of connected pages[2] that, together, supply the required business functionality.

In the Web Dynpro, however, the unit of development is the "component," where a component is a set of related Java programs that, together, form a reusable unit of business functionality. A component may possess zero or more views. In this respect, a Web Dynpro compo-

---

1 For the SAP NetWeaver '04 release, the supported browsers are Netscape V7.0 and higher, or Microsoft's Internet Explorer V6.0 and higher.

2 These pages are usually connected by some persistence layer existing in the Web server.

nent can be thought of as an aggregation of related Web pages. However, there is a lot more to it than that...

1.6 What is the underlying design concept?

1.6.1 The roots of Web Dynpro—Model-View-Controller

SAP's Web Dynpro is built on the foundation of the Model View Controller (MVC) design paradigm originally invented by the Norwegian software designer Trygve Reenskaug[3] while working at Xerox PARC in the late seventies. The first implementation of this design paradigm was with the release of Smalltalk-80.

This was a revolutionary design paradigm because it was the first to describe software components in terms of:

▶ The functional responsibilities each should fulfill

▶ The message protocols to which each component should respond

Nowadays, these concepts are taken for granted, but in the seventies, object-oriented software design was in its infancy, and every step taken was groundbreaking.

Let's start by giving a simplistic overview of how this design paradigm has been implemented in Web Dynpro.

1.6.2 The model

A model is a software component that encapsulates a specific aspect of business processing. A Web Dynpro model is a collection of functional tasks that collectively represent a complete business process. For example, a model could represent all the functional steps that constitute a single transaction in a classical R/3 system.

A model acts as the interface to the business processing layer, providing functionality that is independent of any display client or user communication mechanism. The functionality provided by a model is typically external to the Web Dynpro environment, examples being Web Services, or SAP R/3 BAPIs.

---

3 Pronounced "TRIG-vuh RAINS-cow".

Within a Web Dynpro model, each functional task is known as an executable model object and should be constructed in such a way that:

▶ It runs to completion using only the information supplied to the input side of the interface; i.e., it behaves as an atomic unit of processing.

▶ All errors are handled gracefully.

▶ The interface is always left in a state that accurately reflects the success or failure of execution.

▶ The result set supplied by the functional task is client neutral.

Models should be thought of as black boxes[4] whose internal workings are hidden from view. The only knowledge you need about a model is how to drive its interface.

1.6.3 The view

A view is the user interaction layer. The only functionality a view should contain is that required for the graphical presentation of information to the user. SAP has made several changes to the standard MVC paradigm here. This is because the client layer (typically a Web browser) is separated from the server layer by the stateless HTTP. This means that certain standard MVC concepts cannot be implemented as stated in the original design. Among these are the facts that a Web Dynpro model does not directly notify a view that it has changed, and there are no view hierarchies.

1.6.4 The controller

A controller acts as the functional link between the model and the view. In other words, it is the middleman between the business interaction layer (the model) and the user interaction layer (the view).

The bulk of a Web Dynpro application's functionality should be contained within its controllers.[5] This is the place where validated user data is received from the view and prepared for processing by a model. The model's functionality is then executed, and the controller takes the result set and prepares it for presentation by the view.

---

4 If a Web Dynpro model encapsulates a call to an RFC-enabled ABAP function module such as a BAPI, then the transactional nature of data processing in an R/3 system imposes certain constraints on the design and implementation of such models. These constraints must be understood by Web Dynpro developers, and will be covered in the chapter on the adaptive RFC layer (see Chapter 10).
5 Notice the use of the plural; more about this later.

1.6.5   A more detailed description

As was stated earlier, the previous description is somewhat simplistic; the MVC paradigm has been modified and extended by SAP in several important ways:

1. Web Dynpro controllers come in two distinct varieties—those with a visual interface and those without:

   ▶ Controllers that have a visual interface are referred to as "view controllers."

   ▶ Controllers that have no visual interface are referred to as "custom controllers."

2. The concept of a "component" has been added. A Web Dynpro application consists of one or more components, where a component is a specific arrangement of interdependent custom controllers, view controllers, and models.

> **Caveat confector:**[6] The component is the basic building block of a Web Dynpro application—not the Web page (or view, in Web Dynpro terminology).

A Web Dynpro component consists of the following entities:

▶ **A component controller.**
This is a special custom controller without which a component cannot exist. Because it is a custom controller, it has no visual interface of its own. This controller usually inherits a visual interface from the view controller nominated to act as the default view.

A component controller is not required to have a visual interface. Should you need to write such a component, it will be referred to as a "faceless" component.

▶ **One or more interface controllers.**
A component always provides at least one external interface to expose its functionality. This interface is used when the component functions as the child of another component. The parent component then may only interact with the child through the functionality exposed by the interface controller.

---

6 *Caveat confector* is Latin for "Developer Beware!". This warning will appear when a very important point must be understood.

The visual interface implemented by the interface controller is often the same view nominated to be the component controller's visual interface. This can be composed of a single view or a viewset. Regardless of the composition, the set of views that make up a component's visual interface are known as a "view assembly."

▶ **Zero or more view controllers.**
A view controller is the only controller that has an explicitly defined visual interface. A view controller has exactly one visual interface known as its "layout." Direct interaction between a view controller and a model object is technically possible, but should be discouraged.

▶ **Zero or more custom controllers.**
These are additional custom controllers over and above the component controller. A custom controller is not permitted to have a visual interface, and is always a singleton with respect to its parent component.

The following diagram shows how the different entities within a Web Dynpro component interact.

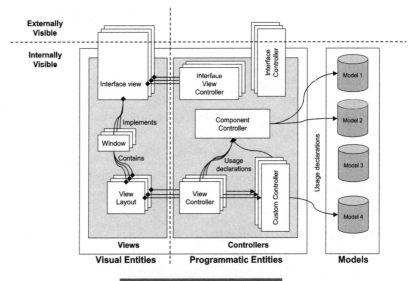

Figure 1.1 Basic MVC Layout of a Web Dynpro Controller

Several important points about Figure 1.1 include:

▶ The multiple occurrences of entities such as windows, view layouts, and view controllers indicate that a Web Dynpro component *can* have more than one of these entities, but does not have to.

▶ The triangular-headed arrows indicate an optional usage declaration in the direction indicated by the arrow. For example, a view controller can declare the use of a custom controller, but a custom controller never declares the use of a view controller; or a component controller can declare the use of a model, but a model never declares the use of a controller.

▶ The square-headed arrows indicate that a fixed association exists between two entities. For example, a view controller will always have exactly one view layout; a window must contain at least one view layout, and implements exactly one interface view.

▶ All controllers within a Web Dynpro component (except a component interface controller) can declare the use of a model.

▶ There is a one-to-one relationship between a window and an interface view.

2   Designing a Web Dynpro application

The development cycle of a Web Dynpro application is much the same as with any other software development, and consists of the following phases:

▶ Analysis phase
▶ Design phase
  ▷ Architecture design
  ▷ Detail design
▶ Implementation phase

These phases are ordered in a top-down manner and their use will be given here only in overview. For a more detailed explanation of how Web Dynpro applications are to be designed, please refer to the online help in the NWDS via the help path **SAP Web AS for J2EE Applications · Development Manual · Developing Web Applications · Web Dynpro · The Development Process**.

2.1   Analysis phase

During the analysis phase, you should determine and describe the application's business requirements. Now, you are concerned only with the "what" of the business process, not the "how."

The results of this phase are known as the analysis model. This is a full, concise, consistent description of the business requirements using language accessible to non-technical readers.

Because the analysis model is not concerned with the "how" of the business process, the description derived here will be independent from any specific technology such as Web Dynpro.

2.2   Design phase

The design phase can be divided into two sub-phases:

▶ Architecture design
▶ Detail design

The basis of the architecture design is the analysis model produced in the previous phase. In the design sub-phase, the global problem-solving strategy for the application implementation is developed.

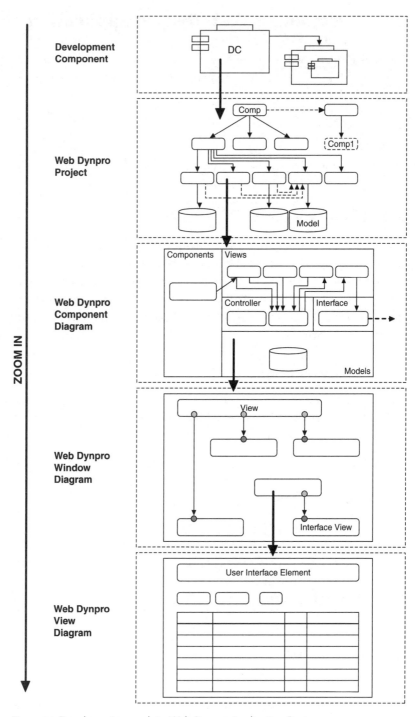

ZOOM IN

Development
Component

DC

Web Dynpro
Project

Comp

Comp1

Model

Web Dynpro
Component
Diagram

Components | Views

Controller | Interface

Models

Web Dynpro
Window
Diagram

View

Interface View

Web Dynpro
View
Diagram

User Interface Element

Figure 2.1 Top-down Approach to Web Dynpro Application Design

The architecture design sub-phase consists of breaking the application down into sub-applications, then breaking the sub-applications down into Web Dynpro components.

The detail design sub-phase then determines the complete definition of the Web Dynpro components. The internal workings of the Web Dynpro components are now determined. This includes view controllers, custom controllers, data structures, methods, events, and event handlers.

2.2.1 Architecture design

The analysis model serves as the basis for the architecture design. Here, you develop an overall problem-solving strategy for the implementation.

It is at this point that you start to connect the units of the analysis model with the larger scale development units known as development components. A development component is a versioned container for holding software developments, and corresponds directly to a self-contained unit of code such as a Web Dynpro project, a Web Service, or a J2EE Container.

For more information on modeling development components, refer to the standard SAP documentation on the Java Development Infrastructure (JDI).

You will also find it useful at this point to create a storyboard of the different screens required by your application. The storyboard is a non-functional mock-up of what each screen should look like. Its purpose is to give a first impression of what the UI will look like, and, more importantly, it provides an end-to-end overview of the flow of business data through the entire application. It also helps as a tool for planning all the navigation routes a user could take when using the application.

The results of the architecture design will be a full description of the major structural units needed to start the detail design.

Here is a summary of the questions you should try to answer in the architecture design sub-phase:

▶ Modeling Web Dynpro development components (DCs):

  ▶ What DCs will be needed to deliver the required functionality? Do new DCs need to be developed? Can existing DCs be reused?

  ▶ What hierarchical arrangement of DCs will be used?

- ▶ What dependencies exist between the DCs?
- ▶ Which public parts are published?
- ▶ Modeling Web Dynpro projects:
  - ▶ Which Web Dynpro components make up the Web Dynpro projects used?
  - ▶ Which Web Dynpro components contain interface views of other Web Dynpro components?
  - ▶ Which models are used in the Web Dynpro projects?
  - ▶ Which Web Dynpro components use which model?
  - ▶ Which Web Dynpro component interfaces are defined in the Web Dynpro projects?
  - ▶ Which Web Dynpro components use which Web Dynpro component interfaces?
  - ▶ Which method calls exist between the Web Dynpro components, and which results are used between the Web Dynpro components?
  - ▶ Which context mappings exist between the Web Dynpro components?

2.2.2 Detail design

The architecture design sub-phase provides you with a full description of the development components and their interrelation. Using this design, the detail design sub-phase provides the detailed description of the architecture on which the implementation is to be based.

Here is a summary of the questions you should try to answer during the detail design sub-phase.

- ▶ Modeling Web Dynpro components:
  - ▶ Which views make up the Web Dynpro components?
  - ▶ Which custom controllers are used in the Web Dynpro components?
  - ▶ Which methods and events are defined within the Web Dynpro components?
  - ▶ In which controllers are the methods and events defined within the Web Dynpro components?
  - ▶ Which context elements are defined within the Web Dynpro components?

- In which controllers are the context elements defined within the Web Dynpro components?
- Which context elements are bound or mapped?
- Modeling Web Dynpro windows:
  - How should the views be arranged?
  - Which navigation paths exist between the views?
- Modeling Web Dynpro views:
  - Which UI elements are contained in the views?
  - How should the UI elements of a view be arranged?
  - To which context elements are the UI elements bound?
  - To which actions are the UI elements bound?

Once these questions have been answered, the graphical window and component modeling tool in the NWDS can be used to start building the application.

2.3 Implementation phase

Lastly, the implementation phase adapts the design decisions to the peculiarities of a particular language. After having made all the difficult decisions in the detail design sub-phase, the decisions for the implementation should add up to only a small part of the work, thus making changes and enhancements easy to implement.[1]

By now, most of the difficult design decisions should already have been made. What remains is the actual construction of the coding units. If the analysis and design phases have been done carefully, the implementation phase should consist largely of typing in your design.

---

1 This is a nice theory, but reality often jumps in at this point and complicates the situation!

3 General architecture

3.1 Web Dynpro Framework

The Web Dynpro Framework (WDF) is a standardized runtime environment that executes as a service within the SAP J2EE Engine. It is within this service that your Web Dynpro applications will run. The WDF provides a series of hook methods within which your application can perform its processing. These hook methods are executed at specific times during the request/response cycle. The processing of the request/response cycle is documented in Chapter 11.

Routine tasks, such as user interface rendering and data retrieval from the HTTP servlet request, are all handled by the WDF automatically.

This significantly reduces the programming effort required in these areas, and allows the application developer to focus his or her attention more on the flow of data through the business process.

3.2 Application

A Web Dynpro application is the entry point to one or more complete business processes and is synonymous with a Uniform Resource Locator (URL). The execution of an application is triggered when the J2EE Engine receives a URL that corresponds to a deployed Web Dynpro application — usually from a browser.

A Web Dynpro application is functionally equivalent to a transaction code in a classical SAP system.

3.2.1 Definition

To define an application, the following information must be known:

▶ The name of the component to be invoked (known as the root component)

▶ Which of the root component's interface views will become the main screen

▶ Which inbound plug to trigger (this plug must be of type `Startup` and is usually called `Default`)

3.2.2 Startup

When a user specifies the URL of an application, the WDF creates and initializes an instance of the root component. Then the inbound plug of the component interface view is fired.

3.2.3 Properties

Each application can be assigned one or more properties. Properties act as control constants that can be used to modify the behavior of the application.

SAP supplies four predefined property names. These are used to control the behavior of the application within the WDF:

▶ Expiration time: `sap.expirationTime`

▶ Default locale: `sap.locale`

▶ Authentication required: `sap.authentication`

▶ Logoff URL: `sap.logoffURL`

The use of these properties is optional. The prefix `sap.` is reserved for SAP-specific values, and should not be used for your own properties.

Custom properties are known as "self-defined" properties and can be used to control specific features of your application.

For instance, if an application displays the details of business documents, you would probably wish to run this application in display mode or edit mode. This behavior can be controlled by creating two applications, each with exactly the same interface view and startup plug, but with different values for the self-defined property `editMode`.[1]

This property would then have a value of `false` for the display-only application, and `true` for the application that provides edit capability. The value of this property can then be examined and appropriate action taken.

3.2.4 Parameters

In contrast to the constant values supplied by application properties, application parameters are variables received from the URL query string. In order to pass variable values into an application, the invoking system should construct a URL with a standard query string.

---

1 The choice of the property name `editMode` is completely arbitrary.

Older versions of Web Dynpro required that all application parameters in the query string be prefixed with the string `app.`. This syntax is still supported, but is no longer necessary.

The inbound plug of the component interface view defines the entry point into your Web Dynpro application, and is a reference to the event handler that will receive control at the start of your application.

Assuming default names are used, then the associated event handler method for this inbound plug will be called `onPlugDefault()`. This is the method to which all query string parameters should be added. Once this has been done, the transfer of parameter data from the query string to the startup event handler is automatic.

You will find the following checklist useful:

1. Identify which interface view controller will be used as the first screen for your application.
2. Identify which inbound plug of the interface view controller will be used as the entry point into your application.
3. On the event handler method for the inbound plug, declare parameters of exactly the same names as the expected query string parameters (these names are case-sensitive).
4. All inbound plug parameters must be of type `String`.

The following situations will not cause errors:

▶ Passing a query string parameter that has not been declared as an inbound plug parameter. The value will be ignored.

▶ Omitting a query string parameter that has been declared as an inbound plug parameter. The inbound plug parameter will be null.

For instance, let's say your application has an interface view controller with an inbound plug of type `Startup` called `StartWithUserName`. As the inbound plug name implies, you want to start your application with a user name obtained from the query string:

```
<WebDynpro_URL>?userName=Harry%20Hawk
```

In this case, your application's interface view controller will have a method called `onPlugStartWithUserName`. Once you have declared a parameter called `userName` of type `String` for this method, as long as the URL contains this parameter, its value will automatically arrive in the startup event handler. See Section 7.9 for more details.

3.2.5 Shutdown

An application can be shut down under two distinct situations. Either the root component calls an outbound plug of type `Exit` on the interface view that started the application, or no user interaction is received within the time limit defined by the application property `sap.expirationTime` (specified in seconds).

The URL to which your browser will be redirected can be defined in the following manner:

▶ Through the `url` parameter of an outbound plug

▶ In the application property `sap.logoffURL`

3.3 Component

Web Dynpro components are reusable building blocks[2] from which complete business processes are built. The creation of a component does not result in the creation of a single Java class, but, rather, a group of classes is created that functions a component.

If we refer to a Web Dynpro component with the abbreviation {n$_c$}, then, in general, when {n$_c$} is created, the following Java classes are generated:

```
{nc}.java
{nc}Interface.java
```

The Java class of the same name as the component is a special custom controller known as the component controller. This class acts as the central point of control for all other controllers within the component.

For a component to be fully reusable, it must present the outside world with an interface to its data and functionality. This is done using a component interface controller.

Once invoked through its interface, the component's interface controller acts as an intermediary between the parent coding entity[3] and the component's internal functionality.

---

2 Reusable only within the scope of their containing Web Dynpro project. To make a component reusable outside this scope, you must create a Web Dynpro Development Component (DC) and add the reusable component to the DC's public part.
3 Which could be either an application or another component.

3.3.1 Lifespan

Since all components are ultimately under the control of an application, the lifespan of a component cannot exceed the lifespan of the application that invoked it.

Component instantiation occurs in two distinct situations. Either, the component functions as:

1. An application's root component, in which case, it is instantiated by the WDF and its lifespan is equal to that of the application

   or

2. A child within some other parent component. In this case, instantiation is controlled by the `Lifespan` parameter in the component usage declaration. This parameter is set to either `createOnDemand`, in which case the child component is instantiated automatically by the WDF, or it is set to `manual`, in which case you are responsible for the instantiation.

Component disposal happens either when the user terminates the application or when the parent component decides that it no longer requires the current instance of the child component and disposes of it manually.

If the user shuts down the client or connects to another Web server, then this action is detected, and the WDF automatically terminates the application, thus terminating all the subordinate components.

3.3.2 Interaction

The only part of a component that is accessible to other components is its interface controller. Although you can write any amount of code you like in an interface controller, that code will be executed only if the component is embedded within another Web Dynpro component.

> **Important:** When a component is invoked by the WDF, the interface component controller is **not** instantiated.

A component, being a reusable unit of code, should make no assumptions about the environment within which it operates. Its internal functionality is always hidden from the enclosing environment. If any data, methods, or events need to be exposed to another component, they must be defined in the component's interface controller.

3.3.3 Reuse

A Web Dynpro component is a self-contained, reusable unit of code within the scope of its parent Web Dynpro project. A component can be reused only as a whole unit and is analogous to an ABAP module pool.

A Web Dynpro component has a well-defined interface structure, and only entities exposed through this interface are visible outside the component.

If you wish to reuse a Web Dynpro component in a totally different development, then you should build your component within a Web Dynpro Development Component (DC), not a Web Dynpro project.

A DC has extra metadata associated with it. This metadata is divided into two parts: the DC definition, and the public parts. The DC definition describes which DCs are required by this DC and the public parts describe which internal objects are going to be exposed to the outside world.

Once a component is added to a DC's public part, a separate JAR file is constructed to provide access to it. This JAR file must be built using a separate build process known as a "DC build."

> **Important:** Just rebuilding your project will not rebuild the interface to the components in the DC's public part; you must perform a "DC build." A DC build is necessary only if you have made a change to coding that lives in the DC's public part. If you have changed some internal area of the DC that is not used in a public part, a DC build is not necessary.

3.4 Controller

A Web Dynpro controller is similar to the MVC concept of a controller in that it usually acts as the binding layer between the model and view layers.

3.4.1 Controller types

Web Dynpro controllers come in two distinct types—those that have a visual interface and those that don't. Those controllers that have no visual interface are known as *custom* controllers, and those with a visual interface are known as *view* controllers.

Custom controllers

Custom controllers should be used sparingly. They are designed to encapsulate a unit of functionality that requires no direct interaction with the user. In practice, you will find that the number of situations in which a custom controller is required is low.

There is, however, one notable exception to this rule. Whenever you create a Web Dynpro component, you are implicitly creating a special custom controller called the component controller. A Web Dynpro component has one, and only one component controller. As with all custom controllers, the component controller has no visual interface, and relies on the existence of one or more view controllers to provide it with a visual interface.

Important: At runtime, a component instance may have one and only one instance of each of its defined custom controllers. In other words, all custom controller instances are singletons with respect to their parent component instance.

Remember that just because you *can* create a custom controller, does not make it a good idea to do so. Before creating a custom controller, ask yourself whether its presence will simplify or complicate the architecture of your component. If possible, always aim for simplicity of design!

Important: If a component contains multiple custom controllers, then the order in which the WDF instantiates them is indeterminate. Do not make any assumptions about the instantiation order!

Component controllers

A component controller is a special form of a custom controller and should be considered the central point of control for a component. Within the scope of a component, the component controller is a singleton class, hierarchically superior to all its view and custom controllers.

View controllers

Controllers that have a visual interface are known as view controllers. These controllers are solely responsible for interaction with the user. That is, they should prepare data for presentation, and then validate the response supplied by the user. Once the data has been validated, it should be passed to a custom controller for processing.

A view controller is created automatically when a view is created, and should be thought of as hierarchically subordinate to a component controller.

For instance, if you require the data from a set of Web Services to be combined into a single result set, then this task should be performed in a custom controller,[4] not a view controller. Then, through context mapping (see Section 6.8), one or more view controllers can obtain the information they require for presentation to the user.

This division of labor between the component controller and the view controllers ensures that good design principles are followed. In other words, the component controller obtains data from some remote system via an executable model object, but does not care how it is to be presented to the user; the view controller simply presents the data it receives from the component controller without caring how it was obtained.

If you follow this design principle, your Web Dynpro application will have its data processing and data presentation layers efficiently decoupled from each other.

Important: View controllers have no public interface; that is, they cannot be reused outside the scope of the component within which they live, and cannot be accessed by other controllers.

3.4.2 Interaction

There are several points that must be clearly understood about the way controllers interact with each other:

▶ Controllers can expose only methods and data that exist in their public interface. A custom controller's context is always part of its public interface and (after a suitable usage declaration) is therefore accessible to other controllers.

▶ For controller A to gain access to the methods and data within controller B, controller A must explicitly declare that controller B is a required controller.

▶ Custom controllers have a public interface, but view controllers do not. Therefore, a view controller can declare the use of a custom controller, but not vice versa. Do not construct your Web Dynpro

---

4 Probably the component controller.

application in such a way that a view controller contains functionality required by a custom controller. If you end up in this situation, then you need to review the architecture of your view controller, and move the functionality in question into the component controller or perhaps a custom controller.[5]

▶ A custom controller can declare the use of any other custom controller within the current Web Dynpro project, or any controller within the public part of a used Development Component (DC).

▶ If the same data is to be displayed on different views, then it should be held in the context of a custom controller (often, this will be the component controller). The data in the custom controller's context can now be accessed by the view controller through a technique called context mapping (see Section 6.8).

3.4.3 Structure

The NWDS generates the following Java classes and interfaces for each type of declared entity. See Chapter 4 for details of the abbreviations used in these tables.

Entity	Naming Convention
Component Controller	${n_c}$ = ${c}$Comp
Component (as seen by the developer)	${n_c}$
Interface	${n_c}$Interface
Messages	
	IMessage${n_c}$
Component Delegates	
Component (as seen by the WDF)	Internal${n_c}$
Interface Controller	Internal${n_c}$Interface
Interfaces	
Component Controller	
External	N/A
Public	IPublic${n_c}$

Table 3.1 Java Classes Generated for a Component

Interfaces	
Component Controller	
Private	IPrivate{n_c}
Interface Controller	
External	IExternal{n_c}Interface
Public	IPublic{n_c}Interface
Private	IPrivate{n_c}Interface

Table 3.1 Java Classes Generated for a Component (cont.)

Entity	Naming Convention
View Controller	{n_v} = {v}View
Controller (as seen by the developer)	{n_v}
Delegate	
Controller (as seen by the WDF)	Internal{n_v}
Interfaces	
View Controller	
External	N/A
Public	N/A
Private	IPrivate{n_v}

Table 3.2 Java Classes Generated for a View

Entity	Naming Convention
Custom Controller	{n_{cc}} = {cc}Cust
Controller (as seen by the developer)	{n_{cc}}
Delegate	
Controller (as seen by the WDF)	Internal{n_{cc}}
Interfaces	
Custom Controller	
External	N/A

Table 3.3 Java Classes Generated for a Custom Controller

Interfaces	
Custom Controller	
Public	IPublic{n_{cc}}
Private	IPrivate{n_{cc}}

Table 3.3 Java Classes Generated for a Custom Controller (cont.)

Entity	Naming Convention
Standalone Component Interface Controller	{n_{si}} = {si}Compl
Controller (as seen by the developer)	{n_{si}}
Delegate	
Controller (as seen by the WDF)	Internal{n_{si}}
Interfaces	
Component Interface Controller	
External	N/A
Public	IPublic{n_{si}}
Private	IPrivate{n_{si}}

Table 3.4 Java Classes Generated for a Standalone Component Interface

3.5 View

Several fundamental features exist that distinguish a view controller from a custom controller:

▶ The only mechanism for user interaction with a Web Dynpro application is through a view controller.

▶ A view is a controller with exactly one visual interface (layout) associated with it.

▶ A view controller is subordinate to, and cannot exist without, the component controller.

▶ A view has a one-to-one relationship with its parent component controller.

▶ A component controller has a one-to-many relationship with its view controllers.

▶ A view controller is reusable *only* within the scope of its parent component controller.

A view controller can interact directly with executable model objects if required, but this style of architecture is not encouraged.

A view layout typically consists of a set of UI elements that can both display application data and receive user input. Typically, you will define a view layout at design time; however, it is perfectly possible to construct a UI layout dynamically at runtime.

A Web Dynpro screen may be composed from any number of view layouts, arranged in a wide variety of ways. The overall screen layout seen by the user is known as the "view assembly," and its contents can be controlled programmatically. All view controller instances are singletons with respect to their parent component instance. You may however, embed the same view several times within the current view assembly as long as only one usage is active at any one time. Should you do this, remember that each use of the view within the view assembly refers to the *same* view instance.

3.5.1 Lifespan

A view controller instance will persist for the duration of time specified by its lifespan parameter. This parameter can have the values "When Visible" or "Framework Controlled."

A view instance can be created for two reasons:

1. Either because it is the default view in a view container or
2. A navigation request to that view has been encountered.

There are three situations is which the view instance can be deleted. These are listed in the chronological order in which they could occur:

▶ First, if the lifespan parameter is set to "When Visible," the view will be deleted when a navigation request is encountered that replaces the current view area with some other view, *and* the view is no longer part of the current view assembly.

▶ Next, if the lifespan parameter is set to "Framework Controlled," the view will be deleted when the framework has no further use for the view. This will never occur while the view is part of the current view assembly.

▶ Finally, a view controller will never exist for longer than the lifespan of its parent component controller. Thus, when a parent component controller comes to the end of its life, any subordinate view controller instances that are still intact will be deleted automatically.

3.5.2 Interaction

A Web Dynpro view controller has been constructed in such a way that, despite being an independent Java class, it cannot function in isolation from its parent component controller.[6]

Because view controllers have no public interface, they cannot directly share information in their contexts with each other. Therefore, if data is to be shared between view controllers, it must exist in a custom controller's context (this will usually be the component controller). Now context mapping can be used to make the data in the custom controller's context available to as many view controllers as required.

It is a general principle that a view controller's context should contain only those nodes and attributes relevant to the data in its layout.

Important: The structure of a view controller's context should reflect the requirements of the UI elements in the layout, not the structure of the data supplied by the model to the custom controller.

Data obtained from a model will be structured according to the result set from the back-end business system. This is rarely suitable for direct display on the user interface; therefore, the custom controller will have to perform some structural transformation on the business data in order to prepare it for display. Depending on the degree of transformation required, you could use either the `WDCopyService` class or, for more complex data transformations, you could implement your own supply function.

3.5.3 Layout

Each view controller has exactly one layout assigned to it.

Typically, you will define the view layout at design time, but it is perfectly possible to have the view controller dynamically build its own layout at runtime. If dynamic UI construction or modification is required, then the coding to perform this task may only live in the view controller's hook method called `wdDoModifyView()`.

---

6 Since the component controller is created automatically by the NWDS, there is no risk of such a situation ever occurring.

3.5.4   Navigation

To navigate from one view to another, you must define entry and exit points. These are known as plugs.

In general, plugs are navigation event triggers. There are two special types of plug—Startup and Exit.

The root component of an application can be entered only through a plug of type Startup. Similarly, if your application requires an explicit exit point, a plug of type Exit must be created.

Startup and Exit plugs may be given any suitable name.

3.6   Model

The MVC design philosophy enforces a strict separation of the business logic from the presentation layer. In Web Dynpro, the business logic is delivered through an executable model object that can encapsulate the following types of functionality:

▶ A remote function call into an SAP system (such as a BAPI)

▶ A Web Service

▶ An Enterprise Java Bean

▶ Another Web Dynpro model previously exported in XMI format

▶ A configuration model[7]

In general, a model should encapsulate a group of business tasks that, taken together, form a complete business transaction.

SAP *strongly* recommends that each model live within its own separate Java package. See Section 5.2 for more details.

3.7   Event handling

Events are the triggers that cause the WDF to perform some sort of processing—often in response to user interaction. Web Dynpro uses of the following trigger types:

▶ Actions

▶ Events

---

7 This type of model is used to implement configuration logic for a Web Dynpro application.

3.7.1 Actions

In an MVC environment in which the view and controller execute on the same host,[8] it is possible for a method within the controller to subscribe directly to an event raised by a UI element within a view. This permits the underlying controller to function in a manner that is closely coupled to the view.[9]

However, such close coupling is not possible in a Web-enabled environment due to the fact that the view layer (a browser) and controller layer (the J2EE Engine) are separated from each other by the stateless HTTP layer. This immediately enforces a coarser level of communication granularity between client and server.

In such an environment, a client-side event raised by a UI element can only invoke server-side processing if an HTTP round trip is initiated. Web Dynpro therefore uses an event abstraction known as an "action" to cause client-side event information to be transported to the server.

You can think of an action as the bridge that takes the event information raised by a UI element in the client, reaches across the stateless HTTP layer, and connects to the corresponding event handler in the view controller.

This design approach provides the following advantages:

▶ A level of abstraction is achieved between the UI element layer and the event handler layer in the view controller. This permits a high degree of independence between the client and the server.

▶ If a complex UI layout requires the use of many different event handlers, a generic action can be created which is shared by a wide set of UI elements. Specific events can then be distinguished from each other by means of action parameters.

▶ Actions are runtime objects that can be enabled and disabled dynamically.

▶ There are two different types of client-side events. These are known as primary and secondary events. Enabling or disabling an action will have different consequences depending on whether the action is linked to a primary or secondary event.

---

8 As in the case of any client-based Java application.
9 Modern software design techniques place major emphasis on the need to decouple the data presentation layer from the data-processing layer. Therefore, close coupling of the view and controller layers is considered undesirable.

- If the action is bound to a primary event, the entire UI element is disabled when the associated action is disabled and vice versa. An example of a primary event is the `onSelect` event of a checkbox. If the action associated with this event is disabled, then you have implicitly disabled the entire UI element. Only primary events will be considered as evaluation candidates during a call to `IWDViewController.requestFocus()`.

- If an action is bound to a secondary event, the entire UI element is not disabled when the associated action is disabled. An example of a secondary UI element event is the `onLeadSelect` event of a table. If the action associated with this event is disabled, the UI element is still open for input, but selecting different rows of the table will not trigger a round trip.

Since actions are the link by which client-side events are replicated on the server, it only makes sense to define an action within a view controller.

If required, the NWDS will automatically create an event handler method within the view controller when an action is created.

3.7.2 Events

Events in the WDF are synonymous with events in the Java world. Using your design time declarations, the WDF will automatically manage the definition, triggering, and handler subscription to such events for you. You also have the option of dynamic event subscription at runtime.

A typical use of such events is the invocation of processing in a view controller after processing in the component controller has been completed. This can be achieved when a method in the view controller subscribes to an event raised by the component controller.

Important: If two or more methods subscribe to the same event, the order in which they will be executed is undefined.

Events can be defined in all controllers except view controllers and interface view controllers.

4   Web Dynpro naming placeholders

Throughout this book, the following set of placeholders is used to identify various named Web Dynpro entities. These placeholders are then combined to form composite names that obey the SAP recommended naming convention for Web Dynpro coding entities.

4.1   Development entities

{a}	Application
{act}	Action
{c}	Component
{cc}	Custom controller
{dc}	Development Component
{m}	Model
{mo}	Model object (referred to by a context model node)
{pi}	Inbound plug
{po}	Outbound plug
{pr}	Project
{rfcm}	RFC module name (defined in ABAP in a remote SAP system)
{rfcm$_{in}$}	Any inbound, structured parameter to an RFC module
{rfcm$_{out}$}	Any outbound, structured parameter to an RFC module
{si}	Standalone component interface
{siv}	Standalone component interface view[1]
{sc}	Software component
{st}	Dictionary simple type
{v}	View
{vs}	Viewset
{w}	Window

---

1 This naming placeholder is required only if a standalone component interface has multiple interface views.

4.2   Context entities

{ca}	Any context attribute
{chn}	Any context child node
{cn}	Any context node
{ctx}	Context name; always the same name as the controller to which it belongs
{mn}	Model node
{ma}	Model attribute
{rn}	Recursive node
{vn}	Value node
{va}	Value attribute

4.3   Generic and composite abbreviations

{dt}	Any data type defined either in standard Java or by the Web Dynpro data dictionary
{dt$_p$}	The data type of UI element property p
{l}	Locale value
{n$_x$}	The name that is formed by the combination of one of the listed placeholders and a naming convention suffix. This value then forms a composite placeholder embedded into the names of the generated coding entities. The subscript x indicates the type of composite name.
{p}	Component usage purpose
{pkg$_n$}	Any part of a Java package name. These parts will be used to form the directory names in the deployed application, and are concatenated to form the full package name for an import statement; e.g., if {pkg$_1$}=com, {pkg$_2$}=sap, {pkg$_3$}=tc, and {pkg$_4$}=webdynpro, then the package name {pkg$_1$}.{pkg$_2$}.{pkg$_3$}.{pkg$_4$} will be com.sap.tc.webdynpro.
{pkg$_{sap}$}	The standard SAP Java package within which all internal Web Dynpro Framework (WDF) classes live. This is currently com.sap.tc.webdynpro.*
{ui}	Any UI element object
{ui$_p$}	Any property of a UI element

{ui_evt}	Any client-side event raised by a UI element
{vnd}	The Java vendor name formed from reversing the order of the first m of the n parts of the package names (where $m < n$). Using the example given for the {pkg_n} placeholder above, the vendor could be formed from reversing the order of the first two parts of the package name to give {pkg_2}.{pkg_1} = sap.com.

4.4 Subscripts for composite placeholders using the SAP recommended suffixes

{n_a}	Application	= {a}App
{n_c}	Component controller	= {c}Comp
{n_cc}	Custom controller	= {cc}Cust
{n_civ}	Component interface view	= {w}InterfaceView
{n_ctl}	A controller of any type	
{n_m}	Model	= {m}Model
{n_pi}	Inbound plug	= {pi}In
{n_po}	Outbound plug	= {po}Out
{n_pr}	Project	= {pr}
{n_si}	Standalone component interface	= {si}CompI
{n_siv}	Standalone component interface view	= {si}{siv}
{n_u}	Component usage	= [{n_c}|{n_si}]]{p}Inst
{n_v}	View	= {v}View
{n_vs}	Viewset	= {vs}Viewset
{n_w}	Window	= {w}

4.5 J2EE Engine placeholders

<SID>	The system ID is a three-character identifier for an installed SAP system, and is an alphanumeric value that must start with a letter, e.g., C11, J2E, or PRD.
<instance_id>	The instance ID is a combination of letters and numbers that is defined at the time your Web Application Server (Web AS) is installed. The specific combination is determined by which processes are installed for that particular Web AS.

For example, the first instance of a standalone J2EE Engine would be called JC00. JC indicates that a Java engine is installed, and 00 indicates that this is the first instance. If a second instance of a standalone J2EE Engine were installed on the same machine, it would typically have an instance ID of JC01.

For a J2EE Engine installed as an add-in to an ABAP Web AS, the instance ID could be something like DVEBMGS00, where each letter indicates that a particular process type has been installed, and 00 indicates that this is the first instance on this machine.

5 Naming conventions

Coding generated by the NWDS will be easier to understand if the following naming convention is used consistently. This convention is designed to provide you with information about the function of each generated coding entity and will help when the structure of a large project needs to be understood.

5.1 General rules for naming

5.1.1 Permitted characters

Since all the Web Dynpro coding described in this book is implemented in Java, the standard naming rules that apply for Java also apply for Web Dynpro, but with certain important restrictions.

Since Java is a Unicode-compliant language, it is possible to create variables that use characters such as ä, é, and ñ, or characters from a non-Roman alphabet. Within Web Dynpro, such characters must not be used! This is because when the Java variable names are included in both the generated form definition (typically HTML or XML) and the embedded scripting language (e.g., JavaScript), the names are not escaped or encoded.

Caveat confector: Web Dynpro coding entity names must use only the characters A..Z, a..z, 0..9 or _. Digits are allowed from only the second position onwards.

Important: You should never use the prefixes wd, WD, or IWD, as these prefixes are used by the NWDS during the generation of internal coding entities. It is likely that you will create a name conflict if you use one of these prefixes.

5.1.2 Length of entity names

When Web Dynpro coding entities, such as components, views, models, and context nodes, are declared, the NWDS will generate various Java source and class files that are placed in specific directories. The path name of these directories is generated from parts that are specified either when the J2EE Engine is installed or when the Web Dynpro application is being designed.

The first location in which these files live is your NWDS workspace directory. The default workspace directories differ depending on whether or not you are developing Web Dynpro projects or Development Components (DCs). These are respectively:

- `<drive>:\Documents and Settings\<user_id>\`
  `Documents\SAP\Workspace`
- `<drive>:\Documents and Settings\<user_id>\.dtc`

Avoiding the path length problem in Windows

This section describes how to avoid a design time problem that does not occur very often, but when it does, you get a rather obscure error message.

Currently, the NWDS is available only for variants of the Windows operating system. Within this OS, there is a built-in limit of 255 characters for a file name (excluding the leading drive and colon characters). If you are not aware of the length to which generated Web Dynpro file names can grow, then it is possible that you could specify a combination of entity names which, when assembled into the generated path name, could exceed 255 characters in length.

Unfortunately, an NTFS directory entry can be created programmatically for a file with a path name longer than 255 characters, but then Windows will not permit any access to the file. The only way to delete such files is to open a DOS prompt and manually issue the `del` command for the offending file.

The first step to avoiding this problem is to shorten the path name to the `Workspace` and `.dtc` directories. This is most easily done at NWDS installation time. Personally, I use the directories `<drive>:\Workspace` and `<drive>:\.dtc`.

In general, the path names of coding entities are generated according to the patterns listed in the following tables. The path names quoted here are not the full list of all possible directory branches. Instead, only those directories have been listed in which Java files with the longest path names are likely to occur. The table rows printed bold indicate sections of the path name over which the user has control.

Directory Subpath	Default Value	Length
path_to_workspace	\Documents and Settings\All Users\Documents\SAP\WorkSpace\	57
project_name	{pr}	≥1
generated_WD_files	\gen_wdp\packages\	18
WD_package_name	\{pkg$_1$}\{pkg$_2$}\{pkg$_3$} .. \{pkg$_n$}	≥2
generated_package_suffix	\wdp	4
generated_class_prefix	\IPrivate	9
WD_controller_name	{n$_{ctl}$}	≥1
inner_class_name.class	$I{cn}Element.class	≥16

Table 5.1 Default Path Name for a Context Node Element within a Web Dynpro Project in the NWDS

Total default path length is at least 108 characters, leaving no more than 147 for user-defined names.

Directory Subpath	Default Value	Length
path_to_DC_workspace	\Documents and Settings\<user_name>\Documents\SAP\.dtc	≥44
software_component_name	\{sc}	≥2
DC_dir	\DCs	4
vendor_name	\{vnd}	≥2
DC_name	\{dc}	≥2
generated_component_dir	_comp\gen_wdp\packages	23
WD_package_name	\{pkg$_1$}\{pkg$_2$}\{pkg$_3$} .. \{pkg$_n$}	≥2
generated_package_suffix	\wdp	4
generated_class_prefix	\IPrivate	9
WD_controller_name	{n$_{ctl}$}	≥1
inner_class_name.class	$I{cn}Element.class	≥16

Table 5.2 Default Path Name for a Context Node Element within a Web Dynpro Development Component in the NWDS

Total default path length is at least 109 characters, leaving no more than 146 for user defined names.

Once a J2EE EAR file has been generated by the NWDS, the deployment process takes all the generated Java class files, and bundles them into a single JAR file called `app.jar`. This is to avoid the possibility of path length problems occurring at deploy time (e.g. if the NWDS and J2EE Engine run on different operating systems).

Directory Subpath	Default Value	Length
`path_to_deployed_apps`	\usr\sap\<SID>\<instance_id>\j2ee\ cluster\server0\apps	≥43
`vendor_name`	\{vnd}	≥2
`DC_name`	\{dc}	≥2
`WD_internal_path`	\webdynpro\public\lib\app.jar	25
Inside `app.jar`		
`WD_package_name`	\{pkg$_1$}\{pkg$_2$}\{pkg$_3$} .. \{pkg$_n$}	≥2
`generated_package_suffix`	\wdp	4
`generated_class_prefix`	\IPrivate	9
`WD_controller_name`	{n$_{ctl}$}	≥1
`inner_class_name.class`	$I{cn}Element.class	≥16
...		

Table 5.3 Default Path Name for Deployed Web Dynpro Casses within the J2EE Engine

The value of `path_to_deployed_apps` in Table 5.3 is the default installation name for a Web AS. It is possible (though unusual) for this path name to be changed at installation time. It is important that the resulting path length of deployed applications is considered before any change is made to the default installation path.

5.2 Naming conventions for coding entities

▶ Applications: {n$_a$} = {a}App
The actual application name {n$_a$}, should consist of the desired name {a}, followed by the suffix App. {a} should describe the business process being delivered.

► **Components:** $\{n_c\}$ ▪ $\{c\}$`Comp`
The actual component name $\{n_c\}$ should consist of the desired name $\{c\}$ followed by the suffix `Comp`. $\{c\}$ should describe some (reusable) unit of functionality within the application.

► **Component interface views:** $\{n_{civ}\}$ ▪ $\{w\}$`InterfaceView`
The creation of window $\{w\}$ automatically causes the component interface view $\{n_{civ}\}$ to be created where $\{n_{civ}\}$ = $\{w\}$`InterfaceView`. Since this name is created automatically, you are not permitted to change it.

The interface view is the component's visual interface and is implemented by the window. It is the means by which the view assembly defined in $\{w\}$ is presented to the client layer.

► **Component usage:** $\{n_u\}$ ▪ $\{n_c\}\{p\}$`Inst` or $\{si\}\{p\}$`Inst`
In order for component *A* to be able to use the data and functionality within component *B*, component *A* must first declare the use of component *B*. The name of the component usage differs from the name of the component in the same way that the name of an object instance differs from the class it instantiates.

Component usage is defined for two situations:

  ► When a component is being used

  ► When a standalone component interface is being used

The usage instance name $\{n_u\}$ should therefore consist of either the component name $\{n_c\}$ or the standalone interface name $\{si\}$, followed by the usage purpose $\{p\}$ and the suffix `Inst`.

► **Custom controllers:** $\{n_{cc}\}$ ▪ $\{cc\}$`Cust`
The actual custom controller name $\{n_{cc}\}$ should consist of the desired name $\{cc\}$ followed by the suffix `Cust`.

► **Inbound plugs:** $\{n_{pi}\}$ ▪ $\{pi\}$`In`
The actual inbound plug name $\{n_{pi}\}$ should consist of the desired inbound plug name $\{pi\}$ followed by the suffix `In`. $\{pi\}$ should start with an uppercase letter.

The inbound plug should be named according to the reason for which the view is being entered.

All inbound plugs have a corresponding event handler in the view controller. This method is named `onPlug`$\{n_{pi}\}$`()`.

▶ **Models:** `{n_m}` ▬ `{m}Model`
The actual model name `{n_m}` should consist of the desired name `{m}` followed by the suffix `Model`.

SAP *strongly* recommends that each Web Dynpro model live in its own Java package; e.g., the package name should conform to a pattern such as `{pkg_1}.{pkg_2}.{pkg_3}.models.{n_m}`.

Failure to adhere to this recommendation could result in erroneous behavior of model objects and possible data loss—especially if the same model is used by multiple Web Dynpro components.

▶ **Outbound Plugs:** `{n_po}` ▬ `{po}Out`
The actual outbound plug name `{n_po}` should consist of the desired outbound plug name `{po}` followed by the suffix `Out`. `{po}` should start with an uppercase letter.

The outbound plug should be named according to the reason for which the current view is being left, not the reason for which the target view is being entered!

▶ **Projects:** `{n_p}` ▬ `{pr}`
The project name `{n_p}` should describe the category of the business processes it contains.

▶ **Standalone component interfaces:** `{n_si}` ▬ `{si}CompI`
The actual standalone component interface name `{n_si}` should consist of the desired name `{si}` followed by the suffix `CompI`.

▶ **Standalone component interface views:** `{n_siv}` ▬ `{n_si}{siv}`
If only one interface view is needed for a component interface, then no manual action is needed here because the suffix `InterfaceView` will be added automatically to the window name `{w}` by the NWDS.

Should multiple interface views be required, then subsequent standalone component interface view names should consist of the standalone interface name `{n_si}` followed by some distinguishing name `{siv}`.

▶ **Views:** `{n_v}` ▬ `{v}View`
The actual view name `{n_v}` should consist of the desired name `{v}` followed by the suffix `View`.

▶ **Viewsets:** `{n_vs}` ▬ `{vs}Viewset`
The actual viewset name `{n_vs}` should consist of the desired viewset name `{vs}` followed by the suffix `Viewset`. The value of `{vs}` will typically be the same as the window `{w}` within which it lives.

SAP does not currently have a recommendation for naming nested viewsets.

► **Windows: {n_w} – {w}**

A window {w} represents an arrangement of one of more views that will form the visual interface for the controller {n_ctl}. The collective name for the set of views making up the user interface is a "view assembly."

A window contains one or more views, and implements a component interface view. There is a 1:1 relationship between a window and a component interface view. From a programming point of view, you gain access to the current view assembly through the window, but from a consumer's point of view (i.e., someone using the component), the view assembly is accessed through the component interface view (see Figure 1.1 in Chapter 1).

Since window {w} does not relate to any developer-modifiable unit of Java coding, it is unnecessary to use any particular suffix in its name.

6   The context

Every controller has exactly one hierarchical data storage structure known as a context.[1] The data held in the context exists only for the lifespan of the controller. Once the controller has been terminated, all data held within its context is lost.

The structure (i.e., the metadata) of a context will typically be defined at design time; however, at runtime, it is perfectly possible not only to modify the contents of the context, but also to modify its structure.

Within the scope of a single component, the context of a custom controller is always part of its public interface, whereas the context of a view controller is always private. This means that a view controller can gain access to the data in a custom controller's context, but a custom controller cannot gain access to the data in a view controller.

Information held in the context of a custom controller can be made accessible to the context of another controller (view or custom) by a technique known as context mapping. Using this technique, two or more contexts can share a reference to the same data. This is the primary mechanism for sharing data between controllers within a single component.

6.1   Context structure at design time

A context is a hierarchical arrangement of entities known as "nodes" and "attributes". A context will always have a parent node known as the root node. The root node is created automatically when the controller is initialized and always has the same properties.

Important: The context root node may not be deleted or modified in any way.

6.1.1   Nodes

A context node is the main abstraction class used for runtime data storage within the WDF. Context nodes are arranged hierarchically and are permitted to have children. The children of a node may be entities known as attributes or other nodes.

---

1   Every controller, that is, except an interface view controller.

A node is a data storage entity within which an element collection is maintained. The exact nature and behavior of the element collection will be discussed in detail later.

From now on, any context node will be generically identified with the abbreviation {cn}, and if {cn} has a node as one of its children, the child node will be referred to as {chn}.

6.1.2 Attributes

An attribute is a hierarchical entity within the context that is *not* permitted to have children. A context attribute cannot exist without being the child of some parent node—be it the context root node itself, or some other node.

We will refer to a context attribute with the abbreviation {ca}.

6.1.3 Terminology concerning nodes and attributes

All context nodes or attributes that have the root node as their immediate parent are referred to as being *independent*. There are certain restrictions placed on the properties of independent context nodes.[2]

All context nodes or attributes that have some other node as their immediate parent are referred to as being *dependent*.

It is possible to create independent attributes in any context of any controller. However, their use should specifically be avoided in component interface controllers (see Section 6.8.4 for more details).

6.1.4 Relationship between nodes and attributes

Any node can have zero or more children, which may be any combination of attributes or other nodes.

The set of children defined for any node form a unit known as an "element." At runtime, the node functions as a collection of such elements. The maximum and minimum number of elements permitted in a node collection is controlled by the `cardinality` property.

All nodes contain an element collection, even if the maximum number of elements within the collection is limited to one.

---

2 For instance, you cannot change the value of singleton flag of an independent node. It will always be set to `true`.

6.1.5   Calculated attributes

To make certain simple but repetitive data formatting tasks easier, a special type of context attribute is available known as a calculated attribute.

This type of attribute differs significantly from a normal attribute in that the data it contains is *never stored* within the node element to which it belongs. Instead, the value is calculated on demand whenever the attribute's accessor method is called.

An example of where a calculated attribute would be useful is assembling a formal greeting from a salutation, a title, and the parts of a user's name.

For example, the greeting "Dear Mr. Silas Greenback" is composed of the salutation "Dear", the form of address "Mr.", the first name "Silas", and the last name "Greenback". If these values have already been stored individually, there is no need to duplicate the data as the assembled greeting.

To assemble these parts into the required greeting, a calculated attribute must invoke some user defined coding in its accessor method. A calculated attribute always has an accessor method defined for it, but a mutator method will be defined only if the read-only flag is set to `false`.[3] The accessor and mutator method names conform to the normal `get(ca)()` and `set(ca)()` naming convention.

Now when a UI element is bound to a calculated context attribute, the accessor method will be called automatically to assemble the parts into the required value—in this case, a greeting.

Important: Implementing a mutator method for a calculated attribute is a potentially complex and, in certain cases, impossible task.

In practice, the majority of calculated attributes will be read-only for the following reasons:

▶ The mutator method must parse and then validate the user's input. Since you are expecting the user to enter a value composed of several parts, the parsing and validation algorithms could easily become very complex. Therefore, the development effort required to implement a mutator method could well exceed the benefit obtained from having such a method!

---

3   Depending on the nature of the data assembled by the calculated attribute's accessor method, writing a mutator method could turn into an excessively complex task!

▶ The functionality of the calculated attribute's accessor method may not be reversible. This would make it impossible for the calculated attribute to have a mutator method.

Caveat confector: There are certain principles concerning the accessor and mutator methods of calculated attributes that must be clearly understood:

▶ The point in time during the phase model (see Chapter 11) at which the calculated attribute's accessor method will run is not generally predictable.

▶ If the WDF is forced to catch an exception raised by the accessor or mutator method of a calculated attribute, then it will terminate your application.

▶ Consequently, all errors must be handled gracefully!

If it really becomes necessary to implement a UI element that *supplies* data to a calculated attribute, then the mutator method should make use of a specific context node with suitable attributes to hold any error messages produced during the validation process.

6.1.6 The element collection

An element is an instance of all the child attributes (ca) and child nodes (chn) that share node (cn) as their immediate parent. The set of elements within (cn) is known as the element collection.

As with any collection, a node's element collection can be accessed using a zero-based index value. It is possible to flag multiple elements as being selected, but only one of the selected elements can ever be processed at any one time. The element currently being processed is referred to as the "lead selection" element.

Each node object has a method (IWDNode.getLeadSelection()) that returns the index of the currently selected element. If this method returns a value of –1, this indicates that no element is currently selected.

Important: It is very important to understand the significance of which element is at the lead selection because this critically affects how singleton child nodes can be accessed. (See Section 6.2.2 for more details.)

The number of elements that may be stored in a node's element collection is controlled by the cardinality property. There are four possible values for this property and it is very important that you fully understand how this property affects the runtime behavior of a context node! (See Section 6.2.1 for more details).

6.1.7 An element's selection status

Each element in the node collection has a boolean flag that indicates its selection status. Within a single node collection, the number of elements that may be selected at any one time is controlled by the selection cardinality property. The selection cardinality can take exactly the same values as the node cardinality, with the one constraint that the selection cardinality may not specify a greater number of elements than are permitted to exist in the element collection.

The set of all selected elements forms a non-contiguous subset of the elements within the node's element collection. Despite being managed by a cardinality property, the subset of selected elements is not a collection in its own right, but merely all those elements that have their selection flags set to true.

6.1.8 Summary of the context at design time

Figure 6.1 shows the design time structure of a context necessary to describe a collection of sales orders, and their associated line items.

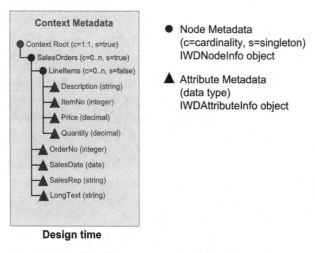

Figure 6.1 The Metadata Structure of a Context Hierarchy

At design time, your context declarations result in the creation of `IWDNodeInfo` and `IWDAttributeInfo` objects. These objects hold the metadata that will define the runtime data.

6.2 Context structure at runtime

At design time, you define nothing more than the context's metadata. This metadata defines what overall structure your data may take on, but the actual data stored within this hierarchy cannot be known until runtime.

Two particular node properties play a critical role in the runtime behavior of your context. These properties are `cardinality` and `singleton`.

Caveat confector: If you do not fully understand the function of the `cardinality` and `singleton` properties, then at runtime, you can arrive at the false impression that data is missing from your context!

6.2.1 The cardinality property

The cardinality property is composed of a pair of values that controls the maximum and minimum number of elements {cn} may contain at runtime.

The cardinality property may have four possible values:

▶ 0..1: Zero or one

▶ 0..n: Zero or more

▶ 1..1: One and only one

▶ 1..n: One or more

The first part of the cardinality describes the minimum number of elements that {cn}'s element collection may contain. This value is either zero or one, and is stored as a Boolean value. This value can be obtained at runtime by calling the method `node{cn}.getNodeInfo().isMandatory()`.

The second part of the cardinality describes the maximum number of elements that {cn}'s element collection may contain. This value is either a 1 or an n (meaning many) and is stored as a Boolean value (false = 1, true = n). This value can be obtained at runtime by calling method `node{cn}.getNodeInfo().isMultiple()`.

If {cn} has a cardinality of 1..<something>, then it can be assumed that after the context has been initialized, there will be at least one element present in the node collection. This element is known as the default element *and cannot be deleted!*

If you attempt to perform some action on a node that would violate the constraints of the cardinality, then you will get a runtime exception in the context, e.g., trying to add a second element to a node of cardinality 0..1, or trying to delete the last element from a node of cardinality 1..n.

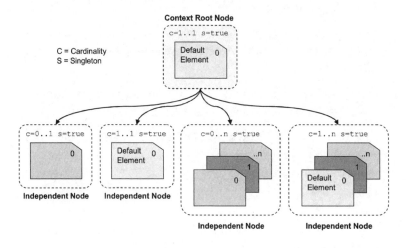

= Element created by an application at runtime
= Element created by the WDF at context initialisation time
= Element at the lead selection

Figure 6.2 How the Cardinality Affects the Number of Elements Permissible in a Node Collection at Runtime

6.2.2 The singleton property

The singleton property critically affects the relationship between the child node {chn} and its parent node {cn}.

If {chn} is declared at design time, the generated interface for this node will vary depending on whether it is a singleton or non-singleton node.

> **Important:**
> ▶ All non-singleton child nodes are associated with their parent node on a per parent *element* basis.

There is a one-to-one relationship between each element in the parent node's element collection and the corresponding child node.

If {cn} has *n* elements in its element collection, then you will have *n* distinct instances of the non-singleton child node {chn}.

Non-singleton child nodes can be created by their respective parent element.

▶ Singleton child nodes, however, are associated with their parent node on a per *node* basis.

Irrespective of the number of elements in the parent node's element collection, *there will only ever be one instance of the singleton child node* {chn}.

The singleton child node holds the data relevant for the element *at the lead selection in the parent node's element collection*.

Singleton child nodes must be created by their parent node. Since there can only ever be one instance of a singleton child node, it is impossible for an *element* in a parent node collection to create a singleton child node.

Figure 6.3 shows how the singleton flag affects the number of instances of {chn} that may exist at runtime.

Since the context root node always has exactly one element, all nodes that have the context root node as their immediate parent must, by definition, be singleton nodes.

Further to this, the definition of a singleton child node {chn} immediately implies that it must be repopulated every time the lead selection in its parent node {cn} changes. This job is performed by declaring a supply function for the singleton child node.

Now, each time the lead selection of {cn} changes, the data in {chn} is flagged as dirty. All supply functions in Web Dynpro are triggered using the concept of lazy access. That is, the supply function will only be executed if the data it provides is actually required.

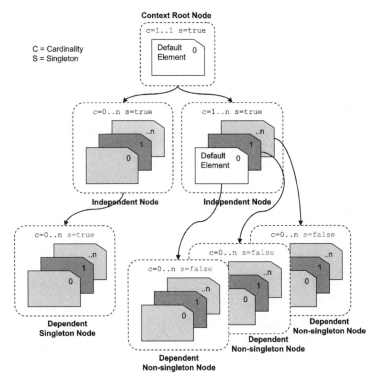

Figure 6.3 The Relationship Between Child Nodes and Their Parents Depends on the Value of the Singleton Property

6.2.3 Selection cardinality

As was stated in Section 6.1.1, all context nodes maintain a collection of elements, where an element is a single instance of all the node's child entities. During the operation of a Web Dynpro controller, it often becomes necessary to mark certain node elements as requiring processing (e.g., after a user has selected multiple rows from a table). The number of elements that may be selected is controlled by the selection cardinality, which may take one of the same four values as the node cardinality.

In the same way that the node's cardinality controls the maximum and minimum number of elements permissible within the node collection at runtime, so the selection cardinality controls the maximum and minimum number of elements that may be selected at any one time.

Unless you say otherwise, a node will have a selection cardinality of 0..1, meaning that you may select zero or one elements at any one time. If such a node were displayed using a table UI element, you would be able to select only one row at a time. However, if you wish to allow the user to select multiple rows, you will need to change the selection cardinality to `0..n`, meaning that zero or more elements may be selected.

6.2.4 Context attributes that can supply data to UI elements

Table 6.1 below lists the data types that can be used to supply data to a UI element. These data types are built in to the Web Dynpro Dictionary and are all defined in the package `com.sap.dictionary`.

Built-in Type	Java Class	Primitive
binary	byte[ ]	Yes
boolean	Boolean	Yes
date	java.sql.Date	
decimal	java.math.BigDecimal	
double	Double	Yes
float	Float	Yes
integer	Int	Yes
long	Long	Yes
short	Short	Yes
string	java.lang.String	
time	java.sql.Time	
timestamp	java.sql.Timestamp	

Table 6.1 Built-in Web Dynpro Dictionary Data Types

The above list represents all the data types that can be visually rendered. Web Dynpro UI elements can be bound only to context attributes whose data types appear in the above list.

Important: Only a select few UI elements can be bound to binary context attributes; these are `OfficeControl`, `FileDownload`, and `FileUpload`. Other UI elements, such as `TextField` or `InputField`, cannot be bound to binary context attributes because there is no general way to parse or format binary data.[4]

---

4 At least not without the additional information supplied by a MIME type.

Context attributes that do not need to be bound to UI elements may be of any available Java class.

6.2.5 Summary of the context at runtime

The metadata shown in Figure 6.1 is now displayed as it could appear at runtime, when actual data has been created by the application.

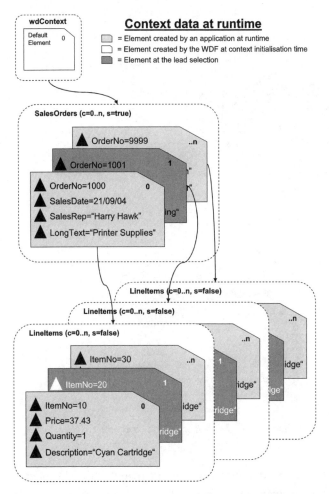

Figure 6.4 Context Structure at Runtime Showing Node LineItems as a Non-singleton Node

Notice that Figure 6.4 shows node LineItems as being a non-singleton node with respect to its parent node SalesOrders. This is shown by the fact that there is a 1:1 correspondence between the *elements* in node SalesOrders and each of the LineItems node instances.

If node `LineItems` is changed to be a singleton, then the runtime structure will change to look like Figure 6.5.

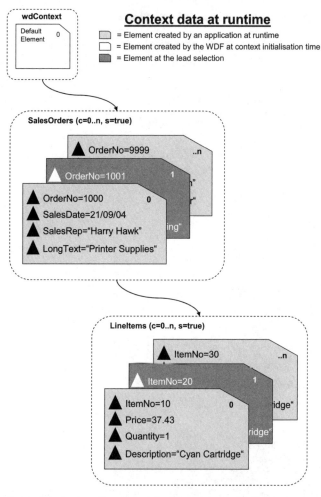

Figure 6.5 Context Structure at Runtime Showing Node LineItems as a Singleton Node

There is now a 1:1 correspondence between the parent and child *nodes* — irrespective of how many elements the parent node contains.

6.3 Should node names be singular or plural?

The name chosen for context node {cn} should reflect the potential number of elements it will contain at runtime. The upper limit is either 1 or many, and is determined by the second part of the node's cardinality.

If a node has a cardinality of `<something>..1`, then there will be, at most, one element in that node collection. Therefore, the node name should be singular.

If, however, the node has a cardinality of `<something>..n`, then the node collection could contain multiple elements. Therefore, the node name should be plural.

6.4 General naming standards

When choosing a name for a context node or attribute, you do not need to include the words "node," "element," or "attribute" within the entity name. If you wish to identify that a certain entity is part of the context, then it is unnecessary to add these words, as they will be added automatically when a typed interface is generated.[5]

If, at design time, node `{cn}` is created with the `typedAccessRequired` property set to `true`, then the NWDS will generate various methods and classes whose names are formed from these words and the supplied name `{cn}`.

Important: All node names must be unique within the entire context because the classes created for these nodes live in the same namespace.

6.4.1 Value nodes: {vn}

A value node name `{vn}` should start with an uppercase letter. You are free to select any meaningful name that obeys the Web Dynpro naming convention for context names.

When a value node is created at design time, you can decide whether a set of typed classes is generated or not. This is done by setting the value of the node property `typedAccessRequired`. The default value is `true`.

See Table 6.2 for a complete list of classes and methods that are generated when `typedAccessRequired` is set to `true`.

---

5 The exception to this rule is when the name of the business data being held by the context contains the word "node," "element," or "attribute." An example of this might be a context node that holds SAP Work Breakdown Structure (WBS) Elements. Here the word "element" is part of the business name and does not have any reference to the Web Dynpro Context.

6.4.2 Value attributes: {va}

A value attribute name {va} should start with an uppercase letter. You are free to select any meaningful name that obeys the Web Dynpro naming convention for context names (see Chapter 5).

All attribute names must be unique within the scope of their parent *node*. Duplicate attribute names may exist within the same context as long as they do not share the same parent node.

6.4.3 Model nodes: {mn}

A model node name {mn} should start with an uppercase letter. You are free to select any meaningful name that obeys the Web Dynpro naming convention for context names (see Chapter 5), but the general convention is to give model node {mn} the same name as the model object to which it will be mapped. The proviso here is that the node name length should be taken into account.

If your executable model object represents an ABAP Remote Function Call (RFC) module, then this function module can have a name that is up to 28 characters long. When various suffixes such as "_Input" or "_Output" are appended to the name, this can create class names that are awkward to work with.

Therefore, model node names will usually be the same as the model object, as long as the name does not become too long to work with. We leave it to your discretion to decide exactly how long "too long" is!

6.4.4 Model attributes: {ma}

Generally speaking, the names of model attributes are inherited from the model object to which the parent model node is bound. You are free to rename model attribute names if you wish, but this is a manual process and is usually only done when a name clash occurs (see Section 10.6), or the generated class name is considered too long to work with conveniently.

Irrespective of whether you choose to inherit attribute names from the model object or you define your own names, all attribute names must be unique within the scope of their parent node.

6.4.5 Recursive nodes: {rn}

A recursive node name {rn} should start with an uppercase letter. You are free to select any meaningful name that obeys the Web Dynpro naming convention for context names.

The only circumstance under which it is permissible to have duplicate node names within a context is when a recursive node is added dynamically at runtime. See IWDNodeInfo.addRecursiveChild(IWDNodeInfo parent) for more details.

6.4.6 Supply functions: supply{cn}()

Any context node {cn} may have a supply function created for it. Supply functions are primarily used to populate singleton context nodes when the lead selection of the parent node changes; however, there is nothing to stop you from writing a supply function for a non-singleton node.

When a supply function is declared, the NWDS will propose a name in the form supply{cn}(). You may alter this name if required, but, for the sake of simplicity and consistency, SAP recommends that the default name be accepted.

Important: When writing a supply function, you should not make any assumptions about either who will call it or when it will be called. The following situations generally act as triggers for the execution of a supply function:

▶ A read request occurs for a context node whose contents are flagged as dirty. Such a call could come either from application code within an action event handler or by the WDF itself.

▶ When data is needed for rendering and the context node has not been accessed before.

Consequently, it is not possible to know from which stage of the phase model (see Chapter 11) the supply function will be called. Therefore, it is not legal to raise a WDNonFatalRuntimeException or to call any of the message manager's raise<msg_type>() methods. If you do, then the content of the singleton child node will probably be left in an undefined state.

As with accessor methods for calculated attributes, there are certain principles that must be understood about supply functions:

- The point in time during the phase model (see Chapter 11) at which a supply function will run is not generally predictable.
- If the WDF is forced to catch an exception raised by a supply function, it will terminate your application.
- All errors must be handled gracefully.

6.5 Classes generated as a result of design time declarations

When a context node or attribute is created, the default behavior of the NWDS is to create a typed set of classes and methods to represent those context entities. If you choose to access the context using only the generic interface, the generation of this typed API can be switched off by setting the node's `typedAccessRequired` property to `false`.

Either way, any context nodes declared at design time are known as "static nodes", and context nodes created at runtime are known as "dynamic nodes".

Caveat confector: The context of a custom controller is publicly accessible, but the context of a view controller is private. Therefore, the following differences exist concerning the scope of the declared classes.

- The context of a custom controller belongs to class `IPublic{n_c}` or `IPublic{n_cc}`.[6]
- The context of a view controller belongs to class `IPrivate{n_v}`.

Assuming that typed access is required, the generated node and element classes will implement different methods depending on whether {cn} has any child nodes, and whether the child node is a singleton node or not.

Table 6.2 shows the methods that are created for node {cn} within component controller {n_c}, but the `IPublic{n_c}` part of the class name can be substituted for `IPrivate{n_cc}` or `IPrivate{nv}` without any loss of generality.

The method names in bold under Context Node will only be created if {cn} has a child node {chn}. Also, the method names in bold under Context Element will only be created if {chn} is a non-singleton with respect to {cn}.

---

6 For any controller, it is perfectly possible to work only with the controller's `IPrivate{n_ctl}` interface.

Generated Class	Method
Context Node	
IPublic{n_c}.I{cn}Node	I{cn}Element create{cn}Element()
	I{cn}Element current{cn}Element()
	I{cn}Element get{cn}ElementAt(int)
	void bind(I{cn}Element)
	I{chn}Node node{chn}()
	I{chn}Node node{chn}(int)
Context Element	
IPublic{n_c}.I{cn}Element	String get{cn}Name()
	void set{cn}Name(String)
	I{chn}Element current{chn}Element()
	I{chn}Element create{chn}Element()
	I{chn}Element get{chn}ElementAt(int)
	I{chn}Node node{chn}()

Table 6.2 Generated Context Classes for Component Controller

6.6 What's the difference between the various types of context nodes?

6.6.1 Value nodes

A value node is the most basic form of node that can exist within a Web Dynpro context. It is one in which all the necessary metadata to define the node attributes either is stored within the node itself or is obtained from a local Java Dictionary object. Value node attributes can be added manually as required and do not necessarily have to represent a pre-defined data structure.

However, if you know that a certain combination of fields will be used frequently across the different contexts in your application, then, rather than repeating the structure declaration for each value node in each context, it is more efficient to create a dictionary structure. Then, when you create a value node, you can obtain the attributes directly from the dictionary structure using structure binding. Under these conditions, the attributes of the value node become fixed, and can only be taken from the dictionary structure.

A value node that uses structure binding may not have any further child *attributes* added to it, but you may add further child *nodes* (which in turn may use structure binding if desired).

When creating a new element for a value node's element collection, the node can create the element object using the metadata stored within it. In a generalized form, the coding looks like this (where {cn} is any context node):

```
I{cn}Element newValueElement = wdContext.
                    node{cn}.
                        create{cn}Element();
```

Important: A value node maintains its own element collection, with each element in the collection holding the actual runtime data.[7]

6.6.2 Model Nodes

A model node is similar to a value node in respect to its API; however, there are three very important differences:

▶ A context model node makes a model object look like any other context node; i.e., it gives the model object an API that is very similar to a value node.

▶ A model node is not considered valid until it is bound to a corresponding model object. Therefore, a model node *always* inherits its metadata from the model object to which it is bound.

▶ The element collection in a model node *does not* hold the actual runtime data! Instead, it holds a collection of references to the relevant model object instances.

When creating the elements of a model node's element collection, you cannot use the exact syntax shown above for a value node. Instead, the createElement() method belonging to a model must be passed an instance of a relevant model object. A reference to this instance is then added to the model node's element collection.

In contrast to a value node, the element collection maintained by a model node is simply a collection of references to model object instances.

---

7 This is true only for an unmapped value node. The element collection of a mapped value node is simply a reference to the element collection of the mapping origin node. More about this later.

The actual runtime data is stored in the model objects, not in the model node's element collection.

For instance, a new element can be added to the model node BAPI_ FLIGHT_GETLIST_INPUT as follows:[8]

```
// Create a new model object instance
Bapi_Flight_Getlist_Input bapiInput =
  new Bapi_Flight_Getlist_Input();

// Using the model object instance, create a new model
// node element
IBapi_Flight_Getlist_InputElement newModelElement =
  wdContext.
    nodeBapi_Flight_Getlist_Input.
      createBapi_Flight_Getlist_InputElement(bapiInput);

// Append the new element to the model node's element
// collection
wdContext.nodeBapi_Flight_Getlist_Input.addElement(bapiInput);
```

Listing 6.1 Adding a New Element to a Model Node

Notice that the create{mn}Element() method of a model node cannot create a new element object on its own: its needs to be passed a reference to an existing model object. The model object is the actual repository for the runtime data, and references to these model objects are maintained in the model node's element collection.

Binding context model nodes to model objects

"Binding" is the name given to the association between a context model node and a model object. Once a context model node has been bound to a model object, the data in the model can be accessed through the standard context API.

When you bind a context model node to a model object, you can elect to transfer some or all of the model object's structure into the context. If certain branches of the model object's hierarchy are not required, there is no need to bind these to the context model node.

It is also possible to extend the structure of a model node by adding further nodes and attributes that are not part of the model object. These

---

8 This is not the only way of adding an element to a model node. The bind() method can also be used.

additional children can be either model or value nodes. The only condition here is that if you add a model node or attribute, it must have an explicit binding to a corresponding entity in a model object.

Important: The structure of a model node can be extended by the addition of child value nodes and attributes. Thus, the children of a model node can be a mixture of nodes and attributes supplied by the model object's metadata, *and* any required additional value nodes and/or value attributes.

The children of a value node, on the other hand, may *only* be value nodes or values attributes.

You may not mix value and model nodes or attributes together if the parent is a value node.

6.6.3 Recursive Nodes

If you wish to represent a recursive data structure within the context, a recursive node is the correct node to use. The simplest example of recursive data within a hierarchical structure is a file system. A directory can contain either files or subdirectories. This definition is then repeated for each subdirectory level down the hierarchy.

Within the context, a recursive node is a special node that has only two properties: `name` and `repeatedNode`. As with any context node, a recursive node must itself have a name, but the `repeatedNode` property is where the recursion is defined. This property holds a reference to some parent node and indicates that, at runtime, the location of the recursive node will be occupied by a node of the type indicated in the `repeatedNode` property.

You should think of a recursive node as a design time placeholder used to indicate that a node will be created at this location at runtime, and will be of the type named in the `repeatedNode` property.

The node name identified by `repeatedNode` must lie on the direct path back to the context root node.

When a recursive node is created at runtime, it is always created as a non-singleton node. This is a hard-coded feature and cannot be changed.

Important: The depth to which recursion will occur is determined at runtime, not design time. At design time, you simply indicate that recursion is possible and leave it to the runtime code to establish exactly how deep that recursion will be.

Consider the following context structure:

Figure 6.6 A Context Structure That Can Represent a Basic File System Hierarchy

The context structure shown in Figure 6.6 is all that is necessary to represent a very simple file system hierarchy. Node `FileSystemNode` has a cardinality of `0..n`, and each element within it will represent either a file or a directory. The recursive node `Subdirectory` has its `repeatedNode` property set to `FileSystemNode`.

The root node of the context is analogous to the root directory of the file system.

If an element of node `FileSystemNode` represents a file, then the recursive node `Subdirectory` will be null; however, if the element represents a subdirectory, the recursive child node `Subdirectory` will be created as a non-singleton node of type `FileSystemNode`. The whole recursive process can now be repeated in the new child instance of `FileSystemNode`.

The following code (see Listing 6.2) will use the recursive context structure shown in Figure 6.6 to create a representation of the simple directory and file structure shown below.

Figure 6.7 A Simple File and Directory Hierarchy

```
public void buildRecursiveNodes() {
  // Get reference to statically defined FileSystemNode
  IFileSystemNodeNode fsNode = wdContext.nodeFileSystemNode();
```

```
// Perform 4 levels of recursion
for (int i = 1; i <= 4; i++) {
    // Create an element in the current FileSystemNode
    IFileSystemNodeElement fsNodeEl =
        fsNode.createFileSystemNodeElement();

    // Set the file name based on the recursion level
    fsNodeEl.setName("File At Level " + i);

    // Bind the element to the node collection
    fsNode.bind(fsNodeEl);

    // Change fsNode to refer to its own recursive child node
    fsNode = fsNode.nodeSubdirectory();
}
}
```

Listing 6.2 Adding a Hierarchy of Recursive Nodes

6.7 Fundamental principles of the context

The behavior of the context is based on the following six fundamental principles:

1. All attributes {ca} and child nodes {chn} of context node {cn} are aggregated into a unit known as an element.

2. The cardinality property controls the maximum and minimum number of elements {cn} may contain at runtime.

   ▶ If {cn} has a cardinality of 1..<something>, element 0 will always be present in its collection. This is known as the default element and *may not* be removed.

   ▶ If {cn} has a cardinality of 0..<something>, element 0 must be explicitly created at runtime.

   ▶ Do not perform any action on a context node that would violate the constraints of its cardinality; e.g., Don't try to delete the default element or add a second element to a node of cardinality 0..1.

3. The singleton flag describes the relationship between the child node {chn} and its parent {cn}. The default value for the singleton flag is true.

   ▶ If {chn} is a singleton with respect to {cn}, then no matter how many elements {cn} contains, there will only ever be one instance of {chn}.

- If {chn} is a non-singleton with respect to {cn}, then for each of the n elements in the parent {cn}, there will be n instances of {chn}.

- The instance of a singleton child node is specific to the element at the lead selection of its parent node. Therefore, the lead selection of parent node {cn} must first be correctly positioned before the singleton child node {chn} can be accessed. Now when {chn} is accessed, its supply function will be called automatically.

- The contents of a non-singleton child node can be referenced directly without needing to reposition the lead selection of the parent node.

4. An unmapped node[9] {cn} maintains its own element collection, but a mapped node does not. Instead, a mapped node maintains a reference to the element collection of its mapping origin node.

5. When iterating around the elements of {cn}, there are two ways to obtain a reference to each element. The method you choose will largely depend on whether or not the node has singleton child nodes.

- If {cn} contains non-singleton child nodes, it is sufficient simply to call method node{cn}.getElementAt(int index). The use of this method does not alter the value of the node's lead selection.

- If {cn} contains singleton child nodes, method node{cn}.setLeadSelection(int index) must first be called to position the lead selection. Then you may call node{cn}.current{cn}Element() if a typed interface has been created, or IWDNode.currentElement() if the generic context API is being used.

6. The selection cardinality controls the number of elements that may be concurrently selected. This value may be any one of the four standard cardinality values, so long as it does not contradict the node's collection cardinality. The following table shows the invalid cardinality combinations:

Collection	Selection
0..1	0..n or 1..n
1..1	0..n or 1..n

Table 6.3 Disallowed Cardinality Combinations

---

9 This includes the context root node whose element collection always contains exactly one element.

6.8   Context mapping

6.8.1   What is mapping?

Context mapping is the mechanism by which information can be shared between the contexts of different controllers. Usually, these controllers live within the same component, but context mapping can also cross a component boundary.

The context node that acts as the data source is known as the "mapping origin," and the context node that obtains data from the mapping origin is known as the "mapped node."

Before context mapping can take place, the controller in which the mapped node lives must declare the use of the controller in which the mapping origin lives.

Caveat confector: Remember that a view controller's context is always private and a custom controller's context is always public. Therefore, for information to be shared between a custom controller and a view controller, the view controller must declare the use of a custom controller—not vice versa!

This feature is a deliberate design decision to prevent a custom controller becoming dependent upon the functionality and data within a view controller. The view controller should be dependent upon the functionality provided by the custom controller.

Important: When a mapping relationship is set up between two nodes in different contexts, the mapped node ceases to maintain its own element collection and, instead, references the element collection of the mapping origin. Any changes made to the data in the mapped node actually update the element collection of the mapping origin. It does not matter which node you update, only the element collection of the mapping origin is ever manipulated.

Since a mapped node does not maintain its own element collection, no runtime data is stored within a mapped node.

For a mapping relationship to exist, both contexts must have a defined node object. That is, if the context of a view controller contains a value node called SalesOrders, and this is mapped to a value node of the same name in the parent component controller, then each context will have a separate node object called `SalesOrders`. What is mapped is a reference to the element collection, *not* a reference to the context node itself. See Section 7.2 for details of the error messages that can arise from this fact.

6.8.2 Selection mapping

Since a context node maintains two cardinality properties (one for the element collection, and one for the selected elements), it is possible to map not only the element collection, but also the selection of elements within that collection. When context mapping is used, the mapped node will always have its element collection mapped to the mapping origin, but you have the choice of whether you want to map the selected nodes as well.

If you choose not to map a node's selection, two independent selection lists will be maintained; one will be the list of selected elements in the mapping origin, and the other will be the list of selected elements in the mapped node. If, for instance, a view controller contains a mapped node that points to a node in the component controller, the selection will typically not be mapped. This is because you will probably want the node selection in the view controller to reflect the user's interaction with the displayed data, rather than a selection made for programmatic reasons within the component controller.

6.8.3 Normal mapping

Unless otherwise specified, all context mapping relationships lie within the boundaries of a single Web Dynpro component. This immediately makes all mapping relationships "internal" to a single component.

The commonest example of this situation is the one where a view controller needs to gain access to the information in the component controller. After the component controller has been declared as a required controller of the view controller, a mapped node can be defined in the view controller that points to a mapping origin in the component controller.

In general, once a custom controller has been declared as required by any other controller, the nodes of its context become available to act as mapping origin nodes. This statement also holds true if a parent component has declared the use of a child component. All the nodes in the context of the child component's interface controller can now act as mapping origin nodes.

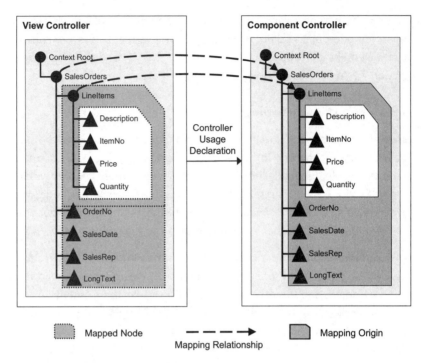

View Controller

Context Root
SalesOrders
LineItems
Description
ItemNo
Price
Quantity
OrderNo
SalesDate
SalesRep
LongText

Controller
Usage
Declaration

Component Controller

Context Root
SalesOrders
LineItems
Description
ItemNo
Price
Quantity
OrderNo
SalesDate
SalesRep
LongText

Mapped Node   Mapping Relationship   Mapping Origin

Figure 6.8 Context Mapping within one Component

6.8.4 External mapping

However, there are certain situations in which a mapping relationship needs to be defined, but the identity of the mapping origin is unknown at the time the mapped node is created. This type of situation exists when the mapped node and the mapping origin lie on different sides of a component boundary.[10]

When writing a reusable component,[11] it is perfectly feasible to define a mapped node in the context of the interface controller that has, as its mapping origin, a node in some context of the parent. In this situation, the mapped node lies in the interface of the child component and the mapping origin lies across a component boundary in some other, as yet undefined, parent component.

This situation is known as "external" mapping.

---

10 This type of mapping relationship can prove very useful when writing a reusable component.
11 A component that will function as the child of some other component.

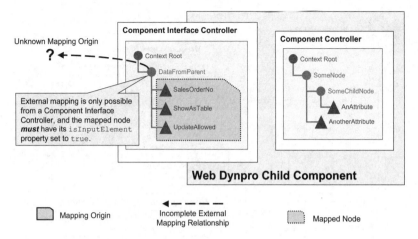

Figure 6.9 External Context Mapping: Part 1

At the time the child component is being written, it is impossible to establish exactly which node in the parent controller will act as the mapping origin—the parent component may not have been written yet! All that can be said is that a mapping origin is required to complete the mapping relationship, and that it will lie outside the boundary of the current component.[12]

Defining the exact identity of the mapping origin is now postponed until the child component is declared for use by a parent component. This is the point at which the parent component must supply the identity of the node that will act as the mapping origin. Only now can the mapping relationship be considered fully established.

This immediately leads to the conclusion that the node nominated to act as the mapping origin for an externally mapped node is specific to the single usage instance of the child component. If you create multiple instances of the same child component, each external mapping relationship can be satisfied by different nodes in the parent component.[13]

---

12 External mapping is possible only for independent nodes in the context of a component interface controller. Independent attributes cannot be mapped externally.

13 If the child component performs a read-only task on the data in the parent context, then one mapping origin node could be shared. But if the child updates the parent context, then multiple child instances will each require their own mapping origin nodes in the parent.

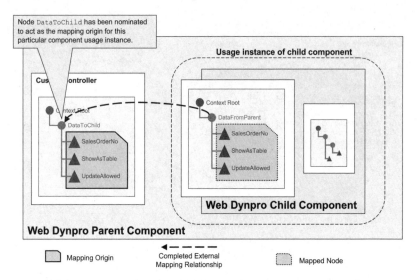

Figure 6.10 External Context Mapping: Part 2

Important: A special property exists only for context nodes of a component interface controller. This is the `isInputElement` property, and it controls whether the context node will be externally mapped or not. If `isInputElement` is set to true, then the node will be mapped to a mapping origin in some other component.

Consider the following two situations in which parent and child components share information via a mapping relationship. We have two components, {c_a} and {c_b}, that will function as parent and child respectively; i.e., in both situations, {c_b} will be regarded as the child of {c_a}.

1. {c_b} contains a mapped node in its component interface controller that has the `isInputElement` property set to true. This immediately indicates that the node acting as the mapping origin lies outside {c_b}. The identity of this node cannot be determined until {c_a} declares a usage instance of {c_b} and identifies a usage specific node to act as the mapping origin.

2. {c_a} both contains a mapped node and creates a usage instance of {c_b}. The mapping origin will lie in the interface controller of {c_b}. Since the usage of {c_b} must be declared when {c_a} is written, {c_b}'s interface now lies within the scope of {c_a}, and can be fully established when {c_a} is written.

Situation 1 uses external mapping.

Situation 2 uses normal (or internal) mapping.

6.8.5 General points about external mapping

▶ An externally mapped node *must* live within the context of a component interface controller and have its `isInputElement` property[14] set to `true`.

▶ External context mapping is possible only for independent nodes of a component interface controller, not independent attributes.

▶ When a parent component declares the use of the child component, any externally mapped nodes in the child component's interface controller must have their mapping references established. This is an extra configuration step during the component usage declaration.

▶ Since external mapping relationships are usage specific, it is entirely possible for there to be different mapping relationships for each usage instance of the child component.

6.8.6 What impact does context mapping have on my coding?

Consider the following situation. A simple Web Dynpro component called `DemoComp` contains a component controller, and a single view controller called `DemoView`. In the context of `DemoComp`, a value node has been declared called `UserPreferences`. In the context of `DemoView`, another value node has been declared that is also called `UserPreferences`. The value node in the view controller has been mapped to its namesake in the component controller.[15]

With this information, we immediately know that the NWDS will create the following Java classes and subclasses:

▶ `IPublicDemoComp`
  A class for the component controller

▶ `IUserPreferencesNode`
  A subclass for the context node in the component controller

▶ `IUserPreferencesElement`
  A subclass for the element of the node in the component controller

---

14 This property exists only for context nodes of a component interface controller.
15 The view controller must explicitly declare the use of the component controller before context mapping can occur.

- ▶ **IPrivateDemoView**

  A class for the view controller

- ▶ **IUserPreferencesNode**

  A subclass for the context node in the view controller

- ▶ **IUserPreferencesElement**

  A subclass for the element of the node in the view controller

Notice that the subclass names for the context nodes and elements are the same in *both controllers*. This is perfectly legal, but you must be careful in the following situation.

Let's say you want to add an element to node `UserPreferences` in the *view controller*. You would use code something like the following:

```
IUserPreferencesElement userPrefEl =
  wdContext.nodeUserPreferences().createUserPreferencesElement();
wdContext.nodeUserPreferences().addElement(userPrefEl);
```

Listing 6.3 Coding to Add an Element to a Context Node

At first, the class name `IUserPreferencesElement` will appear with a wavy red line under it. This indicates that the class name cannot be resolved from any of the currently imported packages, so you need to organize your import statements. This is done by right-clicking the mouse button within the NWDS Java editor, and selecting **Source · Organize Imports** from the side menu.

Now, because of the ambiguity in resolving the class name `IUserPreferencesElement`, you will see the following pop-up window:

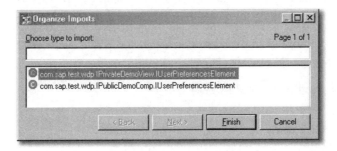

Figure 6.11 Organize Imports Pop-up Window Used to Resolve Class Name Ambiguity

> **Caveat confector:** It is very important that you select the class name for the controller you are currently editing! In the above example, do not select the component controller class containing `IUserPreferencesElement` because it will be considered incompatible with the `UserPreferences` node in the view controller even though they are semantically identical!

6.9 Accessing the context through the typed API

All controllers possess a context,[16] and irrespective of the type of controller in which your code is executing, all contexts operate in the same way.

A context node is the entity through which you can gain access to your runtime information—either because the context node holds the runtime data itself (a value node), or the context node holds references to the runtime data (a model node).

> **Caveat confector:** By default, every node declared at design time has a typed implementation of class `IWDNode` created for it. The following discussion assumes that when you declare your nodes at design time, the node's `typedAccessRequired` property is left at the default value of `true`. If you change this property to `false`, none of the typed classes described below will be generated, and you will have to use the generic context API to access your data (see Section 6.10.1),

An instance of node {cn} can be accessed by calling method `wdContext.node{cn}`. From this node instance, you can then obtain the node's metadata by calling method `getNodeInfo()`. This will return an object of class `IWDNodeInfo`. A node info object contains all the metadata for the specific node and is not type-specific.

Let's say, for example, in your component controller's context you have an independent value node called `SalesOrders` with four value attributes called `LongText`, `OrderNo`, `SalesDate`, and `SalesRep`. Since this node is independent (i.e., it has the context root node as its direct parent), it is forced to be a singleton node. Also, because we have not changed the default cardinality of `0..n`, you know immediately that the node will start life containing zero elements (an empty collection) and may grow to contain as many elements as required.

---

16 Except for an interface view controller.

The value attributes must have their data types set correctly: `LongText` and `SalesRep` are of type `string`, `SalesDate` is of type `Date`, and `OrderNo` is of type `integer`.

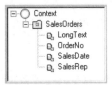

Figure 6.12 Context Value Node

These declarations will cause the following methods to be created:

▶ **wdContext.nodeSalesOrders**
To access the node

▶ **wdContext.createSalesOrderElement**
To create a new element for node `SalesOrders`

▶ **wdContext.currentSalesOrderElement**
To access the currently selected element

Now you have a set of typed accessor methods directly into the context node called `SalesOrder`. Using these methods, you can access the context node, and all the runtime data stored in any attribute in any of its elements.

These methods are generically listed in Table 6.3 in Section 6.7.

6.9.1 Accessing a node element

Using the context shown in Figure 6.12, the elements on node `Sales-Orders` can be accessed as follows:

```
// Access the element at the lead selection of node SalesOrders
ISalesOrdersElement thisSoEl =
wdContext.currentSalesOrdersElement();

// Access the element's attribute values
String       longText  = thisSoEl.getLongText();
java.sql.Date salesDate = thisSoEl.getSalesDate();
String       salesRep  = thisSoEl.getSalesRep();
int          orderNo   = thisSoEl.getOrderNo();
```

Listing 6.4 Accessing the Current Element of Node SalesOrders

The coding in Listing 6.4 has taken a shortcut! Since node SalesOrders is independent, it will be a singleton with respect to its parent node (the context root node); therefore, there can only ever be one instance of this node. Knowing this, we can call the method currentSalesOrdersElement() directly from the context root (wdContext) with the assurance that there is no ambiguity over which SalesOrders node is to be accessed.

> **Caveat confector:** If you want to access node elements that do not lie on the current selection path, then this coding shortcut cannot be taken!

6.9.2 Accessing all elements in a node

It is often necessary to process all the elements in a node collection. This is particularly true if the user is permitted to select multiple rows of a table. Since each table row is represented by a node element, selecting multiple rows will cause the node's isMultiSelected() flag to be switched on for that element.[17] The following code sample shows how such elements can be identified:

```
// Access all the elements of node SalesOrders
ISalesOrdersElement thisSoEl;
int noSalesOrders = wdContext.nodeSalesOrders().size();

// Loop around all the elements in the node
for (i=0; i<noSalesOrders; i++) {
  // Is the current element selected?
  if (salesOrdersNode.isMultiSelected(i)) {
    thisSoEl =
      wdContext.nodeSalesOrders().getSalesOrdersElementAt(i);
    // Do something useful with the selected element
  }
}
```

Listing 6.5 Accessing All the Elements of Node SalesOrders

Now that we want to loop around all the elements in a node, the way in which the elements are accessed must be altered slightly. The get(cn)ElementAt() method exists only for class node(cn). Therefore, even though there is only one instance of node SalesOrders in the context, we must specify the node name to be able to access the elements by their index.

---

17 This assumes that the node has a selection cardinality of <something>..n.

Before obtaining a reference to the node element, we are first testing to see if that element has been selected by the user.

6.9.3 Creating a new node element

Important: Creating a new element in a node is a three-stage process!

Create a new element object using the method `create{cn}Element` available either directly from `wdContext` or from `wdContext.node{cn}`.

Call the various mutator methods to populate the element instance with appropriate values.

Add the element to the node's element collection. This can be achieved by calling either one of `{cn}`'s `addElement()` methods, or one of its `bind()` methods.[18]

Caveat confector: You must ensure that whenever you manipulate an element collection, you do not violate the node's cardinality constraint! You will get runtime exceptions in the context if you attempt either of the following:

▶ Deleting element 0 from a node of cardinality `1..<something>`

▶ Adding a second element to a node of cardinality `<something>..1`

Important: The creation of a new node element does not cause that element to be added to the node's element collection!

The reason for this is that you may wish to maintain the elements in some kind of sort order. Therefore, it would be very inconvenient to have a newly created node appended automatically to the end of an element collection.

Whether maintaining a sorted element collection or not, each new element must be added manually. In generic terms, the coding to add the element created above is as follows:

▶ `wdContext.node{cn}.addElement(newNodeElement);`
Append element to end of collection

---

18 See the class reference section for `I{cn}Node` and `IWDNode` for the difference between `addElement()` and `bind()`.

▶ `wdContext.node{cn}.addElement(idx, newNodeElement);`
  Insert element at position idx of collection

The following code sample will add two elements to the node `SalesOrder`
described above.

```
public void wdDoInit() {
  //@@begin wdDoInit()
  // Create two new element objects for node SalesOrders
  ISalesOrdersElement firstSoEl =
    wdContext.createSalesOrdersElement();
  ISalesOrdersElement secondSoEl =
    wdContext.createSalesOrdersElement();

  // Populate first element
  firstSoEl.setLongText("Printer supplies");
  firstSoEl.setSalesDate(new Date(System.currentTimeMillis()));
  firstSoEl.setSalesRep("Harry Hawk");
  firstSoEl.setOrderNo(100);

  // Populate second element
  secondSoEl.setLongText("Network cabling");
  secondSoEl.setSalesDate(new Date(System.currentTimeMillis()));
  secondSoEl.setSalesRep("Ned Seagoon");
  secondSoEl.setOrderNo(101);

  // Append elements to node collection
  wdContext.nodeSalesOrders().addElement(firstSoEl);
  wdContext.nodeSalesOrders().addElement(secondSoEl);
  //@@end
}
```

Listing 6.6 Adding New Elements to a Context Node

This coding example is simplistic in the sense that hard-coded values are
being added to the context attributes. A more typical situation is one in
which the data to be added to the context is obtained from a model
object.

To make this situation more realistic, the context should be extended to
show how a child node under `SalesOrders` would behave.

Node `SalesOrders` has now had a child value node added of cardinality
`0..n` called `LineItems`. This node, in turn, has four child attributes,
`ItemNo`, `Description`, `Quantity`, and `Price`. `ItemNo` is an `integer`,
`Description` is a `string`, and `Quantity` and `Price` are both `decimal`.

The one critical node property that has not been mentioned here is `singleton`. If we just accept the default value of `true`, this will affect both how the data in the node is managed and which UI elements can be used to display its contents. Refer back to Figure 6.3 to see how changing the singleton flag affects the relationship between a child node and its parent node.

In this example, we will deal with `LineItems` first as a singleton node, and then as a non-singleton node.

Figure 6.13 Context Value Node with Child Node

6.9.4 Treating node LineItems as a singleton node

Declaring child node {chn} to be a singleton means that with respect to its parent node {cn}, you will only ever have one instance of {chn}. This has two immediate consequences:

▶ The node `LineItems` *must* have a supply function.

▶ The `SalesOrders` node *cannot* be displayed using a tree UI element (see Section 7.3).

The coding example given below shows the processing required to add two elements to the `SalesOrders` node, and then four elements to the `LineItems` node that vary depending on which element in `SalesOrders` is selected. Coding is required in four different methods:

▶ **wdDoInit( )**
  Called once at controller initialization time

▶ **supplyLineItems( )**
  Called by `wdDoInit()`

▶ **doNewSalesOrder( )**
  Utility method

▶ **doNewLineItem( )**
  Utility method

Again, the example is simplistic since, in reality, you would probably not hard code the attribute values into the program.

Also observe that the class and package names of the input parameters to `supplyLineItems()` and the two utility methods have been generalized.

```
public void wdDoInit() {
  //@@begin wdDoInit()
  // Create two new SalesOrders elements
  ISalesOrdersElement firstSoEl  =
    wdContext.createSalesOrdersElement();
  ISalesOrdersElement secondSoEl =
    wdContext.createSalesOrdersElement();

  // Populate SalesOrders elements
  wdContext.nodeSalesOrders().addElement(
    doNewSalesOrder(firstSoEl, 100,
                    "Printer supplies",
                    new Date(System.currentTimeMillis()),
                    "Harry Hawk"));
  wdContext.nodeSalesOrders().addElement(
    doNewSalesOrder(secondSoEl, 101,
                    "Network Cabling",
                    new Date(System.currentTimeMillis()),
                    "Ned Seagoon"));

  //@@end
}


public void supplyLineItems(IPrivate{n_c}.ILineItemsNode node,
                            IPrivate{n_c}.ISalesOrdersElement
                            parentElement) {
  //@@begin supplyLineItems(IWDNode,IWDNodeElement)
  // Create four new LineItems elements
  ILineItemsElement lineEl1 = node.createLineItemsElement();
  ILineItemsElement lineEl2 = node.createLineItemsElement();
  ILineItemsElement lineEl3 = node.createLineItemsElement();
  ILineItemsElement lineEl4 = node.createLineItemsElement();

  // Populate the new line item elements based on the order
  // number found in the parent element
  switch(parentElement.getOrderNo()) {
    case 100:
      node.addElement(doNewLineItem(lineEl1, 10,
                                    "Cyan cartridge",
                                    new BigDecimal(90.12),
```

```
                                            new BigDecimal(10)));
        node.addElement(doNewLineItem(lineEl2, 20,
                                            "Magenta cartridge",
                                            new BigDecimal(90.12),
                                            new BigDecimal(10)));
        node.addElement(doNewLineItem(lineEl3, 30,
                                            "Yellow cartridge",
                                            new BigDecimal(90.12),
                                            new BigDecimal(10)));
        node.addElement(doNewLineItem(lineEl4, 40,
                                            "Black cartridge",
                                            new BigDecimal(35.89),
                                            new BigDecimal(10)));
        break;
      case 101:
        node.addElement(doNewLineItem(lineEl1, 10,
                                            "100m reel CAT 5",
                                            new BigDecimal(35.03),
                                            new BigDecimal(4)));
        node.addElement(doNewLineItem(lineEl2, 20,
                                            "RJ45 connectors (50)",
                                            new BigDecimal(5.25),
                                            new BigDecimal(5)));
        node.addElement(doNewLineItem(lineEl3, 30,
                                            "Crimp tool",
                                            new BigDecimal(85.37),
                                            new BigDecimal(1)));
        node.addElement(doNewLineItem(lineEl4, 40,
                                            "40 bay patch panel",
                                            new BigDecimal(130.45),
                                            new BigDecimal(2)));
        break;
      default:
    }
    //@@end
}

public {pkg1}.{pkg2}…{pkgn}.wdp.IPublic{nc}.ISalesOrdersElement
      doNewSalesOrder({pkg1}.{pkg2}…{pkgn}.wdp.IPublic{nc}.
                        ISalesOrdersElement salesOrder,
                        int orderNo,
                        String description,
                        java.sql.Date date,
                        String salesRep ) {
  //@@begin doNewSalesOrder()
  salesOrder.setOrderNo(orderNo);
```

```
salesOrder.setLongText(description);
salesOrder.setSalesDate(date);
salesOrder.setSalesRep(salesRep);

return salesOrder;
//@@end
}

public {pkg₁}.{pkg₂}…{pkgₙ}.wdp.IPublic{nc}.ILineItemsElement
        doNewLineItem({pkg₁}.{pkg₂}…{pkgₙ}.wdp.IPublic{nc}.
                        ILineItemsElement lineItem,
                        int itemNo,
                        String Description,
                        java.math.BigDecimal Price,
                        java.math.BigDecimal Qty) {
    //@@begin doNewLineItem()
    lineItem.setItemNo(itemNo);
    lineItem.setDescription(Description);
    lineItem.setPrice(Price);
    lineItem.setQuantity(Qty);

    return lineItem;
    //@@end
}
```

Listing 6.7 Populating the Singleton Node LineItems Using a Supply Function

Now that the node LineItems has a supply function defined (method supplyLineItems()), the WDF will call it automatically every time the contents are considered invalid. This will most frequently happen when the lead selection in the parent node SalesOrders changes; however, there are other situations that could cause LineItems's supply function to be called; for instance, if the method nodeLineItems.size() is called or the node is forcibly invalidated by calling nodeLineItems.invalidate().

6.9.5 Treating node LineItems as a non-singleton node

Declaring child node {chn} to be a non-singleton means that every element in parent node {cn} will have its own instance of {chn}. This has two general consequences:

▶ The memory requirements can grow rapidly if there are several levels of non-singleton nodes in a hierarchy.

▶ Data must be supplied as a hierarchy of *non-singleton* nodes in order to display it using a tree UI element.

Now that LineItems is a non-singleton node, it does not require a supply function because a one-off node population routine can be called at the start of the controller's processing. This approach stands in direct contrast to the singleton case, in which the contents of LineItems must be replaced each time the lead selection of the parent node changes.

The coding example given above has been modified to account for node LineItems being a non-singleton node. Notice that all the work to populate the context now takes place in wdDoInit(). It is not necessary for LineItems to have a supply function (although there is no reason why a non-singleton node cannot have one).

Methods doNewSalesOrder() and doNewLineItem() are unchanged.

```
public void wdDoInit() {
  //@@begin wdDoInit()
  // Create two new element objects for node SalesOrders
  ISalesOrdersElement firstSoEl =
    wdContext.createSalesOrdersElement();
  ISalesOrdersElement secondSoEl =
    wdContext.createSalesOrdersElement();

  // Populate first SalesOrders element and add it to the
  // SalesOrders node
  wdContext.nodeSalesOrders().addElement(
    doNewSalesOrder(firstSoEl,100,"Printer supplies",
                    new Date(System.currentTimeMillis()),
                    "Harry Hawk"));

  // Create non-singleton child instance of LineItems
  // Notice that the nodeLineItems() method belongs to the
  // parent element not the parent node.  This is possible
  // only for non-singleton nodes.
  ILineItemsNode firstLiNode = firstSoEl.nodeLineItems();

  ILineItemsElement solLineEl1 =
    firstLiNode.createLineItemsElement();
  ILineItemsElement solLineEl2 =
    firstLiNode.createLineItemsElement();
  ILineItemsElement solLineEl3 =
    firstLiNode.createLineItemsElement();
  ILineItemsElement solLineEl4 =
    firstLiNode.createLineItemsElement();

  firstLiNode.addElement(doNewLineItem(solLineEl1, 10,
                                       "Cyan cartridge",
```

```
                                        new BigDecimal(90.12),
                                        new BigDecimal(10)));
firstLiNode.addElement(doNewLineItem(so1LineEl2, 20,
                                        "Magenta cartridge",
                                        new BigDecimal(90.12),
                                        new BigDecimal(10)));
firstLiNode.addElement(doNewLineItem(so1LineEl3, 30,
                                        "Yellow cartridge",
                                        new BigDecimal(90.12),
                                        new BigDecimal(10)));
firstLiNode.addElement(doNewLineItem(so1LineEl4, 40,
                                        "Black cartridge",
                                        new BigDecimal(35.89),
                                        new BigDecimal(10)));

// Populate second SalesOrders element and add it to the
// SalesOrders node
wdContext.nodeSalesOrders().addElement(
  doNewSalesOrder(secondSoEl,101,"Network Cabling",
                  new Date(System.currentTimeMillis()),
                  "Ned Seagoon"));

// Create non-singleton child instance of LineItems
ILineItemsNode secondLiNode = secondSoEl.nodeLineItems();
ILineItemsElement so2LineEl1 =
  secondLiNode.createLineItemsElement();
ILineItemsElement so2LineEl2 =
  secondLiNode.createLineItemsElement();
ILineItemsElement so2LineEl3 =
  secondLiNode.createLineItemsElement();
ILineItemsElement so2LineEl4 =
  secondLiNode.createLineItemsElement();

secondLiNode.addElement(doNewLineItem(so2LineEl1, 10,
                                        "100m reel CAT 5",
                                        new BigDecimal(35.03),
                                        new BigDecimal(4)));
secondLiNode.addElement(doNewLineItem(so2LineEl2, 20,
                                        "RJ45 connectors (50)",
                                        new BigDecimal(5.25),
                                        new BigDecimal(5)));
secondLiNode.addElement(doNewLineItem(so2LineEl3, 30,
                                        "Crimp tool",
                                        new BigDecimal(85.37),
                                        new BigDecimal(1)));
secondLiNode.addElement(doNewLineItem(so2LineEl4, 40,
                                        "40 bay patch panel",
```

```
                                            new BigDecimal(130.45),
                                            new BigDecimal(2)));
    //@@end
}
```

Listing 6.8 Populating the Non-singleton Node LineItems

There are several things to notice about the above code sample:

▶ The coding to create the `SalesOrders` elements is unchanged.

▶ The elements `firstSoEl` and `secondSoEl` must be added to the `Sales-Orders` node collection before any attempt is made to create the respective `LineItems` child node instances. If you try to create a non-singleton child node before the parent element has been added to its node collection, you will get a runtime exception in the context.

▶ The method call to `nodeLineItems()` belongs to the parent *element*, not the parent *node*. This is possible only for non-singleton nodes.

Important:

1. A singleton child node has a one-to-one relationship with its parent *node*, irrespective of the number of elements contained in the parent node. When the lead selection of the parent node changes, all child nodes are flagged as dirty. The supply functions will be called automatically when the child nodes are accessed.[19] The only methods available to create a new instance of a singleton child node belong to the classes `wdContext` and `node{cn}`.

2. A non-singleton child node has a one-to-one relationship with its parent *element*. Therefore, if node `{cn}` contains *n* elements and has a non-singleton child node `{chn}`, there will be *n* separate instances of `{chn}`. In addition to the two methods available for creating a singleton node, a non-singleton node can also be created directly from the parent *element* by calling `wdContext.current{cn}Element.node{chn}()`.

Caveat confector: Regardless of its position in the hierarchy, every node in the context can be accessed directly by calling `wdContext.node{cn}()`. What must be clearly understood is that when the accessor method of an arbitrary node is called, the node instance returned is always the one at the lead selection of each successive parent node.

---

19 Remember that the WDF uses the concept of lazy data access.

If however, you want to access a child node that does not lie on the lead selection path, then two approaches could be taken:

1. For a hierarchy of singleton nodes, start at the root node and perform a step-wise parent-to-child traversal down the hierarchy, setting the lead selection of each node before traversing to the next child.

2. For a hierarchy of non-singleton nodes, the specific child node can be accessed by first obtaining the parent element of the non-singleton node, and then via the instance of the parent *element*, calling the `node(chn)()` method.

6.10 Dynamic context manipulation

There are certain circumstances under which you will need to create context nodes at runtime; such nodes are known as "dynamically defined" nodes, as opposed to the "statically defined" nodes discussed above.[20]

In the previous example, we looked at how the typed context interface is used. Now, we will look at the generic or untyped context interface that must be used when context nodes and attributes are created at runtime. As you will appreciate by now, there is a significant coding convenience provided by declaring your nodes and attributes at design time, since the node and attribute names are built into the generated Java class and method names.

6.10.1 Accessing the context through the generic API

If a node is created at design time with the `typedAccessRequired` property set to `false`, or a node is created dynamically at runtime, there will be no typed interface available. In such cases, the generic context API must be used.

To access a context node generically, you need to know the following:

▶ The name of the node

▶ The index of the element in the parent node

Using the context shown in Figure 6.12, you can access the `SalesOrder` node using the following code:

---

20 The definition of a "statically defined" node assumes that you have left the `typedAccesssRequired` node property set to its default value of `true`.

```
// Get the child node SalesOrders via the generic context API
IWDNode salesOrderNode = wdContext.getChildNode("SalesOrders",0);
```

Listing 6.9 Accessing a Context Node via the Generic Context API

Notice that the node object returned by method `getChildNode()` is of the generic class `IWDNode`.

Since we know that the `SalesOrders` node is an independent node, it must therefore be a singleton. This means that it will be related to element zero in the parent node (i.e., the context root, which only ever has one element!). Hence, the `int` parameter in this case *must be* zero.

If we needed to access a dependent node further down the context hierarchy, then we would first have to ensure that the parent node has been correctly populated; only then would we be able to access the correct child node instance.

We can access the node's element collection in exactly the same way that we did in Listing 6.5. However, the node elements contained within this `IWDNode` node will only ever be of the generic class `IWDNodeElement`; i.e., there will be no typed access to any of the element's attributes. Therefore, we must access the node attributes generically. (The next coding fragment repeats the previous coding and then adds some new statements.)

To access a node attribute held in an `IWDNodeElement` object, you must know the attribute's:

▶ Name

▶ Data type

```
// Get the child node SalesOrders via the generic context API
  IWDNode salesOrderNode =
    wdContext.getChildNode("SalesOrders",0);

// Get the current element of child node SalesOrders
  IWDNodeElement thisSalesOrderEl =
    salesOrderNode.getCurrentElement();

// Get the value of the SalesRep attribute
// Since we know that the SalesRep attribute is of type String,
// we can use method getAttributeAsText(), rather than the more
// generic getAttributeValue() which just returns an Object
```

```
String salesRep =
  thisSalesOrderEl.getAttributeAsText("SalesRep");
```

Listing 6.10 Accessing a Context Node via the Generic Context API

If you don't know the data type of a particular attribute, you can interrogate the node info object associated with the context node. This holds all the metadata for the node, and can supply you with the names and data types of all attributes in the node. This technique is used when context nodes need to be dynamically replicated from one context to another. See Listing 6.19 for more details.

The following example shows the coding needed to access the LineItems node shown in Figure 6.13. Since the child node LineItems could be either a singleton or a non-singleton with respect to its parent node SalesOrders, there are two possible approaches to accessing this child node.

Accessing the singleton node LineItems with the generic context API

If the child node LineItems is a singleton with respect to its parent node SalesOrders, the coding to access LineItems is as follows:

```
import java.sql.Date;

// Get the child node SalesOrders via the generic context API
  IWDNode soNode = wdContext.getChildNode("SalesOrders",0);

// Set the lead selection of node SalesOrders
  soNode.setLeadSelection(<some_element_number>);
  IWDNodeElement thisSoEl = soNode.getCurrentElement();

// Get the attribute's values of the current SalesOrders
  String longText = thisSoEl.getAttributeAsText("LongText");
  int OrderNo =
    ((Integer)thisSoEl.getAttributeValue("LongText")).intValue();
  String salesRep = thisSoEl.getAttributeAsText("SalesRep");
  Date salesDate =
    (Date)thisSoEl.getAttributeValue("SalesDate");

// Get the instance of node LineItems that belongs to this
// SalesOrders element
// The following call to getChildNode() will automatically
// trigger the execution of the node's supply function
  IWDNode liNode =
```

```
soNode.getChildNode("LineItems",soNode.getLeadSelection());

// Loop around all the elements in node LineItems
  for (int i=0; i<liNode.size(); i++) {
    // Get the current LineItems element
    IWDNodeElement liEl = liNode.getElementAt(i);

    // Do something useful with the current LineItems element
  }
```

Listing 6.11 Accessing a Singleton Context Node via the Generic Context API

Notice the following points:

▶ Because node `LineItems` is a singleton with respect to its parent node `SalesOrders`, we must first position the lead selection within node `SalesOrders` before we can obtain the correct element. Hence the call first to method `soNode.setLeadSelection()` followed by the call to method `soNode.getCurrentElement()`.

Caveat confector: Don't think you can sidestep these two statements by simply calling `soNode.getElementAt(i)`.

Method `IWDNode.getElementAt()` does not alter a node's lead selection. Therefore, when you call `soNode.getChildNode("LineItems", soNode.getLeadSelection)`, the child node you get back will be the one related to the element at the lead selection of node `soNode`, which is not necessarily the element returned by `soNode.getElementAt(i)`.

▶ As soon as the lead selection of node `SalesOrders` is changed, the WDF flags any of its singleton child nodes as being dirty. This flag will later trigger the automatic execution of the child node supply functions.

▶ All `string` attributes can be retrieved from the current element using method `getAttributeAsText()`. Attributes of other data types should be retrieved with `getAttributeValue()` and then cast to the appropriate type.

▶ Now that the lead selection of node `SalesOrders` has been positioned, the correct instance of node `LineItems` can be obtained by calling `soNode.getChildNode()`.

Important: If the second parameter to this method is not set to the same value as the node's lead selection, a runtime exception will occur; hence, the use of `soNode.getLeadSelection()` to ensure that this value is always correct.

▶ The call to `getChildNode()` will automatically trigger the WDF to run the supply function[21] for node `LineItems` because its contents have previously been flagged as dirty.

Accessing the non-singleton node LineItems with the generic context API

If the child node `LineItems` is a non-singleton with respect to its parent node `SalesOrders`, the coding to access `LineItems` is slightly different from that shown in Listing 6.11 above. The differences are shown in bold.

```
import java.sql.Date;

// Get the child node SalesOrders via the generic context API
  IWDNode soNode = wdContext.getChildNode("SalesOrders",0);

// Set which element we want to access in node SalesOrders
  int i = <some_element_number>;

// Get the correct parent element of node SalesOrders
// Since the child node LineItems is now a non-singleton,
// we do not need to worry about repositioning the lead
// selection of node SalesOrders
  IWDNodeElement thisSoEl = soNode.getElementAt(i);

// Get the attribute values of the current SalesOrders
  String longText = thisSoEl.getAttributeAsText("LongText");
  int OrderNo =
    ((Integer)thisSoEl.getAttributeValue("LongText")).intValue();
  String salesRep = thisSoEl.getAttributeAsText("SalesRep");
  Date salesDate =
    (Date)thisSoEl.getAttributeValue("SalesDate");

// Get the instance of node LineItems that belongs to
// the SalesOrders element at index i
  IWDNode liNode = soNode.getChildNode("LineItems",i);
```

---

21 We are assuming, of course, that you have actually written a supply function!

```
// Loop around all the elements in node LineItems
  for (int j=0; j<liNode.size(); j++) {
    // Get the current LineItems element
    IWDNodeElement liEl = liNode.getElementAt(j);

    // Do something useful with the current LineItems element
  }
```

Listing 6.12 Accessing a Non-singleton Context Node via the Generic Context API

Notice the differences between accessing a singleton and a non-singleton node:

▶ Since node `LineItems` is now a non-singleton with respect to its parent node `SalesOrders`, there will be multiple distinct instances of node `LineItems` for each element within node `SalesOrders`. Therefore, it is unnecessary to reposition the lead selection of node `SalesOrders` before attempting to access the child node. In this situation, we can access the element directly by calling `getElementAt()`.

▶ The method `getChildNode()` can now be called with any index value we like because the node instance being returned is a non-singleton.

Apart from the two statements in bold, the remaining code is identical.

6.10.2 Dynamic addition of an unmapped context node

First, we will look at how to create context value nodes and attributes at runtime, and then how to access them. Since we are now dealing with dynamically defined nodes, the convenient typed accessor and mutator methods used in the previous examples will not be available. Instead, we will have to use the generic context interface.

The coding example that now follows will dynamically build the context value node and attributes shown in Figure 6.12, and then add exactly the same data as seen in the previous example.

Important: This code will typically be part of a custom controller such as the component controller, since the value node being created is unmapped. Unmapped nodes in custom controllers should be considered the data source for the mapped nodes found in view controllers.

Before the coding details are discussed though...

Caveat confector:

1. It's always simpler to work with context nodes and attributes that have had a typed interface created at design time. Therefore, always ask yourself this question: "Is the extra complexity of dynamic node creation really necessary?" Are you sure that the node cannot be created at design time—even in a generic manner?

   If the answer is that you simply cannot implement the required functionality any other way, then fine; go ahead and create your nodes dynamically.

   If, however, you're just copying the coding out of a book because you think it will make you look smart, don't do it!

   Every line of code you write should contribute towards the overall simplicity of the application, not its complexity.

2. Notice that the coding to create a context node will typically exist in the `wdDoInit()` method of the custom controller. This is because the decision to create dynamic nodes is usually made at controller initialization time, and thereafter the controller works with the created context structure.[23]

Now for the coding:

```
public void wdDoInit() {
  //@@begin wdDoInit()
  // Create the metadata for the new SalesOrders value node
  // Get the metadata object for the context root node
  IWDNodeInfo rootNodeInfo = wdContext.getNodeInfo();

  // Create a metadata object to describe a new independent value
  // node called "SalesOrders"
  IWDNodeInfo salesOrdersInfo =
    rootNodeInfo.addChild(
                "SalesOrders",    // Name
                null,             // Structure reference
                true,             // Is singleton?
                false, true,      // Cardinality
                false, false,     // Selection cardinality
                true,             // Initialize lead selection?
                null,             // Datatype
```

---

22 This recommendation is not a hard and fast rule, but it will make your coding simpler if you follow it.

```
                    null,           // Supplier function
                    null);          // Disposer function

      // Add the attribute metadata to the new node info object
      salesOrdersInfo.
        addAttribute("OrderNo", "ddic:com.sap.dictionary.integer");
      salesOrdersInfo.
        addAttribute("LongText", "ddic:com.sap.dictionary.string");
      salesOrdersInfo.
        addAttribute("SalesDate", "ddic:com.sap.dictionary.date");
      salesOrdersInfo.
        addAttribute("SalesRep", "ddic:com.sap.dictionary.string");

      // Create a new context node using the metadata we just created
      IWDNode soNode = wdContext.getChildNode("SalesOrders",0);

      // Create two new elements in node SalesOrders
      IWDNodeElement soEl1 = soNode.createElement();
      IWDNodeElement soEl2 = soNode.createElement();

      // Populate the two new elements
      soEl1.setAttributeValue("OrderNo",new Integer(100));
      soEl1.setAttributeValue("LongText","Printer supplies");
      soEl1.setAttributeValue("SalesDate",
        new Date(System.currentTimeMillis()));
      soEl1.setAttributeValue("SalesRep","Harry Hawk");

      soEl2.setAttributeValue("OrderNo",new Integer(101));
      soEl2.setAttributeValue("LongText","Network cabling");
      soEl2.setAttributeValue("SalesDate",
        new Date(System.currentTimeMillis()));
      soEl2.setAttributeValue("SalesRep","Ned Seagoon");

      // Add elements to the node collection
      soNode.addElement(soEl1);
      soNode.addElement(soEl2);
      //@@end
}
```

Listing 6.13 Creating and Populating the Unmapped node SalesOrders in the Component Controller

The coding performs the following processing steps:

▶ Before a context node can be created, the metadata that describes that node must first be created. This information is held in IWDNodeInfo objects. To create such an object, you must call the `addChild()` method of the parent node info object. In this case, the context is completely empty; therefore, our new `SalesOrders` node will be an immediate child of the context root node. This makes it an independent node.

Get a reference to the context root node's metadata object using `wdContext.getNodeInfo()`.

▶ Using the context root node as a parent, add metadata information to describe the new node `SalesOrders`. The parameters to the `addChild()` method are used as follows:

  ▶ The first parameter is the name of the new node.

  ▶ The second is a reference to a Java Dictionary structure from which structural metadata information can be inherited if required.

  ▶ The third parameter is a boolean that determines whether the new node is a singleton or not. In our case, we are creating an independent node; therefore, it must be a singleton.[23]

  ▶ The fourth and fifth parameters are boolean values that together determine the node's cardinality.

  ▶ The sixth and seventh parameters are boolean values that together determine the node's selection cardinality.

  ▶ The eighth parameter is a reference to a non-dictionary structured data type.

  ▶ The ninth and tenth parameters are the names of supplier and disposer functions respectively.

▶ Once the metadata for the node has been created, it is now possible to add the metadata describing the node's attributes; this is done using the `addAttribute()` method.

Important: Notice the syntax used to define the data type of the new attributes. If you wish to use data types defined in the Web Dynpro dictionary, you must precede the class name with the string `ddic:`. If, however, you want to use a standard Java class, you must preface the class name with the string `java:`. Failure to use these identifying prefixes will cause a runtime error.

---

23 Try setting this parameter to `false`, and see what happens!

Caveat confector:

A UI element can be bound only to a context attribute whose data type comes from the Web Dynpro dictionary.

Creating a context attribute using the data type `java:java.lang.String` is perfectly okay, but don't expect to be able to bind a UI element to it!

Instead, you must use `ddic:com.sap.dictionary.string`.

Once the `addAttribute()` method has been called for each new attribute, we are ready to create an actual node object in which runtime data can be stored. We are now switching from the manipulation of metadata, to the manipulation of actual data.[24]

▶ Since this node has been created dynamically, the method `wdContext.nodeSalesOrders()` used in the previous examples cannot be called—it doesn't even exist! Therefore, we must use the generic context API for node creation.

The method `{cn}.getChildNode(String, int)` will return an instance of the named child node belonging to the element index. In this case, the parent node is the context root, so `{cn} == wdContext`. Also, the context root node has one and only one element. Therefore, the element number passed to the `getChildNode()` method must be zero (or `IWDNode.LEAD_SELECTION`).

▶ Now that we have a reference to the new node, we can create an element for it. However, we can operate only with the generic, untyped element class of `IWDNodeElement`, so we must call `createElement()`.

▶ A node element of type `IWDNodeElement` will have no specific accessor or mutator methods for the declared attributes, therefore, we must set the attribute values using the generic method `setAttributeValue()`, passing in the name of the attribute and the required value as an object.

▶ Now the elements can be added to the node collection in exactly the same way as before.

As you can see, declaring nodes at design time (with the `typedAccessRequired` property set to `true`) makes the coding much easier because you don't have to use the generic context interface.

---

24 Always maintain a clear distinction between the manipulation of context metadata and actual data.

The coding principles used here to create an independent node can be extended to create the dependent child node `LineItems`. The difference here would be that you must obtain a reference to the metadata of the parent node `SalesOrders` in order to create the metadata for the new node. Don't call `wdContext.addChild()` again, and expect the resulting metadata to have node `SalesOrders` as its parent!

In the case of dynamically created dependent nodes, you will need to pay close attention when setting the value of the singleton flag. If you create a singleton node dynamically, you will also need to specify the name of a supply function. In this situation, you'll have to write a single, generic supply function that can populate all dynamically created context nodes. This means that you must know *a priori* which nodes are likely to be created at runtime, or at least create context nodes in such a way that their content types can be generically identified via their names. This is a much more dynamic approach to context manipulation and, consequently, the situations in which it will be required are more complex. Therefore, it will not be dealt with in any greater detail in this book.

6.10.3 Dynamic addition of a mapped context node

As was explained in Section 6.8, a mapped node does not maintain its own element collection; rather it contains a reference to the element collection of the mapping origin node.

> **Important:** One of the main principles of good Web Dynpro design is that the functional boundaries that exist between a view controller and a custom controller should not be allowed to blur. Maintaining this distinction is going to become even more important now that we're dealing with dynamic context node creation.

The coding example in the previous section dealt with how to create an unmapped context value node. Technically, there is no reason why such code could not be placed in a view controller. Generally speaking, however, a view controller should be designed in such a way that it is concerned only with the *presentation* of business information. The *processing* of business information should be handled in custom controllers. It follows, therefore, that if the context nodes in a view controller contain business information, they will probably be mapped nodes.[25]

Remember, this is a principle of good Web Dynpro design, not a rule!

In this coding example, we will be creating a mapped node dynamically. The usual reason for this type of processing in a view controller is that we wish to display the information in the mapping origin node. Since the mapping origin node has been created dynamically, it follows that any mapping reference nodes must also be created dynamically.

In order to display this information, a chain of references must first be established. Starting from an individual UI element and working back to the mapping origin node, the following chain of references usually exists:[26]

▶ A UI element in a view controller may only be bound to a context node or attribute in its own context.

▶ A view controller's context will often contain nodes that are mapped to a custom controller's context.

▶ Business data is typically derived by a custom controller from a model object, and stored in its local context.

The coding that created the unmapped node in the previous example populates the value node that will act as the mapping origin in step three above. We will now look at the coding to produce the mapped node required in step two. The coding to implement step one is discussed in Chapter 8.

The following functionality is simplistic in the sense that the view controller will examine the context of its component controller and replicate only the independent nodes. Replicating an entire context node hierarchy is possible, but to treat this task in a completely generic manner requires coding that is beyond the scope of this introductory discussion.[27]

```
public void wdDoInit() {
  //@@begin wdDoInit()
  // Get the metadata object for the context root node
  IWDNodeInfo rootNodeInfo = wdContext.getNodeInfo();

  // Get a reference to the root node of the component controller
  IWDNodeInfo compCtx =
    wdComponentAPI.getContext().getRootNodeInfo();
```

25 View controllers will need to maintain their own unmapped nodes to handle such information as user interaction tracking, validation error handling, and drop-down list contents (to name but a few).

26 Again, this is a principle, not a rule!

27 The potential presence of recursive context nodes makes this task much more complex.

```
// Loop around all the independent nodes in the parent context
// replicating whatever is found
for (Iterator compCtxIt =
  compCtx.iterateChildren();compCtxIt.hasNext();) {
  replicateNodeInfo((IWDNodeInfo)compCtxIt.next());
}
//@@end
}
```

Listing 6.14 Generic Creation of Mapped Nodes in a View Controller

In the `wdDoInit()` method of the view controller, the following function-ality takes place:

▶ A reference is obtained to the metadata of the context root node.

▶ By means of a "Required Controllers" declaration,[28] a reference can also be obtained to the metadata of the context root node of the component controller. Within the scope of a Web Dynpro component, the component controller is considered hierarchically superior to all other controllers.

▶ For each independent node in the component controller's context, call the method `replicateNodeInfo()`.

The next coding section shows the implementation of method `repli-cateNodeInfo()`. Just to keep you on your toes, though, the mapping ori-gin of a mapped context node can be defined in three different ways! While the differences may appear pedantic, it will greatly help your understanding of the context if you can appreciate the differences between these techniques. They are:

▶ Specify the mapping origin as a parameter to `IWDNodeInfo.addMapped-Child()`.

▶ The mapping origin parameter is left null in the call to `IWDNode-Info.addMappedChild()`. The required value is now set by calling the `setMapping(IWDNodeInfo, boolean)` method.

▶ The mapping origin parameter is left null in the call to `IWDNode-Info.addMappedChild()`. The required value is now set by calling the `setMapping(IWDContext, String, boolean)` method.

Of these three options, SAP recommends option 2.

---

28 Performed in the **Properties** tab of the view controller.

Important: Method `setMapping()` should be called only once! Do not attempt to alter a node's mapping origin once the mapping relationship has been traversed!

Since the differences relate to the call to method `addMappedChild()` and the statements that immediately follow, only those statements will be listed in the following textboxes. Once these differences have been described, the entire `replicateNodeInfo()` method will be shown using option 2.

The method `IWDNodeInfo.addMappedChild()` is similar to the `IWDNodeInfo.addChild()` method seen in the previous example, but with several important differences. By definition, a mapped node will inherit certain attributes from its mapping origin node, the most obvious of which is the cardinality. Since a mapped node does not maintain its own element collection (it simply points to the element collection of the mapping origin node), its cardinality value will always be equal to the cardinality of the mapping origin node.

The parameters to `IWDNodeInfo.addMappedChild()` are as follows:

▶ The first parameter is the name of the mapped node. This does not need to be the same as the name of the mapping origin node, but for the sake of simplicity, we will use the name of the mapping origin node.

▶ The second parameter is the class of the mapping origin node (now redundant).

▶ The third parameter is a boolean that determines whether the mapped node is a singleton or not. Since we are creating an independent node, this parameter must be set to `true`.

▶ The fourth and fifth parameters are boolean values that control the selection cardinality. For simplicity, we will adopt the same values as the mapping origin node.

▶ The sixth parameter would specify the path name of the mapping origin node. Without this value, the mapping reference is incomplete. The various options for mapped node creation lie in whether you specify a value here or not. We will look at both situations.

▶ The seventh parameter is a boolean that controls whether the mapping origin's list of selected elements is mapped or not.

▶ The eighth parameter is a boolean that controls whether the lead selection is initialized or not.

Technique 1

```
public void replicateNodeInfo(IWDNodeInfo mappingOrigin) {
  //@@begin replicateNodeInfo()
<snip>

  // Create a new node here in the local context based on the
  // values of the mapping reference node
  IWDNodeInfo childNodeInfo =
    wdContext.
      getNodeInfo().
        addMappedChild(mappingOrigin.getName(),
        mappingOrigin.getClass(),
        true,   // Node must be a singleton because it's
                // independent
        mappingOrigin.isMandatorySelection(),
        mappingOrigin.isMultipleSelection(),
        mappingOrigin.getPathDescription(),
        false, // Do not map selection of original node
        true); // Initialize lead selection

<snip>
```

Listing 6.15 Specifying the Mapping Origin as a Parameter to addMappedChild()

Here, all the metadata required to describe the new mapped node is created in a single call to method `addMappedChild()`. Notice the parameter in bold; this is the value required to define the path name to the mapping origin node.

Technique 2

```
public void replicateNodeInfo(
  com.sap.tc.webdynpro.progmodel.api.IWDNodeInfo mappingOrigin) {
  //@@begin replicateNodeInfo()
<snip>

  // Create a new node here in the local context based on the
  // values of the mapping reference node
  IWDNodeInfo childNodeInfo =
    wdContext.
      getNodeInfo().
        addMappedChild(mappingOrigin.getName(),
        mappingOrigin.getClass(),
        true,   // Node must be a singleton because it's
                // independent
```

```
    mappingOrigin.isMandatorySelection(),
    mappingOrigin.isMultipleSelection(),
null,   // Mapping origin must be supplied later
    false, // Do not map selection of original node
    true); // Initialize lead selection

// Map the current node to the corresponding node of the parent
// context
childNodeInfo.setMapping(mappingOrigin, false);
```

⟨snip⟩

Listing 6.16 Calling addMappedChild() with a Null Mapping Origin Parameter Then Adding it by Calling setMapping(): Option 1

Notice that the parameter in bold is now `null`. Since the parameter that defines the mapping origin has not been supplied, the mapped node is unusable until an additional call to `setMapping()` is made. The call to `setMapping()` is now performed by passing in the `IWDNodeInfo` object of the mapping origin node and a boolean to indicate whether the list of selected elements is to be mapped or not.

Technique 3

This technique will not be needed very often, but has been included for completeness.

```
public void replicateNodeInfo(
    com.sap.tc.webdynpro.progmodel.api.IWDNodeInfo mappingOrigin) {
    //@@begin replicateNodeInfo()
```
⟨snip⟩

```
// Create a new node here in the local context based on the
// values of the mapping reference node
IWDNodeInfo childNodeInfo =
    wdContext.
        getNodeInfo().
            addMappedChild(mappingOrigin.getName(),
            mappingOrigin.getClass(),
            true,   // Node must be singleton because its independent
            mappingOrigin.isMandatorySelection(),
            mappingOrigin.isMultipleSelection(),
null,   // Mapping origin must be supplied later
            false, // Do not map selection of original node
            true); // Initialize lead selection
```

```
// Get corrected path name in local context
String pathName = mappingOrigin.getPathDescription();
pathName = pathName.substring(
                pathName.indexOf('.',pathName.indexOf('.') + 1)
                + 1);

// Map the current node to the corresponding node of the parent
// context
childNodeInfo.setMapping(mappingOrigin.getContext(),
                        pathName,
                        false);
```

⟨snip⟩

Listing 6.17 Calling addMappedChild() with a Null Mapping Origin Parameter Then Adding it by Calling setMapping(): Option 2

The bold parameter to `addMappedChild()` is still `null`, which means that the created node info object is still unusable because its mapping origin has not yet been defined. To define the mapping origin, we will now call method `setMapping()` using its alternative signature. Here, we must pass three parameters to `setMapping()`:

▶ An `IWDContext` object identifying in which context the mapping origin lies

▶ The path name of the mapping origin within the aforementioned context, and

▶ A boolean to indicate whether the list of selected elements is to be mapped or not.

Now that the context of the mapping origin and the path name to the mapping origin node are specified separately, you have to be more careful about how the second `String` parameter is constructed. This goes some way to explaining the weird string manipulation that takes place on variable `pathName`.

Important: The example here is rather artificial since you would not really call `setMapping()` with this particular signature in this situation. Nonetheless, it is worth explaining because you will develop insight into the workings of the `IWDNodeInfo.getPathDescription()` method. (This particular signature of method `setMapping()` may be deprecated in future.)

Every node within a context can be uniquely described by a `String` identifier known as the path name. The path name is a dot delimited sequence of identifiers, starting from the component name and working down to the context node. This path name can be represented generically as follows:

`{c}.{n_ctl}.{cn}[.{chn}]`

The `[.{chn}]` syntax indicates that there may be zero or more child nodes occurring in the path name. The exact number will depend on the node's location down the context hierarchy.

For instance, if we assume that the context shown in Figure 6.13 is part of a custom controller called `ShowSalesOrdersCust`, in component `Process-SalesComp`, then the fully qualified path name to child node `LineItems`, under node `SalesOrders`, would be:

`ProcessSalesComp.ShowSalesOrdersCust.SalesOrders.LineItems`

Method `getPathDescription()` belongs to the interface `IWDNodeInfo`, so to obtain the value shown above, you should use the following code:

```
String pathName = wdContext.
                  nodeLineItems().
                    getNodeInfo().
                      getPathDescription();
```

Listing 6.18 Code Fragment to Get the Path Name of the Static Node LineItems

Now, in order to use the value held in `pathName`, you must understand two things:

▶ `getPathDescription()` returns a *fully* qualified value.

▶ The method to which `getPathDescription()`'s value is being passed may require only a subset of the path name.

In our case, the node acting as our mapping origin lies within the same component, therefore the first part of the path name string is redundant. If the component name is missing from the path name, then it is assumed to refer to a node in some local[29] controller.

Also, we are calling `setMapping(IWDContext, String, Boolean)`. The first parameter immediately tells you that the name of the controller has already been identified.[30] Therefore, it is unnecessary to specify the name of the controller in the path name to the mapping origin node.

---

29 By "local," we mean a controller within the same Web Dynpro component.

30 How do we know this? Because there is a one-to-one relationship between a context and a controller. A controller cannot exist without a context, and a context cannot exist without a controller. Therefore, if you know the context name, you know the controller name.

One further little twist! If the call to `{cn}.getNodeInfo().getPath-`
`Description()` is executed in the same component in which the `{cn}` is
found, then the component name will be suppressed automatically, and
the first character of the returned path name will be a dot. So the value of
variable `pathName` shown in Listing 6.18 will be:

`.ShowSalesOrdersCust.SalesOrders.LineItems`

We have already established that both the first and second parts of the
returned path name are surplus to requirements, and that the first part is
stripped off for us. This should now explain the otherwise obscure string
manipulation coding seen in Listing 6.17 above. Using the nested
`indexOf()` calls guarantees that both the component name and the
controller name will be removed.

Method replicateNodeInfo()

Now that the different methods of defining a node's mapping origin have
been clarified, all that remains is to show the coding for the entire
method `replicateNodeInfo()`.

```
public void replicateNodeInfo( IWDNodeInfo mappingOrigin) {
  //@@begin replicateNodeInfo()
  // Reset counters
  attrCount   = 0;
  binarySkip  = 0;
  complexSkip = 0;

  // Create a new node here in the local context based on the
  // values of the mapping reference node
  IWDNodeInfo childNodeInfo =
    wdContext.
      getNodeInfo().
        addMappedChild(mappingOrigin.getName(),
        mappingOrigin.getClass(),
        true,  // Node must be singleton because it's independent
        mappingOrigin.isMandatorySelection(),
        mappingOrigin.isMultipleSelection(),
        mappingOrigin.getPathDescription(),
        false, // Do not map selection of original node
        true); // Initialize lead selection
  // Iterate around the node's attributes
  for (Iterator attIt = mappingOrigin.iterateAttributes();
      attIt.hasNext();) {
    IWDAttributeInfo thisAttr = (IWDAttributeInfo)attIt.next();
    attrCount++;
```

```
// Binary attributes can be bound to the OfficeControl,
// FileUpload, and FileDownload UI elements.  Even then,
// there is no generic mechanism for determining whether the
// binary data is suitable for such a UI element.
// Therefore, this coding example makes no attempt to
// visualize binary attributes, and simply filters them out
if (thisAttr.getDataType().isSimpleType()) {
  ISimpleType st = thisAttr.getSimpleType();

  // Is the data type of this attribute binary?
  if (st.getLocalName().equalsIgnoreCase("binary"))
    // Without additional mimetype information, there is no
    // generic mechanism for determining the suitability of
    // the binary data.
    binarySkip++;
  else
    childNodeInfo.addMappedAttribute(thisAttr.getName(),
                                    thisAttr.getName());
}
// Complex data types cannot be visualized using Web Dynpro
// UI elements without further type-specific processing
else
  complexSkip++;
}
//@@end
}


//@@begin others
static int binarySkip;
static int complexSkip;
static int attrCount;
//@@end
```

Listing 6.19 Method replicateNodeInfo() Used for Generic Node Replication

Method `replicateNodeInfo()` works in the following way:

1. Some static counters are reset. The purpose of these will be explained later.

2. Create a mapped child node in the view controller's context.

3. Now add the metadata describing the node attributes. This is done by creating an iterator on the mapping origin node and then looping around each attribute, creating a corresponding attribute in the local context. There is, however, a complicating factor!

4. Since we are referencing data that already exists in another context, we must examine the data type of each attribute and decide whether it can be visualized or not.

Important:

▶ Only node attributes belonging to package `com.sap.dictionary` can be bound to UI elements.

▶ Within package `com.sap.dictionary`, `binary` data can be visualized only if it contains data suitable for the `OfficeControl` UI element, or is to be transferred using the `FileUpload` or `FileDownload` UI elements.

▶ Data types belonging to package `com.sap.dictionary` are known as simple types.

5. If the node attribute is of a simple data type, it is a potential candidate for visualization. If it is not, then increment the `complexSkip` counter since the data within this attribute cannot be visualized through a standard Web Dynpro UI element without further processing.

6. We will not attempt to determine the suitability of binary data for display. This basic implementation simply filters out such context attributes.

   For each node attribute that is of a simple data type, test to see if it is `binary`. If it is, then increment the `binarySkip` counter. If the attribute is of any other simple data type, then create the metadata for a new attribute in the local node using the details inherited from the corresponding attribute in the mapping origin.

7. The counter variables `attrCount`, `binarySkip`, and `complexSkip` have been made static deliberately. This is so that their values can be accessed from the static method `wdDoModifyView()`. It is within this method that you will need to write the code that creates the dynamic view layout for your dynamic context nodes.[31]

   If required, you can use these counter values to inform the user that there may be context attributes missing from the display because their data types prevent immediate visualization.[32]

---

31 See the section on Dynamic UI Generation.
32 It would be perfectly possible to write a view controller that visualizes complex data types; but such coding would need to examine the structure of the complex data type and react to whatever it finds. This is a highly generic form of coding and is therefore beyond the scope of this introductory text.

7 Coding principles in Web Dynpro

7.1 User-defined code

Within each controller, you are free to add any code you require as long as it lies between a pair of `//@@begin` and `//@@end` comment markers. These markers are created automatically by the code generator within the NWDS and their locations cannot be changed.

Any user-defined code placed outside these special comment markers will be lost during code regeneration.

7.2 Problems with binding UI elements to context nodes

When a view layout is being designed, every interactive UI element must have a context binding of some sort. There are certain runtime situations that may occur in which your input fields may appear in a disabled state or you get a runtime error in the context, such as `Node(<some_node_name>): no active node to map to` or `Mapping reference not found`.

All three situations are caused by the fact that, somewhere in the context, there is either a non-existent node element or a non-existent node.

▶ The simplest situation is the one in which a UI element, such as an input field, is bound to an attribute of a value node of cardinality `0..n`. The first part of the cardinality[1] immediately tells you that when your application first starts, this node will contain zero elements.

If, prior to displaying this screen, you forget to create element zero in the context node, then any input fields bound to attributes in this node will be disabled. This is simply because the node to which the UI element is bound contains no elements; therefore, there is no storage area to receive the user's input. Consequently, the input field will be disabled.

▶ The next situation is slightly more detailed. Imagine your view controller context has an unmapped value node of cardinality `0..n` called `SalesOrders`. This node also has a child node called `LineItems` (also of cardinality `0..n`). Remember that the cardinality of node `SalesOrders` will cause it to start life as an empty collection; i.e., the child node

---

1   Call method `node(cn).getNodeInfo().isMandatory()` to obtain this value.

`LineItems` will not even exist until such time as element zero of its parent node (`SalesOrders`) is created.[2]

At design time, it is perfectly valid to create UI elements in the view layout that are bound to attributes of the child node `LineItems`. However, at runtime, you must ensure that node `SalesOrders` contains at least one element. This element can then act as the parent for the child node `lineItems`.

If you forget to do these data-creation steps yourself, you will end up trying to display the value of a non-existent attribute, belonging to a non-existent element of a non-existent child node! Hence the error, `Node(…): no active node to map to`.

▶ The last situation involves mapping context nodes between different controllers. Imagine that the value nodes for `SalesOrders` and `LineItems` now live in the context of a custom controller (such as your component controller) and not the view controller. Your view controller can gain access to this data by declaring a mapping relationship between its own value node[3] and the corresponding value nodes in the component controller.[4]

If you now create UI elements in the view layout that are bound to the view controller's `SalesOrders` node, the following situation could cause an error to occur:

Again, in the component controller, you forget to add any elements to the `SalesOrders` value node and you completely forget to create the value node `LineItems`. The difference now is that processing to add the data to these node elements is the responsibility of the component controller. The view controller is simply referencing the element collection that exists in the component controller. Mapped nodes do not maintain their own element collections.

Therefore, in order to find the correct value to display in the UI element, a mapping reference from the view controller to the component controller must be traversed. The mapping reference to the child node

---

2 This is a slight oversimplification. If a child node (chn) is a singleton with respect to its parent node (cn), then (chn) can be created, but cannot be populated until (cn) has at least one element. If, however, the child node (chn) is a non-singleton with respect to its parent node (cn), then (chn) cannot even be created until (cn) contains at least one element.

3 The value node in the view controller does not need to have the same name as the value node in the custom controller to which it is mapped. However, it helps greatly with code legibility if the two names are the same.

4 This type of mapping is possible only after you have explicitly stated that the component controller is a required controller for the view controller.

`LineItems` will return a null pointer exception, and this in turn is interpreted as the error `Mapping reference not found`.

See Section 6.8 for more details.

7.3 Building a context node hierarchy suitable for a tree UI element

To make correct use of the tree UI element, it is most important to understand the requirements this UI element imposes on the view controller's context. As has been stated earlier, the structure of data supplied by a model object is rarely suitable for immediate display on the user interface. This is particularly true when using the tree UI element, which requires the context data to be structured in a very particular way. It is almost a certainty that a model object will *not* supply data in this specialized structure!

Here is a perfect example of where a custom controller (such as the component controller) should perform a structural data transformation on the context data to make it suitable for requirements of the UI elements on a view layout.[5]

The properties of trees and tree nodes can be found in classes `IWDAbstractTreeNodeType`, `IWDTreeNodeType`, and `IWDTree`.

The following tree and tree node properties can be bound to context attributes:

Tree	TreeNode
defaultItemIconAlt	iconAlt
defaultItemIconSource	iconSource
defaultNodeIconAlt	ignoreAction
defaultNodeIconSource	Tooltip
minHeight	Text

Table 7.1 Bindable Properties of Tree UI Elements

---

5 It can also be argued that a view controller should receive the raw data supplied by a model object and then perform its own transformation, thus relieving the custom controller of the need to know anything about the requirements of any particular view layout. Both approaches are plausible, and the decision to use one method over another should be judged both on the complexity of the transformation process and the number of views that require the same restructured model data.

Tree	TreeNode
rootText	Design
rootVisible	dataSource
title	expanded
defaultNodeIconSource	tooltip
minHeight	text
rootText	design
rootVisible	dataSource
title	expanded
titleVisible	hasChildren
width	
dataSource	

Table 7.1 Bindable Properties of Tree UI Elements (cont.)

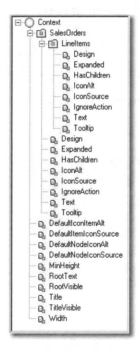

Figure 7.1 A Context Structure Suitable for a Tree UI Element

Depending on your business requirements, it may not be necessary to bind all the properties listed in Figure 7.1, but for the purposes of this illustration, it has been assumed that you want to have full, programmatic control over every aspect of the tree's appearance.

If we assume that we want to display a list of sales orders as a tree, the view controller's context will look something like Figure 7.1.

Important: Notice that the names of the node attributes in the context reflect the properties of the tree UI elements, *not* the attributes found in a sales order. In fact, the only attributes that have anything to do with the business data being displayed are Text and Tooltip. All the other attributes control the appearance and behavior of the tree itself.

We start with the independent node (SalesOrdersForTree) to represent the tree UI element for sales orders. Under this, there is a dependent node (LineItemsForTree) to represent the tree UI element for line items.

In this example, the properties belonging to the entire tree UI element have been created as independent attributes because there is only one tree in this view.[6]

The properties belonging to the tree node UI elements have been created as dependent attributes of node SalesOrdersForTree and LineItemsForTree.

It is *vitally* important that the singleton property of node LineItemsForTree is set to false! Think about how a tree UI element is capable of displaying its information, and then think about the implications of having the child node LineItemsForTree as a singleton node.

If you haven't figured it out, let me explain. First, consider the data held in the element collection of node SalesOrdersForTree. In business terms, it is a collection of sales order headers. Under this is the node LineItemsForTree. This node holds the line items for each sales order. In other words, there must be a whole new instance of child node LineItemsForTree for each element of node SalesOrdersForTree.

Now consider how information can be presented through a tree structure. The parent node of a tree may have, let's say, five children. This corresponds to the node SalesOrdersForTree having five elements in its element collection. A tree UI element allows you to expand each one of

---

6 If you have multiple tree UI elements in the same view layout, then you would need to create a parent node (of cardinality 1..1) for each tree.

these five child nodes and see all their children simultaneously. This immediately implies that each element of node `SalesOrdersForTree` must have its own distinct instance of child node `LineItemsForTree` in existence simultaneously.

Therefore, node `LineItemsForTree` must be a non-singleton with respect to `SalesOrdersForTree`; otherwise, you would only ever be able to see the children of the one element at the lead selection of node `SalesOrders-ForTree`.

As you should now be able to appreciate, this very small configuration step has an enormous impact on the behavior of a context node. This, in turn, can make or break your view layout!

To create the corresponding tree UI elements in a view layout, proceed as follows:

1. Create the context structure shown above in Figure 7.1 — not forgetting to set the singleton flag of node `LineItemsForTree` to `false`.

2. Create a Tree UI element in your layout with a name such as `Sales-OrderTree`.

3. Bind the various properties of the UI element `SalesOrderTree` to the appropriate independent attributes.

4. Bind the `dataSource` property of UI element `SalesOrderTree` to the context node `SalesOrdersForTree`.

5. Add two `TreeNodeType` elements as children of `SalesOrderTree`, calling them something like `SalesOrders` and `LineItems`.

6. Bind the `dataSource` property of the `TreeNodeType` `SalesOrders` to context node `SalesOrdersForTree`.

7. Bind the `dataSource` property of `TreeNodeType` `LineItems` to the context node `LineItemsForTree`.

8. Bind the required properties of each `TreeNodeType` UI element to the appropriate context attributes.

A common mistake is to think that the structure of the `TreeNodeType` UI elements under the tree UI element should reflect the structure of the data being displayed. No! This is not necessary. All you need to do is declare that various nodes will exist somewhere in the tree hierarchy. The response rendering stage of the phase model (see Section 11.11) will then automatically determine the hierarchical position of any given node on the basis of its `dataSource` binding.

All that is required now is that functionality exists[7] that can transform the business data into the structure required by the tree UI element.

To make the tree interactive, it will be necessary to implement the `onAction` event, and possibly also the `onLoadChildren` event.[8]

7.4   Parameter mapping

To ensure that server-side controllers can react intelligently to user actions on the client, it is often necessary to associate parameters with certain client-side events. For instance, when the user selects an item from a dropdown list, the server-side controller needs to know more than just the fact that *an* item has been selected; it needs to know exactly *which* item has been selected. Therefore, when a dropdown list fires its client-side `onSelect` event, the index of the selected item can be received by the server-side action handler.

Important: Event parameter names are hard coded within each UI element.

If an event has an associated event parameter, the UI element will automatically place a value into the event parameter. This part of the coding is done for you automatically; however, you must ensure that the value of the client-side event parameter is received by the server-side action handler.

In the case of the `DropDownByIndex` UI element, the hard-coded parameter is called `index`. You must now add the coding that retrieves the event parameter and passes it to your action handler. This is known as parameter mapping, and is done as follows:

▶ Obtain the name of the parameter associated with the client-side event. This can be found by looking in the javadoc of the relevant UI element. The parameter can be found in the comment above method `mappingOf{ui_{evt}}();`

   i.e., method `IWDCheckBox.mappingOfOnToggle()` has a boolean parameter called `checked`.

▶ Create an action {act} in the view controller.

---

7 Either in the view controller itself, or the custom (component) controller.
8 The `onLoadChildren` event allows you to calculate what the children of a specific node will be at the time the user *first* expands the node.

▶ Define a parameter for the action handler of the same data type as the event parameter.[9] You will often find it helpful to make the server-side action parameter name the same as the client-side event parameter name, though this is not mandatory.

▶ Associate the event parameter with the action parameter.

The UI element shown in Figure 7.2 is a DropDownByIndex, but the principles remain the same for all other UI elements:

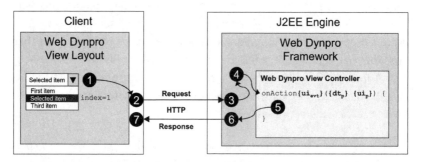

Figure 7.2 How a UI element parameter is passed back to an action handler

1. User selection raises the client-side onSelect event belonging to IWDDropDownByIndex.

2. An HTTP round trip is invoked to process the associated action handler. All available UI parameter values are passed back to the WDF.

3. On the basis of the source mapping declarations, the WDF matches UI parameters with action event handler parameters.

4. The action handler is invoked using any available parameters that match the source mapping declarations.

5. The action handler reacts to the event in an appropriate manner.

6. Control is passed back to the WDF which builds the HTTP response.

7. The client (in this case, a browser) receives the response and renders the processed screen.

---

9 All event parameter output from the client will be of type String. Parameters on action handlers can also be declared to be of type String, but if you want to use the data type specific to the event parameter (typically boolean or int), then you can declare the action parameter to be of the same type as the event parameter, and the WDF will make the conversion automatically.

7.4.1 Basic parameter mapping example

In this example, the `checked` parameter of the `onToggle` event of a checkbox UI element will be associated with a parameter called `checkBoxState` in the corresponding action handler.

▶ Create an action in a view controller to handle the change of state in a checkbox UI element. The checkbox is called `myCheckBox` and will be associated with an action called `HandleCheckBox`.

▶ Define a boolean parameter called `checkBoxState` for the action handler `onActionHandleCheckBox()`.

▶ Place the following coding in the `wdDoModifyView()` method of the view controller. This coding must be executed only *once* during the view controller's lifecycle; therefore, it is imperative that we first check the `firstTime` flag.

```
if (firstTime) {
    // Get a reference to the checkbox UI element
    IWDCheckBox cb = (IWDCheckBox)view.getElement("myCheckBox");

    // Link the client-side event parameter "checked"
    // to the server-side action parameter "checkBoxState"
    cb.mappingOfOnToggle().
        addSourceMapping("checked", "checkBoxState");
}
```

Listing 7.1 Basic Parameter Mapping

Now, whenever this particular checkbox is toggled, the client-side event parameter `checked` that belongs to the `onToggle` event will be passed through to the server-side action handler `HandleCheckBox` as the boolean variable `checkBoxState`.

7.4.2 Action handler generalization

Since the event-to-action parameter mapping is specific to the UI element and not the action, it is perfectly possible to generalize the use of an action handler so that it can respond to events from multiple UI elements. You can extend the first example so that the action handler `HandleCheckBox` can process *any* `onToggle` event from *any* checkbox on the current view.

In order to make an action handler work in this generic manner, you must define an extra parameter for HandleCheckBox that identifies *which* checkbox raised the onToggle event.

This extra parameter has nothing to do with the client-side event itself; therefore, it is completely independent from the client layer. The following code extends the above coding example.

▶ Against the action handler HandleCheckBox, define a new parameter called checkBoxName of type String.

▶ The HandleCheckBox action handler will now process the onToggle events from three different checkboxes.

▶ For each checkbox UI element, you must now define a fixed value for the checkBoxName parameter. In the following example, we will use three checkboxes that all trigger the same server-side event handler. The coding is as follows:

```
if (firstTime) {
    // Get references to all three checkbox UI elements
    IWDCheckBox cb1 = (IWDCheckBox)view.getElement("checkBox1");
    IWDCheckBox cb2 = (IWDCheckBox)view.getElement("checkBox2");
    IWDCheckBox cb3 = (IWDCheckBox)view.getElement("checkBox3");

    // Link the client-side event parameter "checked" to the
    // server-side action parameter "checkBoxState"
    // This parameter is UI-element specific, and therefore
    // identical for all three checkboxes.
    cb1.mappingOfOnToggle().
        addSourceMapping("checked", "checkBoxState");
    cb2.mappingOfOnToggle().
        addSourceMapping("checked", "checkBoxState");
    cb3.mappingOfOnToggle().
        addSourceMapping("checked", "checkBoxState");

    // Now hard code the checkbox names that enable the server-
    // side event to distinguish between each checkbox.
    cb1.mappingOfOnToggle().
        addParameter("checkBoxName", cb1.getId());
    cb2.mappingOfOnToggle().
        addParameter("checkBoxName", cb2.getId());
    cb3.mappingOfOnToggle().
        addParameter("checkBoxName", cb3.getId());
}
```

Listing 7.2 Generalized Action Handler

7.4.3 Further decoupling of the UI

The degree of abstraction between the event parameter and action parameter can be taken a degree further if desired. Rather than hard coding the specific UI element name into a custom action parameter, you could use a reference to a context attribute.

For instance, consider the following situation. You want to display the contents of a context node as a table, but the number of columns to be displayed is unknown until runtime. You also want to give the user the ability to sort the table simply by clicking on a column header. This type of situation calls for a generic action handler that can sort the table based, not on the name of the table column *UI element*, but on the name of the *context attribute* being visualized by that table column. In other words, the information provided to the sort algorithm needs to be the name of the context attribute that will act as the sort key, *not* the name of the table column UI element that is visualizing the information.

This level of disassociation between the table UI element and the sort algorithm allows you to put any table on the screen, made up of any number of columns of any name, and the sort logic will still function.

In this scenario, the standard client-side event parameter `col` (provided by the `onAction` event of `IWDTableColumn`) is ignored because this contains the name of the UI element on which the user clicked. Instead, the name of the context attribute to which the UI element is bound will be used as the parameter value.

The following example describes a situation in which a table of sales orders is displayed, but the number of columns is configurable and therefore not known until runtime. The user can sort the table by clicking on the header of the column he or she wishes to use as the sort key. The name of the action handler that performs the sort is `HandleSortRequest`, and it receives a single `String` parameter called `colAttrib`.

▶ The standard parameter `col` for the table column's `onAction` event must be ignored. This is easy to achieve — do nothing!

▶ Create a new parameter called `colAttrib` of type `String` on the action handler `HandleSortRequest`.

▶ The attributes that will be displayed as table columns live in a context node called `SalesOrders`. In this rather simplistic example, let's say that the attributes of this node are called `CustId`, `CustName`, and `Date`.

▶ In the `wdDoModifyView()` method of the view controller, the following code should be added. In this example, the coding to create the table column UI elements has been omitted, but they are called `tabCol1`, `tabCol2`, and `tabCol3`.

You should associate the context attribute supplying data to the table column with the static parameter `colAttrib`.

```
// Obtain references to the table column UI elements
IWDTableColumn tc1 = (IWDTableColumn)view.getElement("tabCol1");
IWDTableColumn tc2 = (IWDTableColumn)view.getElement("tabCol2");
IWDTableColumn tc3 = (IWDTableColumn)view.getElement("tabCol3");

// Hard code the value of the "colAttrib" parameter to be the dot
// delimited name of the context attribute.
// Notice this is a string value, not an object reference!
tc1.mappingOfOnAction().
    addParameter("colAttrib", "SalesOrders.CustId");
tc2.mappingOfOnAction().
    addParameter("colAttrib", "SalesOrders.CustName");
tc3.mappingOfOnAction().
    addParameter("colAttrib", "SalesOrders.Date");
```

Listing 7.3 Action Handler Using a Context Attribute Name

▶ Now when the action handler `HandleSortRequest` is called, it will receive a `String` containing the name of the context attribute that is to be used as the sort key in the string parameter `colAttrib`.

▶ The action handler must now use the value of the string parameter `colAttrib` to create a reference to the relevant context attribute. The sort algorithm should then be passed this context attribute reference as its sort key.

7.4.4 Advanced parameter mapping example

When processing the events raised by tree nodes, it is vitally important that the action handler know not only the name of the node on which the user clicked, but also the exact element within that node. Therefore, the event-to-action parameter mapping must be done in the following manner.

▶ As with the previous examples, the name of the event parameter raised by the `IWDTreeNodeType` needs to be known. (In the case of this particular interface, the `onAction` event is not defined in `IWDTreeNodeType`, but in the base class `IWDAbstractTreeNodeType`.)

The required event parameter is called `path` and is of type `String`.

▶ Before creating the action parameter, you must identify the name of the generated node element class that the `TreeNodeType` UI element represents.

For instance, the element of context node `WBSElements` in view controller `ShowProjectAsTreeView` will be called `IPrivateShowProjectAsTreeView.IWBSElementsElement`.

In general, for any element of node `{c_n}` belonging to the context of view controller `{n_v}`, the generated class name will always be `IPrivate{n_v}.I{c_n}Element`.

▶ Assuming that the action handler is called `HandleNodeClick`, create a parameter called something like `selectedNodeElement`.

It is most important that the data type of this parameter is *not* `String`! It must be of the data type of the generated node element class identified in the previous step.

▶ As in the previous examples, the event parameter must be associated with the action parameter using the following code:

```
IWDTreeNodeType tn = (IWDTreeNodeType)view.
                     getElement("WBSElements");
tn.mappingOfOnAction().
    addSourceMapping("path", "selectedNodeElement");
```

Listing 7.4 Action Handler Using a Context Node Reference

▶ Now when the user clicks on the displayed node, the client will pass the path name to the context element as a `String` value in the event parameter `path`. Before the value of `path` is transferred to the server-side action parameter `selectedNodeElement`, the WDF recognizes that the parameter to the action event handler is declared as a node element class, and will automatically convert the `String` value held in the event parameter `path` into the object reference required by the action handler.

▶ The action handler method now has an object reference to the exact node element on which the user clicked.

7.5 Efficient use of actions to enable and disable UI elements

Certain UI elements trigger client-side events. In order for these events to be processed on the server, there must be an association between the client-side event and an event handler on the server. This association is performed by instances of class `IWDAction`.

Instances of the class are known as actions, and these can be enabled and disabled at runtime as required by the functionality of your application. As you have seen in the previous section, it is possible to have many different client-side events all associated with the same action; thus, they will all trigger the same generic event handler method. At this point, it would be worthwhile to ensure that you fully understand the difference between a primary and secondary event. If you can't remember, go back and reread Section 3.7.1.

If you wish to stop a user from triggering a particular action (for instance, the user has insufficient authorization), the simplest way to achieve this is to disable the action. This is done by calling the action's `setEnabled()` method and passing it the boolean value `false`.

Now the WDF runtime automatically disables or adapts all UI elements using this action. If the action is associated with a primary event, the entire UI element is disabled for user input. If it is associated with a secondary event, the UI element remains enabled for user interaction. Either way, though, if an action has been disabled, it is impossible for it to be triggered by a UI element.

As you will probably appreciate, this allows you to enable or disable all the UI elements on the screen using a single call to the `setEnabled()` method of the relevant action. Don't fall into the trap of thinking that, to disable a `Button` or a `LinkToAction` UI element, you have to access the UI element object directly within method `wdDoModifyView()` and then disable it explicitly. All UI elements using an action can be enabled or disabled automatically via their associated action object.

 Important: If you disable an action associated with a secondary event, the UI element will remain enabled for user interaction. An example of this is the table UI element. If you have disabled the action associated with the secondary event `onSelect`, the table can still be scrolled, but now the action associated with the `onSelect` event will never be raised.

7.6 Layout managers

The purpose of a layout manager is to provide a structure within which UI elements can be presented. All Web Dynpro UI element containers must implement a layout manager of some sort.

Every Web Dynpro view is represented as a hierarchy of UI elements. This hierarchy is created automatically whenever a view controller is declared, and the view's root UI element has the following properties:

▶ It is always of type `TransparentContainer`.

▶ It is always called `RootUIElementContainer`.

▶ By default, the `RootUIElementContainer` always has the `FlowLayout` layout manager assigned to it.

▶ All UI elements subsequently added to the view become children of `RootUIElementContainer`.

When a layout manager is assigned to a UI element container, at design time a set of property values must be specified for each child UI element that is specific to the layout manager. It is within the layout data object that you specify how that child UI element should appear when rendered with the given layout manager.

7.6.1 Flow layout

The `FlowLayout` is the simplest of the layout managers in that it renders its child UI elements in a simple left-to-right horizontal sequence. If more UI elements have been defined than will fit horizontally across the screen, a new row is created.

As you resize the window within which the `FlowLayout` container lives, you will see the UI elements wrap automatically within the available screen space.

It is not possible to define any form of vertical alignment within a `Flow-Layout` container.

Figure 7.3 UI elements arranged in a container using a Flow layout manager; narrow screen

Figure 7.4 UI elements arranged in a container using a Flow layout manager; wide screen

7.6.2   Row layout

The RowLayout layout manager has been implemented primarily to overcome performance overhead incurred by browsers having to render multiple levels of nested HTML <tables>.

If you wish to subdivide some area of the view into horizontal rows, but you do not require any vertical alignment between the resulting columns, then you should use a RowLayout layout manager. This layout manager should be thought of as an enhanced form of FlowLayout.

Within a row of a RowLayout container, each child UI element will either contain a RowHeadData object or a RowData object. These objects are stored in the aggregation layoutdata and determine whether the UI element will start a new row or just be a row member. The default is that all child UI elements contain RowData objects.

Should you change a child element to contain a RowHeadData object, then you are telling the RowLayout layout manager that this particular element will forcibly start a new row. UI elements nominated to contain RowHead-Data objects will always occupy the left-most position in a row.

A `RowHeadData` object has a set of general properties that apply to all UI elements in the row, that is, all UI elements up until the next `RowHeadData` object.

Once you have specified which UI elements will be that row's `RowHead-Data` objects, the other UI elements in the row are free to rearrange themselves as if they lived in a `FlowLayout` container. Depending on the available screen width, you may very well see the contents of a `RowLayout` container wrapping around to form a new row. As with a `FlowLayout` container, the minimum width at which wrapping stops is imposed by the widest single UI element on the screen.

In Figure 7.5, the outlined UI elements are the ones with a layout data of `RowHeadData`. Notice that there is no vertical alignment of UI elements in corresponding columns.

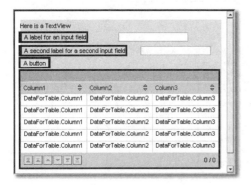

Figure 7.5 UI elements arranged in a container using a Row layout manager

7.6.3   Matrix layout

The `MatrixLayout` layout manager is a further enhancement of the capabilities of the `RowLayout` layout manager.[10]

A `RowLayout` layout manager allows you to specify when new rows should start, but provides no facility for the vertical alignment of elements within the row. This capability is provided by the `MatrixLayout` layout manager.

The `MatrixLayout` layout manager creates a tabular grid on the screen in which the cells are aligned both horizontally and vertically. As with the `RowLayout` layout manager, you still have to specify which child UI ele-

---

10   UI elements arranged in a `MatrixLayout` or `GridLayout` are implemented in a browser using an HTML `<table>`.

ments will be at the start of a new row, but now all the row elements will be vertically aligned into columns.

Using a `MatrixLayout` layout manager, you can produce a grid with a variable number of columns per row.

As with `RowLayout` managed UI containers, each child UI element assigned to a `MatrixLayout` container will contain either a `MatrixData` object or `MatrixHeadData` object. Again, these objects are stored in `layoutdata` aggregation. The default object type is `MatrixData`, but if you wish to start a new row, you must change this to `MatrixHeadData`.

In Figure 7.6, the outlined UI elements are the ones with a layout data of `MatrixHeadData`. Notice that there is now a tabular arrangement of the UI elements.

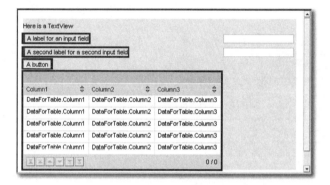

Figure 7.6 UI elements arranged in a container using a Matrix layout manager

7.6.4 Grid layout

The `GridLayout` layout manager divides the view area into a tabular grid with a fixed number of columns. As UI elements are added to a `GridLayout` container, they are positioned within the grid in a left-to-right, top-to-bottom manner.

The number of columns in the grid is determined by the value of the `colCount` property, and the number of rows is dependent upon the number of UI elements added to the container.

To achieve a uniform look and feel across all of your Web Dynpro applications, SAP recommends that the `MatrixLayout` be used in preference to the `GridLayout`.

Important: The time taken for browsers to render a screen can rise if the HTML contains multiple levels of nested `<table>` tags. Since the `GridLayout` and `MatrixLayout` layout managers are implemented in a browser using an HTML `<table>`, if possible you should try to avoid nesting these layout managers within each other.

A better approach when designing a screen layout is to divide the screen into horizontal areas as early as possible. The horizontal subdivisions can be implemented using a `RowLayout` layout manager, and each child added to the row could then be some sort of container such as a `Transparent-Container`. This will avoid the drop in browser rendering performance because you will not be using an HTML `<table>` to provide the major structural subdivisions of the screen.

The view shown in Figure 7.7 is the same layout as seen in the previous figures, but now that the view container is using a Grid layout manager with the `colCount` parameter set to 2, all the UI elements have assigned an arbitrary position in the table, on a left-to-right, top-to-bottom basis. The table UI element has had its `colSpan` parameter set to 2.

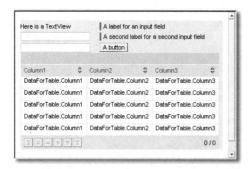

Figure 7.7 UI elements arranged in a container using a Grid layout manager; colCount = 2

This layout is obviously not satisfactory because we want some rows to have only one UI element in them. If you are using a Grid layout manager, then you will need to pad the empty grid cells with invisible UI elements. These can be seen Figure 7.8.

If you require a tabular layout for your UI elements, then SAP recommends that the Matrix layout manager should be used in preference to the Grid layout manager.

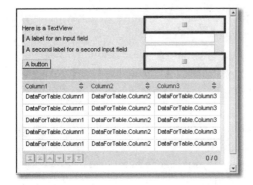

Figure 7.8 UI elements arranged in a container using a Grid layout manager; invisible elements used for padding

7.6.5 Layout Manager Properties

FlowLayout		
Layout Manager Properties	**Data Type**	**Default Value**
defaultPaddingBottom	String	""
defaultPaddingLeft	String	""
defaultPaddingRight	String	""
dcfaultPaddingTop	String	""
wrapping	Boolean	True
Layout Data Properties	**Data Type**	**Default Value**
paddingBottom	String	""
paddingLeft	String	""
paddingRight	String	""
paddingTop	String	""
RowLayout		
Layout Head Data Properties	**Data Type**	**Default Value**
hAlign	WDCellHAlign	LEFT
rowBackgroundDesign	WDCellBackgroundDesign	TRANSPARENT
rowDesign	WDLayoutCellDesign	R_PAD
vGutter	WDLayoutCellSeparator	NONE

Table 7.2 Properties of Layout Manager Classes and Their Associated Data and HeadData Classes

MatrixLayout		
Layout Manager Properties	**Data Type**	**Default Value**
`stretchedHorizontally`	`Boolean`	`True`
`stretchedVertically`	`Boolean`	`True`
Layout Data Properties	**Data Type**	**Default Value**
`cellBackgroundDesign`	`WDCellBackgroundDesign`	`TRANSPARENT`
`cellDesign`	`WDLayoutCellDesign`	`R_PAD`
`colSpan`	`Integer`	`1`
`hAlign`	`WDCellHAlign`	`LEFT`
`height`	`String`	`""`
`vAlign`	`WDCellVAlign`	`BASELINE`
`vGutter`	`WDLayoutCellSeparator`	`NONE`
`width`	`String`	`""`
GridLayout		
Layout Manager Properties	**Data Type**	**Default Value**
`cellPadding`	`Integer`	`0`
`cellSpacing`	`Integer`	`0`
`colCount`	`Integer`	`1`
`stretchedHorizontally`	`Boolean`	`True`
`stretchedVertically`	`Boolean`	`True`
Layout Data Properties	**Data Type**	**Default Value**
`colSpan`	`Integer`	`1`
`hAlign`	`WDCellHAlign`	`LEFT`
`height`	`String`	`""`
`paddingBottom`	`String`	`""`
`paddingLeft`	`String`	`""`
`paddingRight`	`String`	`""`
`paddingTop`	`String`	`""`
`vAlign`	`WDCellVAlign`	`BASELINE`

Table 7.2 Properties of Layout Manager Classes and Their Associated Data and HeadData Classes (cont.)

7.7 Principles for the efficient use of layout managers

1. Wherever possible, try to avoid complex layouts involving multiple levels of nesting.

   When you have the option of nesting UI containers within each other (each with its own layout manager), always opt for the design that results in the fewest levels of nesting. From a performance point of view, it is better to place multiple UI elements directly into one large UI container using a grid or matrix layout (with columns and rows that span where necessary) than to nest transparent containers within the individual cells of the parent container.

2. Only use a transparent container when it is genuinely required. Containers such as the Group control are composite UI elements based on a transparent container. Therefore, it makes no sense to embed a transparent container as the top level child into a Group container, because it already implements one!

3. If vertical alignment is not required, the row layout should be chosen in preference to the grid or matrix layout.

4. If vertical alignment is required, the matrix layout should be chosen in preference to the grid layout. This is not a performance consideration (both layout managers are ultimately implemented using an HTML `<table>`), but it is an easier layout manager to work with. You don't have to specify a column count and you can put as many controls into one row as you like.

5. The matrix layout allows some predefined values for cell padding. The property `cellDesign` can have the following predefined values. The `Standard` option is also referred to as `rPad`.

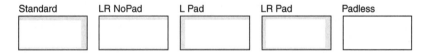

Figure 7.9 The Different Adding Options for the cellDesign Property

7.8 Locale-specific text

7.8.1 Introduction to multilingual support in software products

One of the age old problems with the distribution of software products within geographical regions such as Europe has been that of language support. The French don't want to speak German, the Italians don't want to speak Spanish, and the English (and Americans) can *only* speak English!

This problem has produced a variety of solutions; some vendors distribute entirely new versions of their products with the language-specific text embedded within the executable code, and other vendors have opted to separate the language-specific content from the executable code.

The requirement for multilingual operation has, from SAP's earliest days, been a fundamental design criterion of all its software products. In the R/3 system (and all of its derivative systems), the data stored in its relational database tables is organized in third normal form. This has the direct consequence that business data and the text that describes the business data are always stored in separate tables related by a foreign key.

7.8.2 Internationalization

The word "internationalization" is used to describe either the design process required to make a software product functional in all required languages, or the modification process by which existing software is adapted from single language operation to multilingual operation. The result is a software product in which all language-specific text is external to the executable code that uses it.

Because the word "internationalization" is so long, it is abbreviated to *i18n* — that is, the first letter "i", the last letter "n", and don't bother writing the other 18 letters in the middle!

From now on, we will talk about the "i18n process" or "Web Dynpro i18n" rather than using the full word.

7.8.3 Externalization

Externalization is the process by which hard-coded text strings are removed (i.e., externalized) from a source code file and placed into a `.properties` file. The original source code is then modified to access a generated resource bundle accessor class. Within the NWDS, an Externalize Strings wizard automates the extraction and code modification process.

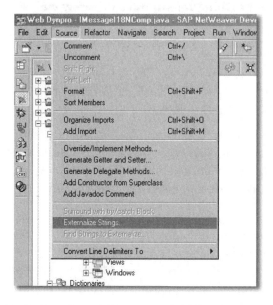

Figure 7.10 Externalize Strings Wizard for Removing Text Strings from Existing Code

For more information on this process, see the standard SAP documentation "Internationalization in the SAP NetWeaver Developer Studio."

7.8.4 Web Dynpro i18n concept

In keeping with the R/3 tradition of separating data from the text that describes the data, the Web Dynpro i18n concept separates text strings from the programs that manipulate those strings. Therefore, Web Dynpro Java class files, metadata files, and dictionary simple types do not contain any language-specific text. The standard Java class `java.util.Resource-Bundle` is used for managing language-specific text at runtime. See the javadoc for more information on the exact details of the operation of this class.

Important: When a Web Dynpro project or DC is created, a language is required such as `British_English` or `Spanish` or `Hebrew`. This language setting serves several purposes:

▶ To inform a translator of the language in which the developer originally wrote the Web Dynpro project or DC.

▶ To determine the original language of all current and future meta-data files in this project.

This value is *not* read at runtime by the WDF when determining the session locale of an application.

Caveat confector:

The project language cannot be changed after a project has been created, and you cannot copy metadata between projects of different languages!

Not all locales recognised by Java are permissible within a Web Dynpro project or DC. The permissible languages are *only* those found in the drop down list seen when a project or DC is created. The reason for this is that internally, SAP uses an R/3 system to serve as a translation engine. This immediately reduces the set of permissible Web Dynpro languages to the subset of languages (or dialects) within which R/3 operates.

Languages not known to R/3 are not permissible in Web Dynpro.

7.8.5 S2X—SAP's use of the XLIFF standard

SAP has taken the XML Language Interchange File Format (XLIFF) and produced a reduced and somewhat modified variant known as "SAP Supported XLIFF" (S2X). SAP's S2X compliant files all use the `.XLF` file name suffix and differ from standard XLIFF in the following ways:

▶ S2X imposes the following restrictions upon standard XLIFF:

  ▷ XLIFF's mechanism for handling alternate translations from different sources, such as a Translation Memory System or a Machine Translation System, has not been implemented.

  ▷ Certain textual content will be encoded using only the lower half of the ASCII character set, i.e., 7-bit ASCII.

▶ S2X extends standard XLIFF in the following areas:

  ▷ Certain XLIFF extensions have been implemented that can accommodate the classification of SAP's software according to software component, development component, and release.

  ▷ Certain XLIFF constraints have been made optional.

An S2X file contains two different types of data: header data and content data.

▶ Header data describes the properties of all the contents stored in the file.

▶ Content data are the text items accompanied by supplementary information, such as unique identifiers, that may be used in reuse or update strategies.

This can be seen in the S2X editor as the tabs **Header** and **Resource Text**. (See Figure 7.13 and Figure 7.14 below.)

7.8.6 Storing language specific text in .XLF files

For each type of entity that can hold language specific content, there will be a corresponding XLF file created. These XLF files will only be created if the developer adds some text, e. g. hard coding a value for the `text` property of a Label UI element.

In general, the following XLF files will be created when language specific content is added:

▶ `{nv}.wdcontroller.xlf`
Action texts in a view controller

▶ `{nv}.wdview.xlf`
UI element text, tooltip and imageAlt values in a view layout

▶ `{w}.wdwindow.xlf`
The value of the window's title property

▶ `{nc}MessagePool.wdmessagepool.xlf`
Component message pool content

▶ `{st}.dtsimpletype.xlf`
Enumeration display texts, field labels, column headers and tooltips for dictionary simple types

Notice that none of the above filenames contains a locale value. During the development of a Web Dynpro application, the developer will only be working in a *single* language—the one specified when the project was created. Consequently, all XLF files generated during the development of the application are assumed to belong to this locale.

7.8.7 Translating XLF files

In the SAP NetWeaver '04 version of the NWDS, there is not yet an IDE based tool for translating XLF files. The creation of an XLF file for any language other than the project default needs to be performed manually. However, this amounts to nothing more than locating the original XLF file in your NWDS workspace directory, and then duplicating it.[11] The important thing to remember is to include the new locale value at the correct position in the file name.

For any new locale {l}, the original file should be copied and renamed thus:

▶ `{n_v}.wdcontroller.xlf` becomes `{n_v}.wdcontroller_{l}.xlf`

▶ `{n_v}.wdview.xlf` becomes `{n_v}.wdview_{l}.xlf`

▶ `{w}.wdwindow.xlf` becomes `{w}.wdwindow_{l}.xlf`

▶ `{n_c}MessagePool.wdmessagepool.xlf` becomes
  `{n_c}MessagePool.wdmessagepool_{l}.xlf`

▶ `{st}.dtsimpletype.xlf` becomes `{st}.dtsimpletype_{l}.xlf`

Once new locale specific XLF files have been created, the project view in the Package Explorer should be refreshed, and then the S2X editor can be used to edit the contents.

7.8.8 Use of the S2X editor within NWDS

SAP has created an editing tool within the NWDS that allows you to edit `.XLF` files in SAP's specific S2X format.

Caveat confector:

The S2X editor is *not* a Web Dynpro specific tool. It has been provided only to fill a functional gap in Eclipse.

The S2X editor should *never* be used to edit language specific content in the project's default language. If you have created your project in German, then all German text belonging to UI elements, dictionary simple types and message pools, should be edited using the standard Web Dynpro tools.

---

11 In the same directory!

Using the S2X editor, it is possible to change the source language of an XLF file, but this change will not cause the filename to be updated (remember, all text belonging to languages other than the project language must have the locale {1} embedded in the file name); therefore, such changes will create inconsistencies within your Web Dynpro project.

If you use the S2X editor to change the XLF file associated with a Web Dynpro view (for instance) *and* you have already opened that view through the normal Web Dynpro editor, then you will not see your text changes in the view layout until you reload the project.

7.8.9 Editing MessagePool XLF files

To edit an XLF file, the SAP NetWeaver '04 version of the NWDS provides an S2X editor. If you double-click on the Message Pool belonging to a Web Dynpro project from the Web Dynpro Explorer menu, you will see a version of the S2X editor applicable for `MessagePools`.

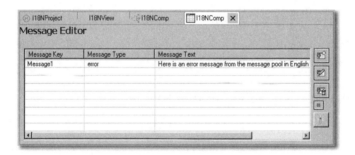

Figure 7.11 S2X Editor for a Component MessagePool

To edit the XLF files associated with view controllers, windows, and dictionary simple types, you should change from the Web Dynpro Explorer view of the project to either the Package Explorer or Navigator views. Here you can expand the `src` directory and locate the XLF files. These files are marked with an 🖥 icon.

The Package Explorer provides the most direct route to the XLF files, and is shown in Figure 7.12.

By double-clicking on the view controller's XLF file (`I18NView.wdview.xlf`) shown above, you will see the editor screens in Figure 7.13 and Figure 7.14.

Figure 7.12 Navigator View of the XLF Files in a Web Dynpro Project

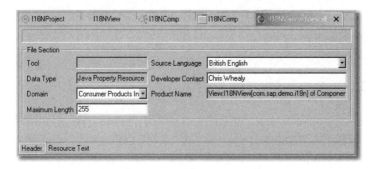

Figure 7.13 The Header Screen in the S2X Editor for a View Controller's XLF File

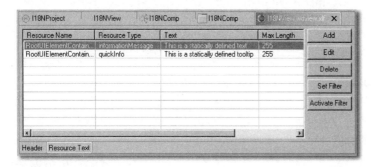

Figure 7.14 The Resource Text Screen in the S2X Editor for a View Controller's XLF File

The application developer can edit all the text resources for his or her project using the S2X editor. As was stated earlier, these XLF files are assumed to contain text that belongs to the language specified when the project was created.

Notice that the view of the S2X editor shown in Figure 7.11 is slightly different from the view seen in Figure 7.14. There is a good reason for this! The view of the S2X editor seen when editing a Message Pool from the Web Dynpro imposes two restrictions:

▶ The available message types are limited to Standard, Warning, Error, and Text because these are the only message types applicable for a Message Pool.

▶ The S2X header information has been suppressed.

However, when the S2X editor is started from either Navigator or Package Explorer views, you will see the full S2X editor, in which both the header information and the full range of message types are accessible.

 Caveat confector: Do not use the S2X editor to change any text belonging to your project's default language! These changes should be made through the Web Dynpro tools in order to ensure the consistency of the underlying XLF files.

7.8.10 Runtime Locale Identification

Within the scope of a project, the locale of a Web Dynpro application can be defined using the application property `DefaultLocale`. This hard coded value will act as the application's default locale unless it is explicitly overridden.

Web Dynpro makes use of the standard fallback process within `java.util.ResourceBundle` to determine which locale value should be used for a particular application.

The following table shows how the fall back process works. The first column indicates the type of user accessing the system. The "Developer" user is the only user for which the `sap.locale` URL parameter is considered legitimate. Once a Web Dynpro application has been developed, the URL parameter `sap.locale` should not normally be used.

If a Web Dynpro application's authentication flag is set to true, then valid user credentials must first be supplied to the WDF before the application can be run. If the user credentials are obtained from the User Management Engine (UME), then the required locale value will be supplied.

User	URL	User Id	Browser	Locale specified in DefaultLocale property	WD system	VM default	Final locale
Developer	pr	de	en	fr	it	ru	pr
Authenticated		de	en	fr	it	ru	de
Anonymous			en	fr	it	ru	en
Anonymous				fr	it	ru	fr
Anonymous					it	ru	it
Anonymous						ru	ru

Table 7.3 Fall back process for locale determination

7.8.11 Locale-dependent text at runtime

There are five main categories of language-dependent text that you could need access to at runtime. The first four categories are the message types that exist within a Message Pool:

▶ Error

▶ Warning

▶ Standard

▶ Text

The first three types are the ones used by the `IWDMessageManager` class and become runtime constants within a generated class `IMessage{n_c}.java`, each message being of type `IWDMessage`.

> **Important:** Only Message Pool messages of type `Standard`, `Warning`, and `Error` are addressable as constants in the generated class `IMessage{n_c}`. Messages of type `text` *do not* appear in this generated class.

Messages of type `Text`, however, are not accessible to the `IWDMessageManager` class; instead, you should use class `IWDTextAccessor`. Messages of type `text` are text strings that either have been created as language-specific texts or have been extracted from existing code using the NWDS Externalize Strings wizard.

The fifth category of locale-dependent texts is those that belong to dictionary simple types. These texts can be accessed through the ISimpleType interface.

Once the application is deployed, the locale-dependent texts are stored in standard resource bundle files.

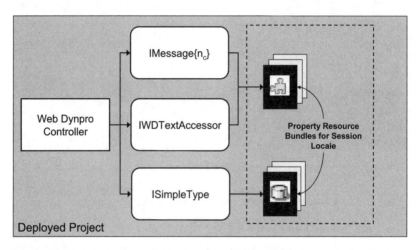

Figure 7.15 The Interfaces needed to Access Locale-Specific Text

The following example assumes that a message called Message1 of type text has been defined in a component's message pool. To access this specific message, you need to use the following code.

```
// Get the text accessor from the current component
IWDTextAccessor textAccessor =
  wdComponentAPI().getTextAccessor();

// Get the message by name from the message pool
String msgFromPool = textAccessor.getText("Message1");
```

Listing 7.5 Code Fragment for Obtaining a Message of Type text from the Message Pool

Remember that the component's message manager has no access to messages of type text, so these types of messages should be used only to supply UI elements. The purpose of the IWDMessageManager interface is to supply the user with informative messages about the success or failure of the application's functionality.

The code fragment below assumes that there is a message called Message2 of type error in the message pool. This message will be reported to the user with no parameters (`null`), and navigation will not be canceled as a result of the error (`false`).

```
// Get the message manager from the current component
IWDMessageManager msgMgr = wdComponentAPI().getMessageManager();

// Issue a warning message using a text constant from the
// generated IMessage{n_c} class
  msgMgr.reportMessage(IMessage{n_c}.MESSAGE2, null, false);
```

Listing 7.6 Code Fragment for Issuing a Message of Type error from the Message Pool

Within any component $\{c\}$, any statically defined text, such as message pool texts or hard-coded text values for UI elements, will be placed into a generated resource bundle file called `Resource{c}.properties`.

This file can be viewed (but must not be edited!) from the Package Explorer view in the NWDS. The general path name is:

$\{pr\}$ • `gen_wdp/packages` • $\{pkg_1\}$ … $\{pkg_n\}.\{n_{ct1}\}.wdp$ • `Resource{c}.properties`

7.8.12 Defining placeholders within a message text

There is often the need to be able to substitute a variable value into a static message string. This can be achieved with numbered placeholders within the text string. The messages are now known as message text patterns.

For instance, if you are writing an application that creates business documents, you will probably want to inform the user what number the newly created document has. Therefore, you would enter the message text into the Message Pool as shown in Figure 7.16.

Message Key	Message Type	Message Text
DocumentCreated	standard	Document {0} has been successfully created

Figure 7.16 A Placeholder in a Text Message

If you wish to have more than one placeholder within the text message, simply increment the placeholder number as shown in Figure 7.17.

Message Key	Message Type	Message Text
DocumentCreated	standard	Document {0} successfully created at {1} on {2}

Figure 7.17 Multiple Placeholders in a Text Message

Where {0} is the document number, {1} is the time, and {2} is the date.

Caveat confector:

All message placeholders must be sequentially numbered integers.

All placeholder values must be supplied as Java strings.

Message text patterns use `java.text.MessageFormat` without using element formats.

The code to issue the above `documentCreated` message must now supply a parameter value:

```
// Get the message manager from the current component
IWDMessageManager msgMgr = wdComponentAPI().getMessageManager();

// Get the document number from somewhere...
  String docNo = getDocumentNo();

// Issue a warning message using a text constant from the
// generated IMessage{nc} class
  msgMgr.reportMessage(IMessage{nc}.DOCUMENT_CREATED,
    new Object[] {docNo}, false);
```

Listing 7.7 Code Fragment for Issuing a Standard Message with Placeholder Parameters

Notice in Listings 7.6 and 7.7 that the class name for the `IMessage{nc}` class has been generalized.

7.9 Accessing any parameter in the query string

Normally, any query string parameters will automatically be mapped to parameters of the same name in the startup plug of the component controller interface view.[12] (Earlier versions of Web Dynpro required that URL parameters be prefixed with `app`. This is no longer a requirement, but the syntax is still supported.)

However, you may find yourself in a situation in which the calling application passes a variable set of parameters in the query string. Under these circumstances, it will probably be easiest to parse the entire query string, rather than attempt to declare all possible query string names as parameters to the startup plug's event handler.

---

12 The startup plug event handler will typically be called `onPlugDefault()`.

You can obtain the entire query string as a `java.util.Map` object using the following code:

```
public void onPlugDefault(IWDCustomEvent wdEvent) {
  //@@begin onPlugDefault(ServerEvent)
  // Get the entire query string as a Map object
  Map qsMap = WDWebContextAdapter.
              getWebContextAdapter().getRequestParameterMap();
  //@@end
}
```

Listing 7.8 Code Fragment for Obtaining a Variable Value from the Query String

This technique is particularly useful when Web Dynpro applications are called from SAP's Enterprise Portal.

8   Dynamic UI generation

8.1   General points about Web Dynpro user interfaces

A Web Dynpro user interface (UI) can be built in such a way that the whole screen layout is usually defined in an entirely declarative manner. That is, at design time, you place UI elements on the view layout and bind their properties to context nodes or attributes. This is known as a static UI definition.

Once the design time declarations have been made, the NWDS generates the necessary Java classes to create the declared layout. The only coding that then needs to be written is that necessary to fill the context with data. Each UI element in the hierarchy then obtains its data from the context by means of its UI element bindings.

The significant point to understand here is that the programmer is separated from the actual UI element objects by the context. At design time, you declare UI elements in your view layout, and bind their properties to suitable context nodes and attributes. Then, at runtime, you place appropriate data into the context to control both the displayed data and the behavior of the UI elements. The WDF is then able to render the entire screen without you needing to interact directly with any UI element object.

Important: For those people with a JSP coding background, you may find this way of working strange at first. The JSP environment is one in which each push button, drop-down list, and checkbox must be coded manually, and is therefore an object over which you have direct control. When you discover that this is not the normal way of working in Web Dynpro, it is easy to draw the initial conclusion that you won't be able to write an interface that does what you want. Not so! You *will* be able to write a highly functional user interface in Web Dynpro, but using a somewhat different design approach.

Important: The UI element hierarchy created at design time can be modified, or even totally deleted, at runtime! The purpose of a declared view layout is to act as a starting point for any modifications that may be required at runtime.

The use of the term "static" here does not indicate that the UI element hierarchy is immutable; rather, it refers to the fact that when the view controller is initialized, you will be starting from a known, fixed layout. If the static view layout is deleted at runtime, it can be reset simply by calling method `IWDView.resetView()`.

Dynamic UI generation stands in direct contrast to static UI generation. A Web Dynpro view containing a dynamic UI layout will have very few (if any) UI elements in its layout at design time. It is now down to the application developer to write the coding necessary to create the UI element hierarchy at design time.

Caveat confector: If you wish to write this type of application, there are several important principles that must be understood. The following sections will discuss all of these principles in detail.

Failure to understand these principles will result in the creation of coding that, at best, will be inefficient and, at worst, will need to be thrown away and rewritten!

8.2 Background information about the design of UI elements

The Web Dynpro design paradigm has been implemented such that there is a *rigorous* separation between the data processing layer and the data presentation layer.[1] The general principle is this:

Every Web Dynpro UI element has a set of properties, many of which can be bound to different context nodes or attributes. Once UI element properties are bound to a context node or attribute, you can directly control the appearance of the UI element without ever touching the graphical object itself. In other words, you perform an indirect manipulation of the UI element via the data held in the context.

Certain UI element properties also function in a manner that may, at first, be unexpected. A good example here is the `length` property of the `InputField` UI element. Many people immediately assume that this property functions in the same way as the `maxlength` property of an HTML `<input>` tag. The following explanation should help you understand why this assumption is incorrect.

---

1 This is very important!

Standard HTML has no metadata repository from which to obtain information about the data it displays. Therefore, an ambiguity exists in the function of two of the ⟨input⟩ tag's parameters: size and maxlength. The first controls the visible length of the UI element, and the second controls the length of the input data.

The ambiguity lies in the fact that the first parameter (size) controls the appearance of the UI element itself, while the second (maxlength) controls the data displayed in the UI element; yet both are *UI element* parameters. This blurred distinction in the use of UI element properties is not permitted in Web Dynpro.

> **Important:** UI element parameters can control only the appearance of the UI element itself, not the data being displayed.

With this distinction in mind, go back to the Web Dynpro InputField UI element and examine what purpose its length parameter could serve. It can control only the visible length of the InputField UI element, not the length of the data it contains. The length of the data displayed by this UI element is determined by the metadata of the context attribute to which it is bound.

So to recap on some UI element design principles:

1. The properties of a UI element control only its appearance.

2. The majority of UI element properties can be bound to context nodes or attributes.

3. The metadata of the information displayed through a UI element is determined by the context node or attribute to which it is bound.

8.3   Accessing existing UI elements in a view layout

Before any attempt is made to construct a view layout programmatically, it is necessary to understand how to access existing elements in a view layout.

Each view layout is constructed as a hierarchy of UI elements. Almost all UI elements form a visible part of the rendered screen; however, there are certain elements that are only structural, and therefore invisible.[2] The

---

2 Such UI elements that are only structural and therefore invisible include transparent containers and layout managers.

most important of these is called `RootUIElementContainer`. This UI element has the following properties:

▶ It is always the root element in a UI element hierarchy.

▶ Its name is hard coded.

▶ It is always of type `TransparentContainer`.

All other UI elements in the view layout will appear as descendants of `RootUIElementContainer`, and each must have a unique name. This name then becomes the easiest mechanism for referencing a UI element in the hierarchy. You don't need to have any knowledge of the UI element's position in the hierarchy in order to access it.

This technique is typically used to access UI elements created at design time.

A second method of accessing UI elements is available, but it is much more involved and should be implemented only where named access is completely impossible. In this situation, not only is the name of the UI element unknown, you will probably also have no knowledge of the hierarchical structure.

Under these circumstances, you must perform a depth-first traversal of the UI element hierarchy.

8.3.1 Accessing UI elements by name

Important: The coding illustrated below can be executed only in method `wdDoModifyView()`. This is the only method in which you have access to the `view` object.

To access a UI element by name, you must know two things:

▶ The UI element's name, and

▶ The UI element's object type

Knowing these values, all you have to do is call method `getElement(String)` of the `view` object and cast the returned object as the appropriate UI element type.

The example below retrieves the UI element called `LastNameInput`, and then requests that it have input focus.

```
public static void
      wdDoModifyView(IPrivate{n_v} wdThis,
                     IPrivate{n_v}.IContextNode wdContext,
                     IWDView view,
                     boolean firstTime) {
  //@@begin wdDoModifyView
  // Get a reference to the UI element LastNameInput
  IWDInputField lastNameInput =
    (IWDInputField)view.getElement("LastNameInput");

  // Set input focus on this field
  lastNameInput.requestFocus();
//@@end
}
```

Listing 8.1 Referencing a UI Element by Name

There are several things to notice about this code sample.

▶ The class names of the input parameters to `wdDoModifyView()` have been generalized, $\{n_v\}$ being the name of this particular view controller. Obviously, you will not see this abbreviation in your code, but rather the name of your view controller!

▶ Although it is not used in this simple example, the boolean value `firstTime` allows you to determine whether you are building the initial presentation of the view layout (`firstTime==true`) or are responding to user input (`firstTime==false`).

▶ The method `view.getElement(String)` will return only a generalized `IWDViewElement` object. This must be cast to the correct object type for you to have access to the UI element's specific accessor and mutator methods.

8.3.2 Accessing UI elements generically

To access UI elements generically, a depth-first traversal of the UI element hierarchy must be performed.

Two approaches can be taken:

▶ **Approach 1** is a simple traversal mechanism and is quite straightforward to implement, but has the disadvantage that it is not fully generic; it can respond only to those child elements returned by the method `IWDUIElementContainer.iterateChildren()`.

▶ **Approach 2** is totally generic, but is more complex to implement. You may also incur slight performance overhead due to the fact that reflection is being used.

> **Caveat confector:** Do not implement a generic UI traversal unless it is really necessary! You will find this method of UI element identification is required only in situations in which you are writing some sort of generic utility component that must parse a UI element hierarchy of unknown structure.
>
> At all other times, you should be able to identify UI elements directly by name!

Approach 1: Simple traversal mechanism

This mechanism performs a recursive, depth-first traversal of only those UI elements returned by method `iterateChildren()` of class `IWDUIElementContainer`.

The important point to understand here is that `iterateChildren()` belongs to class `IWDUIElementContainer`; however, this is not the only class that can hold aggregations of child UI elements. The UI tree can be spanned by other UI element aggregations belonging to non-container elements, such as the `TabStrip`. Therefore, if processing is confined only to those UI elements returned by `iterateChildren()`, it is possible that certain parts of the UI tree will not be traversed.

This approach can be implemented by writing a simple recursive finite state engine, as follows:

▶ The method (called `visit()`) will receive one parameter of type `IWDViewElement`; this is the base class for all UI elements.

▶ If a UI element object is received that is not a container element,[3] then a leaf node has been reached and recursion can terminate.

  ▶ The UI element type must now be identified, and the required processing performed.

  ▶ If you do not explicitly code how the presence of a certain UI element should be handled, then no action is taken.[4]

  ▶ It is here that a special exception can be made if you know you are going to need to handle tab strip UI elements.

---

3 This is a reference to a UI element that is permitted to have children.
4 This is the finite state engine part of the implementation.

▶ If the UI element is a container object, perform any processing necessary for the container, then obtain an iterator of its child elements, and call yourself for each child.

The method described below shows the principles for implementing such a traversal.

```
public static void
        wdDoModifyView(IPrivate{nv} wdThis,
                       IPrivate{nv}.IContextNode wdContext,
                       IWDView view,
                       boolean firstTime) {
  //@@begin wdDoModifyView
  // Start with the root UI element
  visit(view.getRootElement());
  //@@end
}


private static void visit(IWDViewElement e) {
  // Is this UI element a container?
  if (e instanceof IWDUIElementContainer) {
    // Yup. If necessary, do something to the container
    IWDUIElementContainer elCont = (IWDUIElementContainer)e;
    elCont.<some_method>;

  // Visit each child element
    for (Iterator it = elCont.iterateChildren(); it.hasNext();) {
      visit((IWDUIElement)it.next());
    }
  }
  // Nope, implement a finite state engine to identify each UI
  // element that needs to be processed
  else if (e instanceof IWDButton) {
    // Instruct all button UI elements to obtain their icon
    // source from SomeNode.SomeAttribute in the context
    ((IWDButton)e).bindImageSource("SomeNode.SomeAttribute");
  }
  else if (e instanceof <UI_element_class>) {
    // Do something to the UI element ...
  }
  // Finally, handle the special case of a tab strip
  else if (e instanceof IWDTabStrip) {
    // Do something to the tabstrip itself
    IWDTabStrip tabStrip = (IWDTabStrip)e;
    tabStrip.<some_method>;
```

```
    // Do something to each tab, then recursively process the
    // contents of tab strip
    for (Iterator it = tabStrip.iterateTabs(); it.hasNext();) {
      IWDTab tab = (IWDTab)it.next();
      tab.<some_method>;

      // Visit content using recursive call to visit()
      visit(tab.getContent());
    }
  }
}
```

Listing 8.2 Simple Traversal of a UI Element Hierarchy

Notice that a tab strip UI element must be handled as a special case of a UI element that contains an aggregation of child elements, but is itself not a UI element container.

Approach 2: Generic traversal mechanism

If you wish to be able to respond in a completely generic manner to any aggregation of UI elements, the depth-first traversal mechanism must be extended. Now reflection must be used to determine the capabilities of each UI element in the hierarchy.

This form of implementation does not require that any UI elements be treated as special cases.

Caveat confector: Before you implement this type of coding, ask yourself: "Why am I doing this?" If it is because you are writing some sort of utility component that must behave in a completely generic manner, then fine; generic behavior is a fundamental part of your component's functionality, and therefore this style of coding is appropriate.

However, if you are simply copying the coding out of this book because you think it will make you look smart, then don't do it! You will not be contributing towards the overall simplicity and clarity of the application.

To implement coding that operates in a completely generic manner, the traversal mechanism must be neutral to the following situations. It must be able to process all UI element aggregations irrespective of:

- ▶ Whether the current element is a container element or not
- ▶ The method name by which the aggregation is returned

The required logic works as follows:[5]

Every UI element class has methods that will return an aggregation of UI elements. If the aggregation has a cardinality of single, then the method will be named `get<Aggregation>()` if the aggregation has a cardinality of multiple, then the method will be named `iterate<Aggregation>()`.

Step 1: Using reflection, examine each UI element class and obtain a list of its methods.

Step 2: Examine all the method names to see if they start with either `iterate` or `get`. This will identify which aggregation type is being returned.

Step 3: If we have found a method that returns an aggregation, does it return another UI element? That is, is the returned object derived from class `IWDViewElement`?

Step 4: All the methods satisfying the name criteria in step 2 and the return type criteria in step 3 are now invoked.

Step 5: Recursively process the UI elements returned from each call.

The following utility class (courtesy of Armin Reichert) will perform the necessary generic traversal of a UI element hierarchy.

```
// This template class provides a depth-first, generic traversal
// of a UI element hierarchy.
public class UITreeVisitor {
   private Map aggregationsByClass = new HashMap();
   private Set visited = new HashSet();

   public void beforeVisitChildren(IWDViewElement e) {
     // Do something useful before visiting the view element's
     // children
   }

   public void visitElement(IWDViewElement e) {
     // Do something useful with the current UI element.  This
     // processing is best implemented as a finite state engine
   }
```

---

5   Stay with me on this one…

```
public void afterVisitChildren(IWDViewElement e) {
  // Do something useful after the view element's children
  // have been visited
}


// Traverse all UI aggregations under the given view element
public final void visit(IWDViewElement e) {
  // Record visit to this element in a HashMap
  visited.add(e);

  visitElement(e);
  beforeVisitChildren(e);

  // Find all the methods of the current element that return UI
  // element aggregations. These aggregations could have single
  // or multiple cardinality.
  List aggregations = getOutgoingAggregations(e.getClass());

  // Process each method
  for (Iterator it = aggregations.iterator(); it.hasNext();) {
    // Get a reference to the next method
    Method m = (Method)it.next();

    // Does this method return an aggregation of multiple
    // cardinality?
    if (m.getName().startsWith("iterate")) {
      // Yup, so invoke this method process all the child UI
      // elements recursively
      try {
        // Loop around the child UI elements in the iteration
        for (Iterator targets = (Iterator)m.invoke(e, null);
          targets.hasNext();) {
          IWDViewElement child =
            (IWDViewElement)targets.next();

          // Visit the child (as long as we haven't been here
          // before)
          if (!visited.contains(child))
            visit(child);
        }
      }
      catch (Exception x) {
        // Shouldn't ever arrive in here...
      }
    }
    else {
```

```
      // Nope, so this method must return a single UI element
      try {
        // Call the method to see what we get
        IWDViewElement child = (IWDViewElement)m.
                                      invoke(e, null);

        // Visit the child (as long as we haven't been here
        // before)
        if (!visited.contains(child))
          visit(child);
      }
      catch (Exception x) {
        // Shouldn't ever arrive in here either...
      }
    }
  }

  afterVisitChildren(e);
}


// Returns the list of outgoing aggregations for the given view
// element class.  This information is cached for efficiency.
// An empty list will be returned when a leaf node is
// encountered.  This behavior defines the termination
// condition for recursion.
private List getOutgoingAggregations(Class clazz) {
  // Have we already encountered this class before?
  if (aggregationsByClass.containsKey(clazz)) {
    // Yup, so return the results from the cache
    return (List)aggregationsByClass.get(clazz);
  }
  else {
    // Nope, so find the methods of this class that all return
    // one or more UI elements
    List aggregations = collectOutgoingAggregations(clazz);

    // Store the method list to avoid having to repeat the
    // above processing
    aggregationsByClass.put(clazz, aggregations);

    return aggregations;
  }
}


// Build a list of outgoing aggregations for the given view
// element class using reflection.
```

```
private List collectOutgoingAggregations(Class clazz) {
  List result = new ArrayList();

  // Get a list of all the methods in this element class
  Method[] methods = clazz.getMethods();

  // Now check to see what each method does...
  for (int i = 0; i < methods.length; ++i) {
    // Does the method name start with "iterate"?
    if (methods[i].getName().startsWith("iterate"))
      // Yup, we can safely assume that this method returns an
      // aggregation of UI elements of multiple cardinality
      result.add(methods[i]);

    // Does the method name start with "get"?
    if (methods[i].getName().startsWith("get")) {
      // Yup, check the method's return type
      Class returnType = methods[i].getReturnType();

      // Is the return type ultimately derived from an
      // IWDViewElement?
      if (IWDViewElement.class.isAssignableFrom(returnType))
        // Yup, we can safely assume that this method returns
        // an aggregation of single cardinality (i.e., one UI
        // element).
        result.add(methods[i]);
    }
  }

  // Return a list of methods that, when called, will all
  // return an aggregation of one or more UI elements
  return result;
  }
}
```

Listing 8.3 Generic Traversal of a UI Element Hierarchy

This traversal mechanism will be able to navigate through a UI element hierarchy of any arbitrary structure. All that you need to implement is the finite state engine processing within method `visitElement()` to do something useful when UI elements of a particular type are encountered.

8.4 The principles of dynamic view construction

8.4.1 Before you start...

Before embarking upon an application design that uses dynamic view construction, consider carefully whether it would be possible to break up your view layout into declarative units that can be interchanged dynamically. This approach is preferable to building the entire view layout dynamically. However, if after careful consideration of your application's requirements, you conclude that it is not possible to declare your view layout at design time, then it can be constructed at runtime.

> **Caveat confector:** Dynamic UI construction must be used carefully. If this approach is used inappropriately or without a full understanding of the consequences, it is possible that you will introduce performance overheads that can be removed only by rewriting your view controller!

In some circumstances, a table UI element will function as a very good "dynamic" display, without actually needing to be created at runtime. For instance, if you are displaying the line items of a sales order, and you would like the amount of information on the screen to expand and contract as the number of line items changes, then the following is a good alternative to creating UI elements at runtime:

1. Create a table UI element on your view layout at design time.

2. Bind the table to a suitable context node.

3. Bind the `visibleRowCount` property of the table UI element to a context attribute.

4. Now, as the number of elements in the line items node varies, you can programmatically alter the context attribute controlling `visibleRow-Count`. Thus, the table will expand and contract as required.

8.4.2 The fundamental principles of dynamic view layout construction

1. Wherever possible, construct as much of the view layout as possible at design time.

2. Place as little code as possible into method `wdDoModifyView()`.

3. Prior to entering method `wdDoModifyView()`, the view controller's context must contain the necessary nodes, attributes, and runtime data.

This task must *not* be performed in `wdDoModifyView()`. See Chapter 11 for why this is so.

In addition to the business data to be displayed, the context should also contain nodes and attributes that can be used to control the behavior of the UI elements themselves. This principle remains true irrespective of whether the context has been declared at design time or built dynamically at runtime.

Either way, by the time you build the UI element hierarchy in method `wdDoModifyView()`, the context must have been fully prepared for read-only use.

4. Construct the view layout in method `wdDoModifyView()` only when the boolean parameter `firstTime` is true. Assuming that some sort of user interaction will occur with the view, method `wdDoModifyView()` will probably *not* need to reconstruct the view layout after each user interaction.

   If `firstTime` is false, then try to avoid UI element hierarchy manipulation.

5. During this construction process, you will need to assign values to the various properties of each UI element. This can be done either directly, by calling method {ui}.set{ui$_p$}, or indirectly by calling method {ui}.bind{ui$_p$}. The difference here is that the {ui}.set{ui$_p$} method assigns a fixed value to property {ui$_p$}, whereas method {ui}.bind{ui$_p$} instructs the UI element to obtain a value for property {ui$_p$} from the context.

Important:

▶ This principle remains true irrespective of whether the UI elements were created at design time or runtime.

▶ The call to method {ui}.bind{ui$_p$} is the recommended approach because UI manipulation can now be performed via the context, i.e., from outside method `wdDoModifyView()`.

6. All subsequent modifications to UI element behavior should be controlled by manipulating the context, not the UI element object.

If you follow these principles, you will ensure that your view layout is constructed in a manner that will provide the highest possible performance at runtime. For instance, if you continually use the {ui}.set{ui$_p$} method, you'll encounter the following consequences:

- ▶ If multiple UI elements all share the same property value (say the `visible` property), you will need to call the `{ui}.set{ui_p}` method for each individual element.

- ▶ You will only ever be able to alter the value of that property in method `wdDoModifyView()`.

Both of these consequences result in the violation of the principle that as little coding as possible should be placed in method `wdDoModifyView()`.

> **Important:** There are two dangers that are often not recognized by people writing a dynamically constructed view layout. The first has an impact on performance, and the second on code flexibility.

1. All too often, dynamic view layouts are constructed in which the entire UI element hierarchy is rebuilt every time method `wdDoModifyView()` is called; i.e., the design does not consider the value of the boolean parameter `firstTime`. This architecture should be avoided if possible.

2. If you wish to change the appearance of your screen, you will need to rewrite part or all of the functionality in method `wdDoModifyView()`.

However, SAP fully recognizes that not all application requirements can be fulfilled by a view layout containing a static UI element hierarchy. If you must construct your view layout dynamically, make sure you follow the principles listed above.

8.4.3   Controlling UI element behavior from the context

Most of the properties of a UI element can be bound to either a node or an attribute of the context. The behavior of the UI element can then be controlled by manipulation of the context. Properties such as `visible`, `enabled`, and `readOnly` are the ones you will typically use for dynamic alteration of a user interface.

The properties `enabled` and `readOnly` are boolean and don't affect whether a UI element is visible; they simply control whether the user can interact with it. However, if you want a UI element to be completely removed from the rendered screen, then you should change the `visible` property. This property takes three possible values held in the built-in type `Visibility`.

- ▶ `VISIBLE`
  Visible on the screen, but the user cannot necessarily interact with it

▶ **BLANK**
   Invisible but present on the screen

▶ **NONE**
   Completely absent from the screen

The `visible` property of a UI element must be bound to a context attribute of type `Visibility`. A context attribute can be assigned this data type as follows:

▶ Create a dependent context attribute called, say, `InputVisibility`.[6]

▶ The default data type for any context attribute is `string`. Change this by clicking on the ellipses button that appears to the right of the data type field.

▶ In the pop-up window, the radio button should be set to "Dictionary Simple Type." Expand the tree node "Local Dictionary."

▶ Expand the tree node `com.sap.ide.webdynpro.uielementdefinitions`, and select `Visibility`.

▶ Create your UI element in the view layout, and bind the `visible` property to this context attribute.

From the coding in your view controller, you will now be able to control the value of this context attribute using the values found in the `WDVisibility` class.

8.5 Dynamic Construction of a UI element hierarchy

The dynamic construction of a UI element hierarchy will typically be required when you have to display a context of unknown structure. Under these circumstances, it is not possible to create much of a UI layout at design time, because some (or even all) of the nodes in the view controller's context have not yet been defined.

Before implementing the dynamic construction of a UI element hierarchy, make sure you understand the following restrictions:

▶ You are only permitted to access UI elements in the view layout from the `wdDoModifyView()` method of the view controller.

▶ By referring to Chapter 11, you will see that `wdDoModifyView()` runs near the end of the request/response cycle. By the time the phase model processing has reached this step, all controller contexts should

---

6 This name is completely arbitrary.

be *stable*. That is, the processing performed within method `wdDoModi-fyView()` should not perform any actions that modify the context![7]

▶ Third, `wdDoModifyView()` is a static method! This is the result of a deliberate design decision made to discourage developers from storing references to UI element objects as instance members.

Do not store references to UI element objects and then attempt to manipulate them outside `wdDoModifyView()` (in event handlers, for instance). Every time `wdDoModifyView()` is called, all references to UI element instances will be overwritten!

Now that you have an understanding of the hierarchical structure of UI elements in a view layout, the dynamic construction approach will be easier to understand. This approach is typically required when you wish to create a UI element layout based on information whose structure can only be known at runtime.

Important: The solution documented here has its limitations! The following example deals only with a simple context structure. It is possible to write a totally generic context viewer, but to discuss such an application adequately would occupy too much space, and it is not the purpose of this book to discuss a specific application.

Consider the following situation:

A view controller context may contain an independent child node called `SalesOrders`. If this node exists, then it needs to be displayed as a table.[8] For the purposes of this example, we will assume that if the context node is absent at design time, the corresponding table UI element will also be absent from the view layout at design time.[9]

The task now is to create a view layout that can respond to a context of unknown structure. It is necessary, therefore, that the `wdDoModifyView()`

---

7 Due to the WDF's lazy data access mechanism, it is still possible that supply functions for context nodes could be executed during `wdDoModifyView()`. This would only happen if the node's contents were being accessed for the very first time during the current request/response cycle.

8 Each node attribute becomes a table column, and each node element becomes a table row.

9 It is entirely possible to declare a table UI element at design time, but to leave its `dataSource` property unbound. The caveat here is that before the screen can be rendered, you must ensure that either the `dataSource` parameter is correctly bound, or the table UI element is removed from the view.

method examine the structure of the context and generate UI elements according to what it finds.

> **Important:** If the context node `SalesOrders` had been created at design time, then a typed accessor method would have been created called `wdContext.nodeSalesOrders()`. However, in our situation, this method does not exist, so the generic accessor method `wdContext.getChildNode()` must be used instead. This method requires two parameters: first, the name of the node to be accessed, and, second, an integer identifying the lead selection of the parent node.[11]

The following example will examine the context for independent nodes and place any nodes it finds in collapsible tray UI elements. The following types of displays will be constructed depending on the number of elements found in the node collection:

▶ **Zero elements**
An appropriate text message will be displayed.

▶ **One element**
The single element will be displayed as a pair of label/input field columns.

▶ **Many elements**
The node will be displayed as a table.

Several utility methods have been created; the first will display any node (`showNode()`). This then examines the contents of the node and calls either `showNodeAsColumns()`, or `showNodeAsTable()`.

One important point to realize is that since method `wdDoModifyView()` is static, any methods it calls must also be static. Since it is not possible to declare a static method from the Methods tab in the controller editor screen, any utility methods required by `wdDoModifyView()` have to be defined between the `//@@begin others` and `//@@end` markers found at the end of the view controller's source code.

`wdDoModifyView()` is the second to the last stage of the phase model in which user-defined coding can be executed. Every view controller that is part of the current view assembly will have its `wdDoModifyView()` method called irrespective of any previous errors that may have taken place.

---

10 For independent nodes (i.e., nodes that have the context root as their parent), this value will always be zero, because the root node has one and only one element—element zero.

The following code is divided into different sections. Each one will be discussed separately.

```
public static void
        wdDoModifyView(IPrivate{nᵥ} wdThis,
                       IPrivate{nᵥ}.IContextNode wdContext,
                       IWDView view,
                       boolean firstTime) {
  //@@begin wdDoModifyView
  // It is only necessary to build the UI element hierarchy once
  if (firstTime) {
    nodeCounter = 0;

    // Get a reference to the root UI element in the view layout
    // hierarchy.  It is safe to assume that this element will
    // always exist, will always be of type
    // IWDTransparentContainer, and will always be called
    // RootUIElementContainer
    IWDTransparentContainer tCont =
      (IWDTransparentContainer)view.getRootElement();

    // Every UI element container must have a layout manager
    // assigned to it.  The layout manager defines how the child
    // UI elements will be arranged within this container.  Since
    // a layout manager cannot exist independently from a
    // container element, the act of calling the container's
    // createLayout() method both creates a new instance of the
    // layout manager and assigns it to the UI element container.
    tCont.createLayout(IWDRowLayout.class);

    // Loop around as many independent nodes as can be found in
    // the context
    for (Iterator indNodeIt =
           wdContext.getNodeInfo().iterateChildren();
         indNodeIt.hasNext();) {
      nodeCounter++;

      // Get the next independent node info from the iterator
      IWDNodeInfo indNodeInfo = (IWDNodeInfo)indNodeIt.next();

      // Call showNode() to create a visual representation of the
      // current node

      showNode(tCont, view,
        wdContext.getChildNode(indNodeInfo.getName(),0));
    }
```

```
     // If the context contains no nodes, then display an
     // appropriate message
     if (nodeCounter==0) {
       IWDTextView tv =
         (IWDTextView)view.createElement(IWDTextView.class,
                                    "EmptyContextTextView");
       tv.setText("The context is empty!");
       tv.setDesign(WDTextViewDesign.HEADER2);
       tCont.addChild(tv);
     }
   }
//@@end
}
//@@begin others
   static int nodeCounter;
//@@end
```

Listing 8.4 Generate a Dynamic UI Layout by Traversing the Independent Context
Nodes

The following processing steps takes place in `wdDoModifyView()`:

1. The processing is only to take place if this is the first time `wdDoModify-View()` has been called

2. A node counter is initialized.

3. A reference is obtained to the `RootUIElementContainer` object. This UI element will contain all subsequent additions to the view layout.

4. A layout manager is assigned to the entire view layout.

5. Via the `wdContext` object, we can obtain a reference to the context root node's metadata. This is the object returned by `wdContext.getNo-deInfo()`. From this, we can obtain an iterator on the metadata for all the independent child nodes in the context.

6. It must be stressed that this iterator returns objects that describe context metadata—not actual data! When working with both context nodes (`IWDNode` objects) and context node metadata (`IWDNodeInfo` objects), you must not confuse the two object types!

7. Iterate around all the objects under the context root, casting each as an `IWDNodeInfo` object.

8. The `nodeCounter` variable serves to give a numerical value to each node. This is only necessary for making each UI element name unique.

9. Utility method `showNode()` is now called. This generic method examines whatever node it is passed, and creates an appropriate visual representation for it. Method `showNode()` is passed a reference to the `RootUIElementContainer`, the WDF defined `view` object, and a reference to the current node object in the iteration.

10. Once the iterator has been processed, if the `nodeCounter` variable still equals zero, the context was empty, and an appropriate message is displayed.

The coding of the third parameter in the call to `showNode()` requires some explanation:

Because we have no idea what any of the context nodes are called, we cannot use any of the typed accessor methods available for nodes created at design time; therefore, we must access the context generically. This requires the use of the `getChildNode()` method. Every context node object implements this method, and it will return the instance of the named child node for the particular element of the parent collection. In general, you can retrieve an instance of child node {chn} from its parent node {cn} by the following coding:

```
IWDNode childNode = {cn}.getChildNode("Name of {chn}",
                            <element index in {cn}>);
```

In this case, we need to reference an independent node (an independent node has the context root node as its immediate parent). Therefore, there are two things to note:

▶ Access to the context root node is provided through object wdContext.

▶ The call to method `getChildNode()` must specify with which element in the parent node the child node is associated. The context root node can only ever have one element (its cardinality is hard coded to 1..1), therefore, the element number *must* be zero.

The `showNode()` method operates in the following way.

```
//@@begin others
private static void showNode(IWDTransparentContainer tCont,
  IWDView view, IWDNode thisNode) {
  // Get the metadata for the current node
  IWDNodeInfo thisNodeInfo = thisNode.getNodeInfo();
  // Create a collapsible tray in which to display the node
  IWDTray theTray = (IWDTray)view.
                  createElement(IWDTray.class,
                          "NodeTray" + nodeCounter);
```

```java
theTray.setDesign(WDTrayDesign.FILL);

// A tray UI element must have a descriptive caption in its
// header. A caption is a distinct UI element in its own right.
IWDCaption trayCaption = (IWDCaption)view.
                          createElement(IWDCaption.class,
                                        "NodeTray" +
                                        nodeCounter +
                                        "Caption");
trayCaption.setText("Node " + thisNodeInfo.getName());

// Add the caption to the tray
theTray.setHeader(trayCaption);

// How many elements does the context node contain?
switch (thisNode.size()) {
// Empty node collection
case 0:
  IWDTextView tv = (IWDTextView)view.
                    createElement(IWDTextView.class,
                                  "NoData" + nodeCounter);
  tv.setText("Node " + thisNodeInfo.getName() +
             " has no elements");
  theTray.addChild(tv);

  break;
// One element in node collection
case 1:
  // Configure the Tray UI element to have a layout manager of
  // RowLayout
  theTray.createLayout(IWDMatrixLayout.class);
  showNodeAsColumns(view, thisNodeInfo, theTray);

  break;
// Many elements in node collection
default:
  // Add table UI element to tray UI element
  theTray.addChild(showNodeAsTable(view, thisNodeInfo));
}

// The visual representation of the node to the transparent
// container
tCont.addChild(theTray);

// Loop around as many dependent nodes as can be found for this
// node
```

```
for (Iterator chnIt = thisNode.getNodeInfo().iterateChildren();
     chnIt.hasNext();) {
  nodeCounter++;
  // Store the next iterator object as an IWDNodeInfo
  IWDNodeInfo chnInfo = (IWDNodeInfo)chnIt.next();

  // Call showNode() to create a visual representation of the
  // current node
  showNode(tCont, view,
           thisNode.getChildNode(chnInfo.getName(),
                                  thisNode.getLeadSelection())));
  }
}
```

Listing 8.5 Method showNode() Builds a UI Layout Appropriate for the Node It Has Been Passed

First, notice that the `showNode()` method is defined between the `//@@begin others` and `//@@end` comment markers found at the end of the view controller's source code. This is the only place in the controller coding where you may define a static method.

The following processing takes place in `showNode()`:

▶ We have been passed a reference to the specific node object to be displayed. This is a reference to the actual runtime data. However, we need to know about the node's metadata; therefore, we call the `getNodeInfo()` method on the node object.

Important: Every node object `{cn}` has an associated metadata object. This can be obtained by calling `{cn}.getNodeInfo()`. However, if you have a node info object, it is not possible to obtain an instance of the related node object since there are potentially many different objects based on this one metadata object. In other words, there is no such method as `IWDNodeInfo.getNode()`.

▶ A Tray UI element is created and its design property is set.

▶ Every tray UI element has a mandatory child caption object. This object is defined, its text value is assigned from the node info object, and then the caption is added to the tray.

▶ Now the number of elements in the current node is examined, and the following actions taken:

  ▷ Zero elements: Display text message

- ▶ One element: Show node element as label/input field pair of columns

- ▶ Many elements: Show node elements as a table.

▶ Once an appropriate visual representation has been created for the current node, another iterator is obtained on the current node's child nodes. This iterator is now processed and showNode() is called recursively for each child node.

▶ Notice on the recursive call to showNode() that the same getChildNode() method is being used, but with two important differences.

- ▶ The method belongs to the current node being processed, not wdContext.

- ▶ We must obtain the appropriate child node instance for whichever element is at the lead selection of the current node. This will not necessarily be element zero. The element at the lead selection is controlled automatically by which table row the user has clicked on.

This form of processing will produce a sequence of tray elements down the screen that corresponds to the top-to-bottom, left-to-right traversal of the node hierarchy.

The last two methods to be discussed are the utility methods that take a node and display it either as a pair of label/input field columns, or as a table.

```
private static void showNodeAsColumns(IWDView view,
                                      IWDNodeInfo attrInfo,
                                      IWDTray theTray) {
// For each attribute, create a label/input pair of fields
for (Iterator attrIt = thisNodeInfo.iterateAttributes();
     attrIt.hasNext();) {
  IWDAttributeInfo attrInfo = (IWDAttributeInfo)attrIt.next();

  // Create a label UI element and set its text to be name of
  // the attribute
  IWDLabel lab = (IWDLabel)view.
                  createElement(IWDLabel.class,
                                attrInfo.getName()+ "Label");
  lab.setText(attrInfo.getName());

  // Set the layout data to be the start of a new matrix row
  // and switch off the vertical bar to the left of the label
  // text
  lab.createLayoutData(IWDMatrixHeadData.class);
```

```
lab.setDesign(WDLabelDesign.LIGHT);

// Add the label to the tray container
theTray.addChild(lab);

// Create an input field UI element and bind it to the
// relevant context attribute
IWDInputField inFld = (IWDInputField)view.
                    createElement(IWDInputField.class,
                            attrInfo.getName() +
                            "Input");
inFld.bindValue(attrInfo);

// Make the input field read-only and set the layout data to
// be a matrix cell
inFld.setReadOnly(true);
// Since MatrixData is the default layout for this layout
// manager, setting this value is not strictly necessary
inFld.createLayoutData(IWDMatrixData.class);

// Add the input field to the tray container
theTray.addChild(inFld);
  }
}
```

Listing 8.6 Method showNodeAsColumns() Displays a Node as a Pair of Columns

showNodeAsColumns() should be called only if the node it is to display contains a single element. The processing works as follows:

▶ Using the node metadata object (IWDNodeInfo), you can obtain the corresponding metadata object (IWDAttributeInfo) for each node attribute.

Remember we are dealing here entirely with the metadata stored in node info and attribute info objects. We are not working with actual runtime data. Be careful not to get the two confused!

▶ For each attribute, create a label UI element and set its text to the name of the current attribute info object.

▶ Add the label to the tray UI element.

▶ Create an input field to display the actual data.

▶ Bind the input field to the current attribute info object. This action establishes the link between the UI element and the appropriate context attribute. This is how the runtime data will appear in the UI element when the screen is rendered. If this step is not performed, you'll get a runtime error from the response rendering stage of the phase model.

▶ Setting the readOnly attribute to true is optional.

▶ Add the input field to the tray UI element.

```
private static IWDTable showNodeAsTable(IWDView view, IWDNodeInfo
   childNodeInfo) {
IWDTableColumn tabCol;
IWDCaption     tabColCap;
IWDInputField  cellEditor;

// Create a table object and bind its dataSource property to
// the current node info object
IWDTable tab = (IWDTable)view.
                createElement(IWDTable.class,
                              childNodeInfo.getName() +
                              "Table");
tab.bindDataSource(childNodeInfo);

// Iterate around the attributes of this node turning each one
// into a table column
// Each UI element object must be given a unique name
for (Iterator attIt = childNodeInfo.iterateAttributes();
     attIt.hasNext();) {
  // Create a table column object. All table columns must have
  // a caption element as their headers and some sort of
  // element as their cell editors. A column may have only one
  // type of UI element as its cell editor.
  IWDAttributeInfo thisAttrib = (IWDAttributeInfo)attIt.next();
  tabCol = (IWDTableColumn)view.
            createElement(IWDTableColumn.class,
                          "ColumnFor" + thisAttrib.getName());

  // Define a column caption, set the text, and add it to the
  // column.
  tabColCap = (IWDCaption)view.
               createElement(IWDCaption.class,
                             "CaptionFor" +
                             thisAttrib.getName());

  tabColCap.setText(thisAttrib.getName());
  tabCol.setHeader(tabColCap);

  // Define an input field to be the cell editor for this
```

```
    // column and associate it with this column
    cellEditor = (IWDInputField)view.
                    createElement(IWDInputField.class,
                    "CellEditorFor" +
                    thisAttrib.getName());
    // Bind cell editor to the path of the context attribute
    cellEditor.bindValue(thisAttrib);
    tabCol.setTableCellEditor(cellEditor);

    // Finally, add the column to the table
    tab.addColumn(tabCol);
  }

  return tab;
}
// static variable declarations
  static int nodeCounter;
//@@end
```

Listing 8.7 Method showNodeAsTable() Displays a Node as a Table

Method `showNodeAsTable()` operates in a similar manner to `showNode-AsColumns()`, but there are some important differences.

▶ Create a table UI element and bind its `dataSource` property to the current node info object. This supplies the UI element with the metadata of the columns it will (potentially) display.

A table UI element is a composite UI element. That means it is constructed from child UI elements whose existence is mandatory! A table UI element is composed of one or more table column UI elements, which, in turn, are composed of a caption UI element and a cell editor.[11] The cell editor is any interactive UI element in which the data for that column is to be displayed.[12]

▶ As with `showNodeAsColumns()`, `showNodeAsTable()` obtains an iterator of the attribute metadata for the current node.

▶ Create a table column UI element for the current attribute.

▶ Create a caption UI element, set its text property to the name of the current attribute, and add it to the table column UI element.

---

11 Two other optional UI elements can be used in a table: `MasterColumn` and a `ToolBar`.
12 A table column can have only one type of cell editor.

▶ Nominate a UI element to be the cell editor. You have a wide choice of UI elements that can be used here. In this case, we'll use an `Input-Field`.

A cell editor can be any one of a `Button`, `Caption`, `CheckBox`, `DropDown-ByIndex`, `DropDownByKey`, `FileDownload`, `Image`, `InputField`, `LinkTo-Action`, `LinkToURL`, `ProgressIndicator`, `RadioButton`, or `TextView`.

▶ Once the cell editor has been added to the table column UI element, and the table column added to the table UI element, the processing for that one node attribute is complete.

▶ Once all the node attributes have been processed, the completed table UI element is returned to the calling method.

9   The Common Model Interface[1]

As stated earlier, the design paradigm upon which Web Dynpro is based is Model View Controller. So far, the view and controller parts of a Web Dynpro component have been described, and the model part has been used but not fully described. This is because the model objects are implemented through their own abstraction layer known as the Common Model Interface (CMI).

The CMI serves as an interface definition for any runtime framework or application that wants to make the business logic within some remote system (such as R/3 or a Web Service provider) available to a higher application layer. Therefore, the CMI is a highly versatile layer that can supply functionality to *any* consumer layer, i.e., a batch processing facility or, in our case, the WDF.

The introduction of CMI as an intermediate abstraction layer means that any consumer layer is completely decoupled from the specific model implementation (like Adaptive RFC or Web Service). The consuming layer need only reference the CMI in order to gain full access to the underlying business logic.

The current implementation of the CMI is mainly driven by the needs of the Web Dynpro context, so it focuses on the following areas:

▶ Data transport to and from the model layer

▶ The metadata needed to build generic functionality

▶ Event processing to enable change management

It does not yet provide additional services that are common to other model implementations like transaction handling, locking, or messaging.

9.1   CMI terms and definitions

9.1.1   Model

A model is the collective name for an aggregation of model classes. The model should be considered the whole, whereas model classes are the parts out of which the whole is constructed. Each model class within the model implements the CMI to expose business data and metadata (at least via reflection) to the consuming layer.

---

1   From an article written by Frank Weigel.

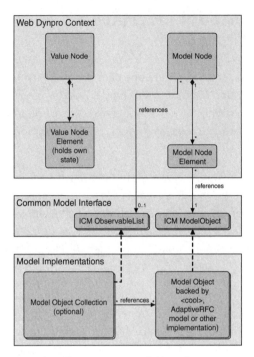

Figure 9.1 The Common Model Interface

The model itself will then hold information beyond that supplied simply by the individual model classes—such as connection information, transaction status, and messages.

A model may contain either typed model classes or generic model classes (see below). In some rare cases, a model can contain both typed *and* generic model classes.

Important: The CMI is *not* responsible for the consistency of data within the model. A model must guarantee its own data consistency!

9.1.2 Model class

A model class is the main data abstraction class for the CMI in much the same way that a context node is the abstraction of a typed data collection. It represents a single type of data within a model. Each model class exposes a set of properties similar to the attributes of a context node. Where model classes differ from context nodes is in the fact that model classes can perform specific relationship roles with each other that are not restricted to the simple parent-child relationships seen in the context.

For instance, since model class {rfcm}_Output represents the typed data on the output side of the executable model object {rfcm}_Input, it performs the relation role of "Output". This role would be generically identified using the relation name {rfcm}_Input:Output:{rfcm}_Output.

9.2 Access from a CMI object to the underlying business logic

The CMI defines two mechanisms by which the underlying business logic can be accessed:

▶ Typed access
▶ Generic access

9.2.1 Typed access

A typed CMI model class allows access to the underlying business logic through typed accessor and mutator methods. This is much like a Java Bean or a context node where typedAccessRequired == true.

The typed access interface of CMI has the following requirements:

▶ The structure of a model and its model classes must be at least partially known at design time. This design-time information must be supplied as metadata available to the model consuming layer, such as Web Dynpro.

▶ CMI defines some naming rules for how the design time metadata maps to the Java runtime implementation of the model.

▶ A CMI typed access class is not required to implement any mandatory Java interfaces.

One significant advantage of a typed model class is that applications can program against models in a completely type-safe manner. Using both this metadata and the CMI-defined naming rules, Web Dynpro is able to bind context model elements to model classes, and also generate "glue" code to connect the two layers together.

9.2.2 Generic access

A generic CMI class is one in which the structure of a model is not necessarily known at design time. This concept is very similar to the generic context API.

Each runtime implementation of a model class must extend CMI specific interfaces that allow the model's consumer to interrogate the model's metadata at runtime, and to access and modify model attributes and relations by their names only.

Since no metadata is available for generic classes at design time, Web Dynpro can use only dynamic binding between context model nodes and CMI model objects at runtime. On the other hand, no generation step is needed to create the "glue" coding mentioned for typed classes.

Applications can use either the CMI interfaces or the actual model implementation depending on their needs.

Use of typed access is usually preferable because it provides design-time convenience (code completion) and safety (compiler checks). On the other hand, generic frameworks or generic application components might prefer generic access as it is independent from actual types (except the generic CMI interfaces).

To allow maximum flexibility, a model implementation can use either typed or generic classes or even mix them.

These interfaces are defined in the packages under `com.sap.tc.cmi`; see the SAP NetWeaver Developer Studio help for details.

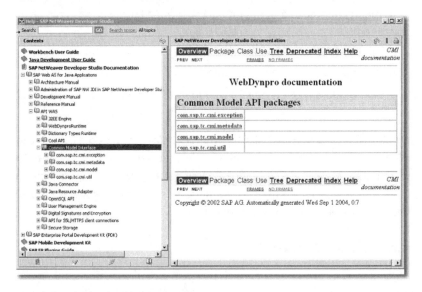

Figure 9.2 Javadoc for the CMI Interface

10   The Adaptive RFC layer

Many customers using Web Dynpro will already be users of one or more existing SAP systems; for instance, you may have an R/3 Enterprise, CRM or a BI system. In order for an external program to interact with the business functionality found in SAP systems, the ABAP based functionality must be invoked by means of a remote function call (RFC). The most well known RFC modules are the so called BAPIs.[1]

10.1   General introduction to BAPIs

For those readers not familiar with the internal workings of an SAP system, a BAPI is a unit of ABAP coding known as a function module. Each function module is a member of an aggregation known as a function group. All function groups are designed in such a way that their member function modules perform tasks related to the same business process.

In addition to each function module having its own private variable declarations, function modules can share information with each other by means of variables common to the function group. Standard SAP function modules make frequent use of this technique.[2]

The average SAP system contains around 50,000 function modules contained within approximately 8,000 function groups. Of these 50,000 function modules, some 9,500 are callable from outside the SAP system,[3] with a variable proportion of that being BAPIs.[4]

10.1.1   What is a BAPI?

Superficially speaking, a BAPI is simply an ABAP function module that can be invoked from outside the SAP system. However, a much stricter set of criteria must be met before a function module can truly be described as a BAPI. The ABAP function module must:

▶ Be delivered by SAP.[5]

▶ Have a name that starts with BAPI_[6]

---

1 BAPI stands for Business Application Programming Interface.
2 This information sharing feature only applies when function modules are called from the same ABAP session.
3 I.E. They are known as RFC modules.
4 The proportion of function modules in an SAP system that are BAPIs varies with the type of system—BI, CRM, APO etc.
5 Customers are welcome to write RFC modules that function exactly like BAPIs, but the burden of support for such modules lies with the customer, not SAP.
6 A customer written function module must start with the letter Z or Y.

- ▶ Maintain a static interface through different versions of the SAP system.

- ▶ Be a remote enabled module (I.E. it can be invoked from outside the SAP system).

- ▶ Not cause an ABAP session change by invoking a direct database update or an ABAP COMMIT statement.

- ▶ Run to completion without any need for secondary user interaction.

- ▶ Handle all errors gracefully (I.E. not raise any ABAP exceptions).

- ▶ Be written to implement the method of an SAP business object.[7]

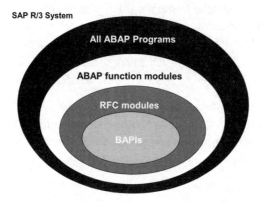

Figure 10.1 BAPIs are an inner subset of the set of ABAP function modules

10.1.2 The interface of an ABAP function module

Figure 10.1 shows that within the set all ABAP programs, there is the set of coding entities known as ABAP function modules. Within this subset, there is the subset of RFC modules; these ABAP function modules can be invoked from outside the R/3 system. Within the set of RFC modules, there is a further subset of RFC modules that conform to the BAPI design criteria.

Irrespective of its functionality or visibility, the interface of every ABAP function module within an SAP R/3 system conforms to a standard design. Therefore, the following explanation of the interface of an ABAP function module will also hold true for all RFC modules and all BAPIs.

All ABAP function modules can make use of 5 distinct types of parameter. Some are use only for input, some are used only for output, and some are bi-directional. These parameter types are:

---

7 Customer written RFC modules will probably not need to fulfil this requirement.

- **IMPORTING parameters**

  As the name implies, `IMPORTING` parameters define those value that are only used on the inbound side of the function module's interface. These parameters are either single fields or scalar structures.

- **EXPORTING parameters**

  As the name implies, `EXPORTING` parameters define those value that are only used on the outbound side of the function module's interface. These parameters are either single fields or scalar structures.

- **TABLES parameters**

  `TABLES` parameters define any tabular structure in the function module's interface. The structure of these parameters is defined using an ABAP dictionary structure and at runtime, may contain zero or more rows.

  All `TABLES` parameters are bi-directional. This means that you may pass data into a function module in one of the `TABLES` parameters, the function module can then modify the contents, and pass the same table back containing completely different data.

  Important: For this reason, a Web Dynpro model object will maintain an inbound and outbound version of all `TABLES` parameters.

- **CHANGING parameters**

  `CHANGING` parameters define the function module's bidirectional scalar parameters. That is, they behave as if they were both `IMPORTING` and `EXPORTING` parameters.

  Standard SAP BAPIs tend not to use `CHANGING` parameters.

- **EXCEPTIONS**

  `EXCEPTIONS` are labels used to identify that some type of abnormal termination has occurred within the function module.

  Exceptions are triggered by using the ABAP statement `RAISE`, but the use of this statement has been explicitly excluded from SAP's definition of a BAPI. This is because upon executing a `RAISE` statement, the function module will terminate immediately, thus violating the principle that a BAPI should run to completion, handling all errors gracefully.

  The use of the `RAISE` statement could also leave the function module's interface in an inconsistent state.

Important: Whilst it is not necessary for a Java Web Dynpro programmer to be able to program in ABAP, it is very important that the interface presented by an ABAP function module is understood. The different parameter types will be represented as proxy objects within the generated model, and in order to understand the generated objects, you must understand the interface of the underlying ABAP function module.

Important: If you are a Java developer with no prior experience of an SAP system, then in order to have a full understanding of the interface with which you are working, you should learn how to do the following in an SAP system:

► Logon to an SAP system[8]

► Use transaction SE37 (Function Module Builder) to:

 ▸ Examine the interface of a function module

 ▸ Run the function module with appropriate test data

 ▸ Examine the output from a function module

► Use transaction SE12 (ABAP Dictionary) to examine the fields in a table or data structure

► Use transaction SE16 (Data Browser) to display the contents of a database table

The above skills should be considered the minimum level of SAP competence required by all Web Dynpro developers. (These skills are very basic and can be taught in a matter of hours).

Beyond this, extra skills related to the actual SAP application area in which you are working may also need to be acquired.

10.2 Custom written RFC modules

During the course of the analysis phase of your Web Dynpro project, it is likely that you will encounter a situation in which the required functionality cannot be supplied by a standard BAPI. Under these circumstances,

---

8 The user id used in this situation must have at least S_RFC and S_DEVELOP authorisation.

a decision must be made on how to proceed. There are various options available, each having their own advantages and disadvantages.

1. Adjust the functional requirements of your application to fit the functionality delivered by the standard BAPIs.

   Advantages: Your custom written Web Dynpro application will only make use of standard SAP delivered functionality, and will therefore be free from any side effects after an upgrade.

   Disadvantages: The missing functionality may be fundamental to the success of the Web Dynpro application; therefore, it cannot be excluded from the project scope.

2. If a standard BAPI can be identified that partially delivers the required functionality, then this can be used as the starting point for a customer developed wrapper RFC module.

   Advantages: You are already half way to a solution. The wrapper RFC module will have an interface that is a superset of the BAPI's interface; the extra fields being those necessary to drive the enhanced functionality found in the wrapper RFC module.

   The wrapper RFC module should first call the standard BAPI, then once this has completed successfully, the extra functionality is performed.

   Disadvantages: More development effort is required. ABAP development skills will be required in addition to Java Web Dynpro development skills.

3. If no standard BAPI can be identified that even comes close to the required functionality, then a customer written RFC module must be developed.

   Advantages: You have complete control over the delivered functionality.

   Disadvantages: More development effort is required. ABAP development skills will be required in addition to Java Web Dynpro development skills.

   Your custom developments are not guaranteed to work after an SAP upgrade. The burden of responsibility for migrating custom developments to an upgraded SAP system lies entirely with the customer.

Caveat confector: If either option 2 or 3 is implemented, then important design principles must be adhered to during the development of custom RFC modules. These principles are documented in the SAP Online help (*http://help.sap.com*) under the heading "BAPI Programming Guide" (Component CA-BFA) and "RFC Programming in ABAP" (Component BC-MID-RFC).

Failure to adhere to these BAPI design principles will result in your Web Dynpro application being unable to manage the data in the SAP system correctly. For instance, you will experience problems with Web Dynpro's ability to manage ABAP lock objects, if you are not aware of the association between a JCo session and an ABAP session.

A Web Dynpro application is not concerned about whether the RFC module it invokes is a standard BAPI, an SAP delivered RFC module, or a custom written RFC module. In addition to this, since the set of BAPIs in an SAP system is a subset of the set of all RFC modules; from this point onwards, we will refer to all ABAP function modules invoked by Web Dynpro as *RFC modules* rather than restricting the discussion simply to BAPIs.

10.3 Background to the adaptive RFC layer

Interaction between external programs and the ABAP world of SAP systems has been provided by the Remote Function Call (RFC) communication layer since version 2.0F of R/3. From a technical point of view, the RFC layer is built upon the Common Programming Interface for Communication protocol (CPI-C), which in turn, sits upon the TCP/IP layers.

In earlier versions of the RFC interface, external programs had to work directly with the RFC layer. This was fine if you were a C programmer, but for languages like Java, implementation was not possible without using native OS libraries to make the RFC calls for you.

10.3.1 The Java Connector (JCo)

The JCo layer was developed to provide efficient access to R/3 systems from Java via RFC on all supported SAP platforms. The JCo interface was not typed, but provided a generic interface at the level of RFC semantics.

The JCo layer tolerates changes in the interface structure because fields are accessed through a named lookup, rather than a simple offset and length, based on runtime metadata.

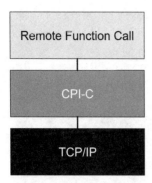

Figure 10.2 Basic RFC Architecture

Nevertheless, the only metadata available was restricted to what the RFC layer provided. This did not include ABAP dictionary metadata such as label texts or ValueSets. Also, the JCo layer implemented a programming model similar to JDBC, which proved quite complex due to the structured nature of RFC module calls and their various structured parameters.

10.3.2 The Enterprise Connector

In order to simplify the use of the JCo layer, a typed interface containing a 1:1 representation of the RFC function and all of its structures and tables was required. This was provided by the Enterprise Connector Framework (formerly known as the Java Connectivity Builder).

This layer was built on the JCo layer, but worked on the basis of a static interface definition created via the import of metadata at design time. This meant that within the external program, there was a static representation of the RFC module's interface containing only the offset, length, and primitive data type of each field *as it was defined at the time the interface was imported*. The byte stream exported from the SAP system was then subdivided using this hard coded offset and length information.

This type of interface seriously restricted the flexibility of the external program because it had no access to the information in the ABAP Dictionary. This produced the following limitations:

▶ ABAP Dictionary fields and data structures could only be represented by primitive data types.

▶ No support for standard extensibility features found in the ABAP Dictionary such as the .APPEND[9] structure.

---

9 Pronounced "Dot Append".

▶ No support for different versions of dictionary structures found in different versions of SAP systems.

▶ No availability of interface metadata at runtime.

Consider the ABAP Dictionary structure in Figure 10.3.

Figure 10.3 ABAP Dictionary structure used in an RFC module interface

If this structure appeared in the interface of an RFC module, the then Enterprise Connector would have generated accessor method using static offset and length values, such as those shown in the following pseudo-implementation.

```
String getId()        { return bytesAsString(0,10); }
String getLastName()  { return bytesAsString(10,50); }
String getFirstName() { return bytesAsString(60,50); }
```

Listing 10.1 A pseudo-implementation of the accessor methods typical of the older static Enterprise Connector interface

If the interface to the ABAP function module was changed in *any* way, then the static Enterprise Connector object became incompatible with the new byte stream, and the external program would typically suffer a fatal runtime error!

This meant that because the Enterprise Connector was not aware of any new fields in the interface, it was unable to keep running after the interface changed.

The JCo layer contains the ability to access any part of the interface structure, but since the Enterprise Connector only held a static definition of the interface, it made no use of this functionality, and was therefore unable to react to modifications that took place in the interface after design time.

What was needed was a mechanism for passing the full interface definition available in the JCo layer, up to the application layer at runtime. This would then allow the application to respond to changes in a function module's interface at runtime. In order to achieve this, it would be necessary both to provide typed access to the interface, and to supply interface metadata at runtime.

The adaptive RFC layer supplies this required functionality.

10.4 Introduction

The Adaptive RFC (aRFC) layer is an application layer that sits on top of the JCo communication layer. Its purpose is to provide a dictionary based, adaptive interface to the byte stream received at the JCo communication layer. It has been built in such a way that it can automatically adapt to certain modifications in an RFC module's interface.

This dictionary based access to one or more RFC module interfaces is encapsulated within a generated class hierarchy known as a model. An aRFC model may contain as many RFC module interfaces as you require. Whilst no technical limits exist on the number of RFC modules that may be encapsulated within a model, there are certain practical and functional limits that you should impose upon the size of a model. These will be discussed in the following sections.

Important: Notice that the aRFC layer is adaptive – not dynamic! If you include a whole new TABLES or IMPORTING parameter in your RFC module, then the aRFC layer will not be able to adapt to the presence of this new structure. Nevertheless, such a change will not prevent the RFC module working with the original functionality.

What the adaptive RFC interface can handle is the arrival of a new field within an existing structure. The aRFC layer can adapt to modifications such as:

▶ Addition of new fields to `.APPEND` structures in standard SAP tables.[10]

▶ Field length changes

▶ Label text changes

▶ Value set changes

Using the example in Figure 10.3 above, you will notice that the fields of the ABAP structure `WDY_DEMO_ADDRESS` are based on the following ABAP dictionary components (the last of which is a `.APPEND` structure)

▶ `WDY_DEMO_NAME`

▶ `WDY_DEMO_FIRSTNAME`

▶ `WDY_DEMO_TITLE`

▶ `WDY_DEMO_STREET`

▶ `WDY_DEMO_CITY`

▶ `WDY_DEMO_ZIP`

▶ `WDY_DEMO_COUNTRY`

▶ `WDY_DEMO_PHONE`

▶ `WDY_DEMO_STATE`

▶ `WDY_DEMO_APPEND`

Each Web Dynpro model has its own dictionary in which are held the unique set of structures that define the interfaces of all the RFC modules in the model. When a Web Dynpro model is generated for an RFC module that uses structured parameters in its interface, the ABAP Dictionary structures are replicated as Java Dictionary Simple Types within the model's dictionary. This means that all the metadata defined in the ABAP Dictionary is available via the model's dictionary both at design time (through the Web Dynpro Perspective of the NWDS) and at runtime. You now have runtime access to such metadata as the:

▶ `Field label`

▶ `Column heading`

▶ `Tool tip`

---

10 The use of `.APPEND` as a field name within an ABAP dictionary table allows another dictionary structure to be included at that point in the table definition. This mechanism allows customers to extend SAP standard tables without having to register the change as a modification of an SAP standard dictionary structure. The structure being `.APPEND`ed is considered free for modification by the customer.

▶ Value set

▶ Field length[11]

> **Important:**
>
> ▶ A model should be designed to represent a self contained unit of business functionality. The business functionality will frequently be broken into discrete steps;[11] with each step providing an atomic unit of processing.
>
> In database terms, you should design a model to contain only those processing steps that form a single logical unit of work. Once the functionality of a model has completed (using as many steps as necessary), a database commit (or rollback) should be issued. This topic will be discussed in greater detail in Section 10.10.
>
> ▶ You cannot construct a Web Dynpro model from RFC modules that live in *different* SAP systems!
>
> ▶ RFC modules should be grouped into Web Dynpro models according to their common functionality.

The RFC module (part of whose interface is shown in Figure 10.4) has been imported into a Web Dynpro Project using the model name of AddressModel.

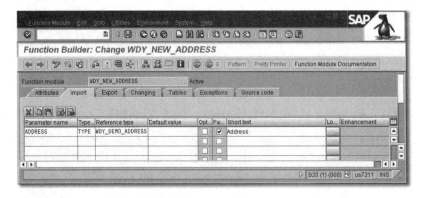

Figure 10.4 ABAP Dictionary structure WDY_DEMO_ADDRESS used to define an RFC module's IMPORTING parameter

---

11   In the case of an aRFC model, each step corresponds to an RFC module.

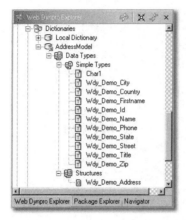

Figure 10.5 Dictionary structures created after a model import

If you look back at Figure 10.3 and Figure 10.5, you will see how the model generator takes the ABAP Dictionary Component Types and creates a corresponding Simple Type in the Java Dictionary. These are then aggregated into the structured type of the same name as the ABAP dictionary structure. Therefore, the ABAP dictionary structure Wdy_Demo_Address appears under the Structures node, and the different ABAP component types (upon which the fields in Wdy_Demo_Address are based) appear under the Simple Types node.

All access to the RFC module's structured parameters now takes place using the information held in the model's dictionary.

The .APPEND structure WDY_DEMO_APPEND contains a single field of type CHAR1 called DUMMY. This is because a .APPEND structure is not permitted to contain zero fields.

10.5 Explanation of Generated Model Classes

The name of an aRFC model is user definable. According to the SAP naming convention for such objects, the model name {n_m} should consist of the desired model name {m}, with the suffix Model.

{n_m} = {m}Model

In the example in Figure 10.6, the desired model name is Address; therefore, the resulting aRFC model should be called AddressModel. This naming convention must be adhered to manually; it is not enforced by the IDE!

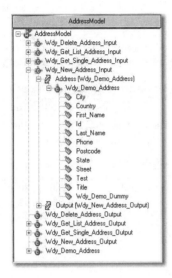

Figure 10.6 Hierarchy within a model object

The various parameters types used in a model object can be identified by the different icons:

▶ 🌐
  A non-executable model class

▶ 🌐
  An executable model class

▶ 🖉
  A structured parameter (often bi-directional)

▶ 🔖
  A scalar parameter

Four RFC modules have been imported into this model:[12]

▶ **WDY_GET_LIST_ADDRESS**
  Return a table of all known addresses

▶ **WDY_GET_SINGLE_ADDRESS**
  Return details of a single address

▶ **WDY_NEW_ADDRESS**
  Create a new address

▶ **WDY_DELETE_ADDRESS**
  Delete an address

---

12   See Appendix A for the ABAP coding listings.

10.5.1 Model object hierarchies

For each of the RFC modules, an {rfcm}_Input and an {rfcm}_Output class have been created, where {rfcm} is the name of the RFC module.

All structured parameters are represented as distinct classes (each constructed from fields defined as Dictionary Simple Types). Each time {rfcm} uses a parameter defined by one of these structure, that structure class will appear under the corresponding {rfcm}_Input or {rfcm}_Output class (or both if the parameter is bi-directional).

The class hierarchy within a model can be represented generically as follows:

```
{n_m}
    {rfcm}_Input
        {rfcm_in}
        Output
                {rfcm}_Output
                        {rfcm_out}
    {rfcm}_Output
        {rfcm_out}
```

The names {rfcm_in} and {rfcm_out} represent the parameter names as defined in the ABAP interface, not the names of the ABAP dictionary data types upon which they are based.

Notice that class {rfcm}_Output occurs both individually, and as a child of {rfcm}_Input. This is because the data coming out of the RFC module is represented by its own distinct class; but at the same time, output from an RFC module cannot be generated without there first being a corresponding input object![13] Therefore, the {rfcm}_Output class always appears as a child of {rfcm}_Input.

Important: This concept remains true irrespective of whether the RFC module requires input parameters or not.

When you bind a context model node to a model object, the ABAP structured parameter names (icon) will be replicated into the context as node names, and the ABAP field names (icon) will be replicated as attribute names.

---

13 The RFC module's functionality is invoked by calling the execute() method that can only be found in class {rfcm}_Input.

Due to the CHANGING and TABLES parameters of an RFC module being bi-directional, duplicate parameter names will be found on both the input and output sides of the interface. In these situations, the ABAP dictionary structures used in these parameter types will appear both as children of the {rfcm}_Input and {rfcm}_Output classes.

Within a model's class hierarchy, parameters are identified using their ABAP parameter names (🔧 icon), then under each of these, you will see the model class icon 🔩 that identifies the Java class representing the ABAP dictionary structure for that parameter.

10.5.2 Executable and non-executable model objects

The model object hierarchy shown in Figure 10.6 contains both execut-able and non-executable model objects. These can be distinguished by their icon. Notice that all model objects that define the input side of an RFC module's interface are executable (I.E. they have the 🔩 icon next to them). All the other model objects are non-executable (I.E. they have the 🔩 icon next to them).

The reason for this is that within the interface of an RFC module (or any model type for that matter), there are both structured and scalar param-eters. Each of the structure parameters is represented by a separate class, but that class on its own, does not fully describe the RFC module's inter-face. Therefore, these classes are non-executable.

In order to describe the interface fully, a set of these model objects are aggregated together, with each object satisfying some relation role within the interface. Once the entire interface has been constructed from these smaller, non-executable parts, an executable model object can be created ({rfcm}_Input).

Important: The executable model object is the parent for all other model objects in the hierarchy, and it is the only object in which you will find an execute() method.

10.6 Using model objects in a Web Dynpro controller

A model object is declared for use within the scope of either a Web Dyn-pro Project or a Web Dynpro Development Component (DC). When you wish to make use of a model object, the first task is to declare the use of the model object under the Used Models node of your Web Dynpro

Project or DC. Having done this, all controllers will have access to that model object.

10.6.1 Model objects and the context

Model nodes are usually declared within the context of a custom controller—probably the component controller.[14] The easiest way to declare both a context model node and bind it to a model is through the Data Modeller. Figure 10.7 shows the Data Modeller screen once various models have been dragged into the context of a custom controller. This action both creates the model node in the target context, and invokes the model binding functionality.

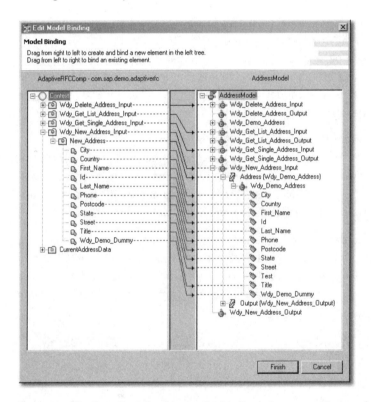

Figure 10.7 The Data Modeller showing the binding between a context model node and a model

---

14 Try to adhere to the principle that view controllers should not interface directly with model objects; however, this is a principle of a good design, not an absolute rule!

Important: Notice that the context node `Wdy_New_Address_Input` has a child node called `New_Address`. However, this child node is bound to a model class called Address, not `New_Address`. This is an example of where a context node has had to be renamed manually, because all node names in a context must be unique, irrespective of their position in the hierarchy.

Using the model classes shown in Figure 10.6, you will end up with a context that looks similar to Figure 10.8.

Figure 10.8   A model object and its corresponding context model node

In the context editor of the controller, you will see your context hierarchy on the left, and the available model objects on the right. Figure 10.8 shows the context editor after the model nodes have been created and bound to their corresponding model classes.

Due to the fact that many RFC modules use bi-directional parameters, when you bind a model node to such a model class, you will always have to rename one of the parameters manually. It is common practice to append the string "_Output" to node names on the output side of the interface.

Important: This is a general principle that must be followed when binding a context model node to a model object. Any bi-directional RFC module parameters (RFC module TABLES or CHANGING parameters) will occur twice in the model object hierarchy, and one of those occurrences will always need to be renamed manually during the node mapping process.

10.6.2 The relationship between the contents of a model object and its corresponding context model node

An aRFC model is a Java proxy object that, through the CMI, represents a set of functionally related ABAP RFC modules in some SAP system somewhere. Each {rfcm}_Input object within the model should be considered the primary source for all interaction with RFC module {rfcm}.

When a context model node is bound to a model object, you are simply providing your Web Dynpro application with a standardised API to that model object. In other words, you are making a model object look as if it is a node in a context. However, binding a model node to a model object has certain consequences about which you must have a clear understanding:

Caveat confector:

▶ A model node's element collection only holds references to model object instances. This stands in direct contrast to the element collection of a value node in which actual runtime data is stored.

▶ If a hierarchical relationship needs to exist between two or more model objects, then the association between the parent and child model objects must be created by calling the appropriate mutator method of the parent model object.

▶ Adding a model object to the element collection of a child model node does not associate it with the model object in the parent model node's element collection.

The following coding scenario will demonstrate not only the use of model objects and context model nodes at runtime, but also the importance of the above caveats.

10.7   A simple example using context model nodes at runtime

This sample application is one in which basic address maintenance is performed. This application lives in a project called `AdaptiveRFC`, and has a single application called `AdaptiveRFCApp` and a single component called `AdaptiveRFCComp`.

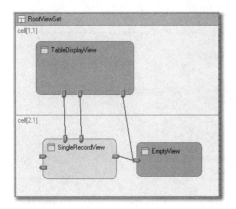

Figure 10.9 Window diagram of the Adaptive RFC application showing the inbound and outbound plugs

Figure 10.9 shows that the screen is composed from a horizontal viewset. In the top view (`TableDisplayView`), a table of address details is displayed, and in the bottom view (which is initially empty—`EmptyView`), an address details view (`SingleRecordView`) appears when the user either selects an existing address from the table, or decides to create a new address.

Address Data

	Firstname	Last Name	City	Zip	Country
■	Elwood	Blues	Chicago	60613	US
□	Jake	Blues	Calumet City	60409	US
□	Fred	Flintstone	Bedrock	12345	US
□	Harry	Hawk	London	W1 4QB	UK
□					

⇤ ⇞ ⇡ 1 of 4 ⇣ ⇟ ⇥

◀ Display previous address ‖ Create new address ‖ Display next address ▶

Figure 10.10 Layout of TableDisplayView

If the user presses the **Create new address** button, then the view shown in Figure 10.11 below will appear. The same view is reused for display purposes when the user hits either of the **Display previous address** or **Display next address** buttons.

Figure 10.11 Layout of SingleRecordView. New entry

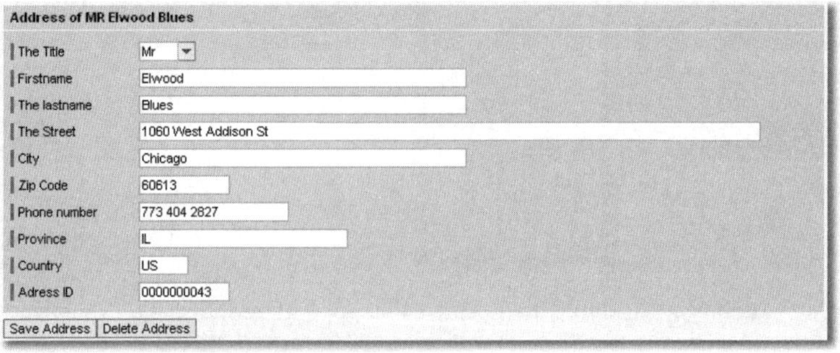

Figure 10.12 Layout of SingleRecordView. Display/Maintain entry

10.7.1 **Preparing the context at design time**

The context of the component controller for AdaptiveRFCComp is shown above in Figure 10.8. The model nodes have been created in the Data Modeller by dragging each {rfcm}_Input class from the model, and dropping it on the context. All duplicate node names have been renamed manually.

(Incidentally, why do the output classes Wdy_Delete_Address_Output and Wdy_New_Address_Output have no "plus" icons next to them?)[15]

The context also contains a value node called CurrentAddressData, which is of type Wdy_Demo_Address. This means its metadata is identical to the structured parameters returned by the RFC modules. The purpose of this value node is to act as a holding area for the address data being either displayed or created.

---

15 This is because the Java classes that represent these RFC modules only write data to the input side of the interface. They do not read any data from the output side of the interface. This in turn, indicates that these RFC modules do not return any data.

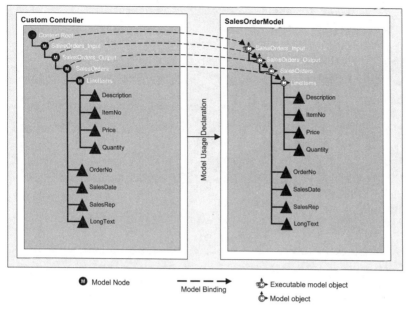

| ● Model Node | ━ ━ ━ → Model Binding | ⇒◉ Executable model object |
| | | ◉ Model object |

Figure 10.13 Binding a context model node to a model object

Component controller coding

Caveat confector: When programming with context model nodes and model objects, you must make a clear distinction in your mind between coding that manipulates the context model node, and coding that manipulates the model object to which it is bound.

If you get the two types of object muddled up, then you can get some very confusing results!

When the component AdaptiveRFCComp is instantiated, the first task that must be performed is the preparation of the model objects for use via the context. This preparation need only to take place once per component lifecycle; therefore, it can be placed in method wdDoInit() of the Adap-tiveRFCComp component controller.

```
public void wdDoInit() {
  //@@begin wdDoInit()
  // Create the reference to the component's message manager
  msgMgr = wdComponentAPI().getMessageManager();

  // Create instances of the RFC module proxy objects
  // These objects always describe the input side of the RFC
  // module's interface. The output side of the interface is
```

```
// always represented as a child of the input side.
getAddressListInput   = new Wdy_Get_List_Address_Input();
getSingleAddressInput = new Wdy_Get_Single_Address_Input();
deleteAddressInput    = new Wdy_Delete_Address_Input();
newAddressInput       = new Wdy_New_Address_Input();

// Bind model objects to the corresponding context model nodes
wdContext.nodeWdy_Get_List_Address_Input().
        bind(getAddressListInput);
wdContext.nodeWdy_Get_Single_Address_Input().
        bind(getSingleAddressInput);
wdContext.nodeWdy_Delete_Address_Input().
        bind(deleteAddressInput);
wdContext.nodeWdy_New_Address_Input().bind(newAddressInput);

// Create an instance of the specific model object to hold new
// address information. This corresponds to the IMPORTING
// parameter ADDRESS for RFC module WDY_NEW_ADDRESS
Wdy_Demo_Address theAddress = new Wdy_Demo_Address();

// Associate the model object for the new address information
// with the model object representing the input side of the
// WDY_NEW_ADDRESS RFC module. This correctly establishs a
// parent/child relationship between these objects
newAddressInput.setAddress(theAddress);

// Read all available addresses
readAddressData();
//@@end
}


//@@begin others
private Wdy_Get_List_Address_Input    getAddressListInput;
private Wdy_Delete_Address_Input      deleteAddressInput;
private Wdy_Get_Single_Address_Input getSingleAddressInput;
private Wdy_New_Address_Input          newAddressInput;

private IWDMessageManager              msgMgr;
//@@end
```

Listing 10.2 Coding to prepare the context model nodes of component Adaptive RFC

Notice that three principal tasks are being performed here:

1. The proxy objects for each RFC module are first instantiated. These proxy objects are executable model objects and represent the entire input side of each RFC module's interface.

Notice that the object instances are declared between the `//@@begin`
`others` and `//@@end` markers that occur at the end of the source code.
In this application, we only need one instance of each RFC module
proxy object; therefore, to avoid having to pass object references
around as parameters, we can declare class wide objects for use
throughout the entire instance.

2. Each of the model object instances created in step one are then bound
to the corresponding context model nodes. This action replaces the
model node's element collection with the object being bound. See the
class reference entry for `IWDNode.bind()` for more information on the
behaviour of this method.

3. Of the four RFC modules called by this application, only one (`WDY_NEW_`
`ADDRESS`) requires input in the form of a data structure. Therefore it is
also necessary to create a model object for the structured input parameter `ADDRESS` of RFC module `WDY_NEW_ADDRESS`.

Once the model object representing the structured field `ADDRESS` has
been created (called `theAddress`), it is associated with the parent
model object (called `newAddressInput`). The executable model object
for RFC module `WDY_NEW_ADDRESS` now knows that it has a child object
representing the `IMPORTING` structure called `ADDRESS`. See both Figure
10.8 and Appendix A to compare the structure of the context and the
structure of the RFC module interface.

Avoid making an easy mistake!

If you do not have a good understanding of the relationship between
model objects and the context model nodes to which they are bound,
then it is likely that you will fail to spot the error in the following code.

The `wdDoInit()` method shown in Listing 10.2 has been repeated below,
but with a couple of small, but highly significant changes.

```
public void wdDoInit() {
  //@@begin wdDoInit()
<snip>
  // Create an instance of the specific model object to hold new
  // address information. This corresponds to the IMPORTING
  // parameter ADDRESS for RFC module WDY_NEW_ADDRESS
  Wdy_Demo_Address theAddress = new Wdy_Demo_Address();

  // Add a new element to the ADDRESS model node to hold the
  // input parameters
```

```
INew_AddressElement newAddrEl =
wdContext.nodeNew_Address.createNew_AddressElement(theAddress);
wdContext.nodeNew_Address.addElement(newAddrEl);

// Read all available addresses
readAddressData();
//@@end
}
```

Listing 10.3 Incorrect coding attempting to prepare the context model nodes of component Adaptive RFC

Whilst these changes may seem plausible, they will result in a runtime error! This error is due to misunderstanding of how the elements of a model node's collection relate to actual model objects. The following line of reasoning is usually the cause:

1. Object `newAddressInput` is an executable model object that represents the entire input side of the RFC module `WDY_NEW_ADDRESS`.

2. Model object `theAddress` represents the `IMPORTING` parameter `ADDRESS` of this RFC module.

3. I need to ensure that model object `theAddress` is recognised as the child of model object `newAddressInput`.

4. In the context, model node `Wdy_New_Address_Input` has had model object `newAddressInput` bound to it.

5. Model node `New_Address` is the child node of model node `Wdy_New_Address_Input`.

6. Therefore, if I add model object `theAddress` to the element collection of model node `New_Address`, it will become the child of model object `newAddressInput` because the parent model object lives in the parent model node `Wdy_New_Address_Input`.

Oops!

The logic is fine right up until the last step, when an illogical conclusion is drawn from otherwise logical information. The fault lies in the failure to realise that context model nodes only hold references to model objects, not the actual data contained within the model objects. Therefore, for a parent/child relationship to exist between two model objects, the mutator method `{mo}.set{rfcm_{in}}()` or `{mo}.set{rfcm_{out}}()` must be called.

This relationship cannot be established by adding elements to model node element collections!

In our example, the vital missing statement is:[16]

```
newAddressInput.setAddress(theAddress);
```

Syntactically speaking, the highlighted code in Listing 10.2 is perfectly correct, and will genuinely add an element to the child model `New_Address`. If you were then to populate `newAddrE1` with data and execute the RFC module, you would get a runtime error saying that the mandatory parameter `ADDRESS` has not been supplied.

The consequence of all this is that the highlighted statements in Listing 10.3 serve no useful purpose, and should be replaced by the single statement shown above.

Using model objects at runtime

The following stages were required to prepare the model objects and context model nodes for use:

1. Instantiate the executable model objects (in this case, these are the `{rfcm}_Input` objects)
2. Bind these objects to the correct model nodes in the context
3. Associate all parent and child model objects with each other

Steps two and three in the above list do not necessarily need to be done in this order.

Now in order to show the use of the model objects, we will go through the coding that first displays a list of all the addresses, and then we will look at the coding to create a new address.

Using the principles discussed in Section 3.4, all interaction with the model objects will be confined to the component controller. In turn, the data supplied by the model objects will be available to the view controllers through context mapping.

As you can see from the component diagram in Figure 10.15, both view controllers have declared that they require the use of the component controller. This means that both `TableDisplayView` and `SingleRecordView` have access to all the data in the component controller's context and it methods.

---

16   Once this association has been made between the model objects, the context can be synchronised with the model objects by calling the `invalidate()` method of the relevant context model node.

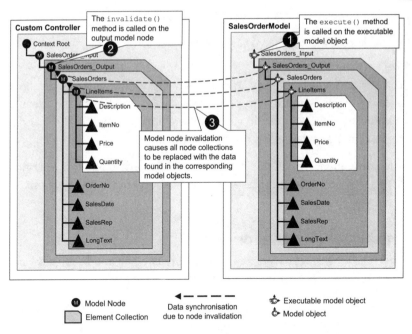

Figure 10.14 After a model object has been executed, the context model node must be synchorinised with the new data in its model object

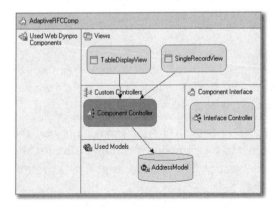

Figure 10.15 Diagram view of component AdaptiveRFCComp

The coding in Listing 10.4 to Listing 10.8 follows on immediately from that in Listing 10.2. Standard methods such as wdDoExit() and wdDoPost-Processing() have been omitted from these listings because they have not been implemented. The following user defined methods have been declared:

- ▶ **readAddressData( )**
  Reads all available addresses

- ▶ **readSingleAddress( )**
  Read the address data for the given address id

- ▶ **createNewAddress( )**
  Create a new address using the data in node currentAddressData

- ▶ **deleteAddress( )**
  Delete the address data for the given address id

- ▶ **doErrorMsg( )**
  Utility method to handle any model object execution errors

```
public void readAddressData( ) {
  //@@begin readAddressData()
  try {
    // Invoke the RFC module to return a list of addresses
    getAddressListInput.execute();
    // Synchronise the context node representing the output
    // side of the RFC interface with updated model object
    wdContext.nodeAddressList_Output().invalidate();
  }
  catch (Exception e) { doErrorMsg(e); }
  //@@end
}
```

Listing 10.4 Method readAddressData()

```
public void readSingleAddress(java.lang.String id) {
  //@@begin readSingleAddress()
  // Store the address id in the inbound side of the model
  // object's interface.  This could be done via the context, but
  // the coding is shorter and easier to understand if the model
  // object is accessed directly.
  getSingleAddressInput.setId(id);

  try {
    // Invoke the RFC module to return a single address
    getSingleAddressInput.execute();
    // Synchronise the context node representing the output
    // side of the RFC interface with updated model object
    wdContext.nodeSingle_Output().invalidate();

    // Copy the returned address information from the context
    // model node to the value node acting as a temporary holding
    // area
```

```
      WDCopyService.
        copyCorresponding(
          wdContext.currentAddressElement(),
          wdContext.currentCurrentAddressDataElement());
    }
    catch (Exception e) { doErrorMsg(e); }
      //@@end
    }
```

Listing 10.5 Method readSingleAddress()

```
public void createNewAddress( ) {
    //@@begin createNewAddress()
    // Get references to the current (only!) element in the
    // temporary holding area, and the current element in the
    // New_Address node
    ICurrentAddressDataElement addrSrcEl =
      wdContext.currentCurrentAddressDataElement();
    INew_AddressElement addrDestEl      =
      wdContext.currentNew_AddressElement();

    // Copy the data from the holding area to the RFC module input
    // parameter called ADDRESS
    WDCopyService.copyCorresponding(addrSrcEl, addrDestEl);

    try {
      // Invoke the RFC module to create an address
      newAddressInput.execute();
      // Synchronisation is not necessary here because this
      // particular RFC module produces no output

      // Re-read address data to refresh display
      readAddressData();
    }
    catch (Exception e) { doErrorMsg(e); }
    //@@end
}
```

Listing 10.6 Method createNewAddress()

```
public void deleteAddress(java.lang.String id) {
    //@@begin deleteAddress()
    // Store the address id in the inbound side of the model
    // object's interface.  This could be done via the context, but
    // the coding is shorter and easier to understand if the model
    // object is accessed directly.
      deleteAddressInput.setId(id);
```

```
  try {
    // Invoke the RFC module to delete the address
    deleteAddressInput.execute();
    // Synchronisation is not necessary here because this
    // particular RFC module produces no output

    // Re-read address data in order to refresh display
    readAddressData();
  }
  catch (Exception e) { doErrorMsg(e); }
  //@@end
}
```

Listing 10.7 Method deleteAddress()

```
public void doErrorMsg( java.lang.Exception e ) {
  //@@begin doErrorMsg()
  // Get the error message for the current locale
  String msg = e.getLocalizedMessage();

  // If there isn't one, then get the locale independent message
  if (msg == null || msg.length() == 0) msg = e.getMessage();

  // If there isn't one of these either, then get the string
  // representation of the exception
  if (msg == null || msg.length() == 0) msg = e.toString();

  // Issue the exception message as a warning through the message
  // manager
  msgMgr.reportWarning(msg);
  //@@end
}
```

Listing 10.8 Method doErrorMsg()

Notice that a common set of steps exists in each method that invokes a model object's functionality. RFC module {rfcm} is represented by class {rfcm}_Input. This class is then instantiated as model object {mo}. Using these abbreviations, the following steps can be seen in each method:

1. Supply data to the correct instance of class {rfcm}_Input. This can be done either by manipulating the context model node to which the model object is bound,[17] or by direct manipulation of the model object. Direct access to the model object makes the coding easier to read.

---

17 This is only possible after the model object {mo} has been bound to the context model node.

2. Within a `try/catch` construct, invoke the RFC module either by calling `wdContext.node{mn}().modelObject().execute()`,[18] or directly by calling `{mo}.execute()`.

3. After the model functionality has completed, the model node representing the output side of `{rfcm}`'s interface must be invalidated. Calling method `wdContext.node{mo}_Output.invalidate()` will cause all references in the model node's element collection to be discarded and resynchronised with the new data found in the model object. This process is performed recursively down the context hierarchy, starting from the invalidated node.

4. The exception processing implemented in the `catch` clauses is simplistic in this example, but is illustrative of the use of a message manager object. The message manager will display as many error messages as required when the component's view assembly is next rendered.[19]

10.7.2 View controller coding

Coding for view TableDisplayView

The functionality of the view shown in Figure 10.10 is very simple. Consequently, the context is simple, and requires very little coding.

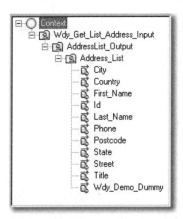

Figure 10.16 Context for view TableDisplayView

Notice here that context mapping has only been performed for the `Address_List` node on the output side of RFC module `WDY_GET_ADDRESS`'s

---

18 Again, invoking an executable model via the context can take place only if the model object has been bound to the context model node.
19 A message manager is a singleton with respect to a Web Dynpro component.

interface. This is the only information required in the view layout; therefore, no other node mappings are required.

The only methods that have been implemented in this view controller are the following four UI action handlers:

▶ **New**
Create a new address entry

▶ **Previous**
Skip to previous address

▶ **Next**
Skip to next address

▶ **SelectionChange**
User clicks on row in table UI element

These action handlers are responsible for firing the following outbound plugs (see Figure 10.11):

▶ **OutDisplayNew**
Trigger navigation to an initialised `SingleRecordView`

▶ **OutDisplaySingle**
Trigger navigation to a populated `SingleRecordView`

```
public void onActionNew(IWDCustomEvent wdEvent ) {
  //@@begin onActionNew(ServerEvent)
  wdThis.wdFirePlugOutDisplayNew();
  //@@end
}
```

Listing 10.9 Event handler for new address

This event handler simply fires an outbound plug to invoke the display of view `SingleRecordView` in an initialised state.

```
public void onActionNext(IWDCustomEvent wdEvent ) {
  //@@begin onActionNext(ServerEvent)
  int thisEl = wdContext.nodeAddress_List().getLeadSelection();
  int elCnt  = wdContext.nodeAddress_List().size();
  // Prevent variable jumpTo from going off the end of the
  // element collection
  int jumpTo =
    thisEl == -1 ? 0 : (thisEl + 1 == elCnt ? thisEl : ++thisEl);

  wdContext.nodeAddress_List().setLeadSelection(jumpTo);
  wdThis.wdFirePlugOutDisplaySingle(
```

```
          wdContext.currentAddress_ListElement().getId());
  //@@end
}
```

Listing 10.10 Event handler to show next address

When attempting to display the next element in a collection, it is very important that the value of the lead selection is not incremented off the end of the node's element collection! Hence, the ternary operator has been used to provide a compact range check for the new index value jumpTo.

Once the lead selection of node Address_List has been correctly incremented, the outbound plug is fired to invoke the display of view SingleRecordView in a populated state.

```
public void onActionPrevious(com.sap.tc.webdynpro.progmodel.api.
IWDCustomEvent wdEvent ) {
  //@@begin onActionPrevious(ServerEvent)
  int thisEl = wdContext.nodeAddress_List().getLeadSelection();
  // Prevent variable jumpTo from going off the beginning of the
  // element collection
  int jumpTo =
    thisEl == -1 ? 0 : (thisEl - 1 < 0 ? 0 : --thisEl);

  wdContext.nodeAddress_List().setLeadSelection(jumpTo);
  wdThis.wdFirePlugOutDisplaySingle(
          wdContext.currentAddress_ListElement().getId());
  //@@end
}
```

Listing 10.11 Event handler to show previous address

When attempting to display the previous element in a collection, it is very important that the value of the lead selection is not decremented below zero. This is because a lead selection value of -1 means that no element is currently selected. Again, the ternary operator has been used to provide a compact range check for the new index value jumpTo.

Once the lead selection of node Address_List has been correctly decremented, the outbound plug is fired to invoke the display of view SingleRecordView in a populated state.

```
public void onActionSelectionChange(com.sap.tc.webdynpro.
  progmodel.api.IWDCustomEvent wdEvent ) {
  //@@begin onActionSelectionChange(ServerEvent)
```

```
if (wdContext.currentAddress_ListElement() != null)
   wdThis.wdFirePlugOutDisplaySingle(
            wdContext.currentAddress_ListElement().getId());
//@@end
}
```

Listing 10.12 Event handler to show previous address

Whenever a user clicks on a row in a table UI element, it is possible to trap this event by assigning an action to the table's `onLeadSelect` event. In this case, the action happens to be called `SelectionChange`, hence the event handler method is call `onActionSelectionChange()`.

As long as there is an element to display (this could also be determined by testing that `wdContext.nodeAddress_List.getLeadSelection() != -1`) then fire the outbound plug to display the details of the selected table row. This invokes the display of view `SingleRecordView` in a populated state.

Coding for view SingleRecordView

The context of view `SingleRecordView` is just as simple as the context of `TableDisplayView`, except this time a mapped *value* node is used instead of a mapped *model* node. If a UI element is bound to an attribute of mapped node, then that UI element can both receive data from, and supply data to the mapping origin node.

Figure 10.17 The context of controller SingleRecordView

The independent attribute `HeaderText` is a calculated attribute that supplies the text seen at the top of the Group UI element in Figure 10.11 and Figure 10.12. This means that no data is stored in `HeaderText` at runtime; instead, its associated accessor method (`getHeaderText()`) is called every time the attribute's value is required (in this case, the accessor method will be called automatically by the Response Rendering stage of the Phase Model. See Section 11.11 for more details).

Since context mapping is being used here, no action is required at component initialisation time. Consequently, the standard hook method `wdDoInit()` contains no coding.

The view controller `SingleRecordView` has two different declared actions:

▶ **Save**
Save the current address details

▶ **Delete**
Delete the current address details

```
public void onActionSave(IWDCustomEvent wdEvent ) {
  //@@begin onActionSave(ServerEvent)
  wdThis.wdGetAdaptiveRFCCompController().createNewAddress();
  //@@end
}
```

Listing 10.13 Event handler for action Save

In keeping with the design principle that a view controller should not interact directly with a model object, the address details are saved by calling the appropriate method in the component controller. Context mapping ensures that the data entered by the user through the view's UI elements is automatically available to the component controller.

```
public void onActionDelete(IWDCustomEvent wdEvent ) {
  //@@begin onActionDelete(ServerEvent)
  String id =
    wdContext.currentCurrentAddressDataElement().getId();

  wdThis.wdGetAdaptiveRFCCompController().deleteAddress(id);
  wdThis.wdFirePlugOutHideMe();
  //@@end
}
```

Listing 10.14 Event handler for action Delete

The Delete action handler must conform to the same design principle as the Save action handler. The action handler in the view controller does not interact directly with the model object; instead, it calls the appropriate method in the component controller to delete the address details.

After this has completed, the outbound plug is fired to hide view `Sin-gleRecordView`.

View controller `SingleRecordView` has the following inbound plugs (see Figure 10.11):

▶ **InCreateNew**
Cause the view layout to be initialised

▶ **InDisplaySingle**
Read the address details for the specified address id.

```
public void onPlugInCreateNew(IWDCustomEvent wdEvent ) {
  //@@begin onPlugInCreateNew(ServerEvent)
  initAddressData();
  //@@end
}
```

Listing 10.15 Initialise the view when the InCreateNew inbound plug is fired

This plug is fired in response to a user's request to create a new address. Therefore, each element in the context node to which the UI elements are bound must be initialised (see Figure 10.17):

```
public void onPlugInDisplaySingle(IWDCustomEvent wdEvent,
                               String id ) {
  //@@begin onPlugInDisplaySingle(ServerEvent)
  wdThis.wdGetAdaptiveRFCCompController().readSingleAddress(id);
  //@@end
}
```

Listing 10.16 Inbound plug InDisplaySingle

This plug is fired in response to a user's request to display the details of a specific address. This address is identified by the parameter `id`. As has been seen before, the view controller does not interact directly with the model object, but calls the appropriate method in the component controller to read the address data.

There are two other methods that must briefly be shown; `initAddress-Data()` and the accessor method for the calculated attribute `HeaderText` called `getHeaderText()`.

```
public void initAddressData() {
  //@@begin initAddressData( )
  IWDNodeInfo     nodeInfo =
    wdContext.nodeCurrentAddressData().getNodeInfo();
```

```
IWDNodeElement elem       =
    wdContext.currentCurrentAddressDataElement();

// Initialise attribute values using the default value of the
// simple type
for (Iterator iter = nodeInfo.iterateAttributes();
    iter.hasNext();) {
    IWDAttributeInfo attrInfo = (IWDAttributeInfo)iter.next();

    elem.setAttributeValue(attrInfo.getName(),
        attrInfo.getSimpleType().getDefaultValue());
}

// The ABAP data type NUMC is currently represented as a Java
// String.  The only drawback is that in ABAP, NUMC fields have
// an initial value of "all zeroes", whereas a string has the
// initial value of "" (empty string).  Therefore, the
// getDefaultValue() method will not return the correct initial
// value for this data type.
wdContext.
    currentCurrentAddressDataElement().setId("0000000000");
//@@end
}
```

Listing 10.17 Method initAddressData()

In order to initialise a context node in a generic manner, it is necessary to examine the data type of each attribute, and then assign the appropriate initial value for that data type. This functionality assumes that all the attributes of the context node are of a Simple Type.

An iterator is obtained to return the metadata of the node's attributes, and then each attribute in the element is reset to the default initial value for its data type. This coding does not require a nested loop, because there will only ever be at most, one element in the node (cardinality = 0..1).

Lastly, since the id field is of data type String, its initial value will be "", but this field is interpreted as an ABAP type NUMC by the RFC module.[20] Therefore, the correct initial value is all zeroes.

```
public String getHeaderText(IPrivateSingleRecordView.
            IContextElement element) {
```

---

20 NUMC means numeric character. ABAP fields of this type are stored as fixed length character strings that may only contain digit characters.

```
//@@begin
// getHeaderText(IPrivateSingleRecordView.IContextElement)
String msg;
ICurrentAddressDataElement addrEl =
  wdContext.currentCurrentAddressDataElement();

if (wdContext.nodeCurrentAddressData().isEmpty())
  msg = "Address entry not possible";
else if(addrEl.getFirst_Name() == null)
  msg = "Enter new address";
else
  msg = "Address of "+addrEl.getTitle()+"
    "+addrEl.getFirst_Name()+" "+addrEl.getLast_Name();

return msg;
//@@end
}
```

Listing 10.18 Accessor method for calculated attribute HeaderText

This accessor method first checks that the node actually has an element in it! If it does not, then it will be impossible for the user to enter any data through the UI, because there is no element in the context node in which information can be stored. Under these circumstances, any UI elements bound to context attributes that do not exist at runtime will be disabled for user input.

If there is an empty element, then we must be entering a new address, hence the "Enter new address" message. Otherwise, construct the header text from the title, first name, and last name.

10.7.3 Look at what has *not* been done

Do you notice what type of coding is missing from all of these methods? Someone with a JSP coding background will probably have noticed that at no time has any interaction with user interface objects taken place!

By now, you should be able to answer the following question:

Q: How does the data get from the model object onto the screen without any code being written?

A: Well, you have written some code—you just did it declaratively rather than explicitly. Three declarations have been made that create the required chain of connections.

1. The model object is bound to a context model node in the component controller. The component controller then invokes the model functionality and after the `invalidate()` method has been called for the `{rfcm}_Output` model node, the data within the model object is available to the context.

2. The data in the component controller's context acts as the mapping origin for the mapped nodes in both view controllers.

3. The context nodes in the view controller have UI elements directly bound to them, which causes data to be supplied automatically to the screen renderer.

So in this example, only a single line of code needs to be written, namely the call to the `invalidate()` method. This synchronises the references in the model node's element collection, with the new data in the model object. After that, the WDF automatically transports the data from the model object through to the UI elements on the screen.

10.8 Adapting to changes in an RFC interface

In this particular situation, we have two view controllers, both of which are displaying information derived from a model object. Since the `Table-DisplayView` is only showing a tabular overview, it is unnecessary to modify this view layout when the RFC module's interface changes.

However, the `SingleRecordView` displays all the details of the selected address. Therefore, we will have to add some coding to this view controller in order to handle any changes in the RFC module's interface. As with all the other areas of Web Dynpro programming that we have dealt with, there are some fundamental principles that must be understood.

▶ The view layout will be composed of UI elements that are handled in two different ways:

  ▶ The static set of UI elements declared at design time that requires no programmatic adjustment.

  ▶ The dynamic set of UI elements known only at runtime. The UI element hierarchy will need dynamic modification to account for these new fields.

▶ Adaptation can only take place for fields within `.APPEND` structures of ABAP tables.

▶ The static view layout created at design time must be designed in such a way that the area used for field display can expand in response to changes in the RFC module's interface.

If you refer back to Figure 10.3, you will notice that the last field in structure WDY_DEMO_ADDRESS is a .APPEND field called WDY_DEMO_APPEND.[21] Also, notice that the only field in this structure is a CHAR1 field called WDY_DEMO_DUMMY. This field was omitted from the static UI layout seen in Figure 10.12 because it carried no useful information. This field cannot be dropped from the structure of WDY_DEMO_APPEND, so we will have to implement coding that suppresses its display.

Important: The aRFC layer assumes that all interfaces changes are additive!

Now the .APPEND structure WDY_DEMO_APPEND has been modified to include six new fields.

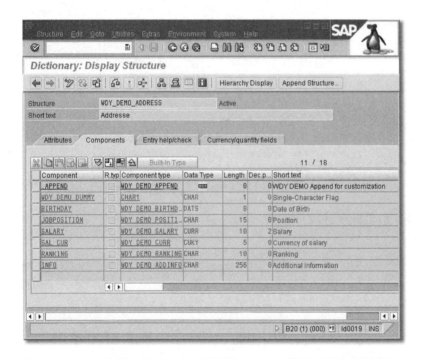

Figure 10.18 New fields added to the .APPEND structure WDY_DEMO_APPEND

---

21 The .APPEND syntax appearing in an ABAP table definition indicates that the fields found in the dictionary structure (in this case WDY_DEMO_APPEND) are to be included at this point in the table.

To account for these changes in the RFC module's interface, we do not need to re-import the model object; but what we do need to do is write some code that generically handles additional fields. The aRFC layer will query the SAP system, and discover that the structure of the interface has changed. It will then adapt the relevant dictionary structures to fit the new interface, and supply this modified definition to the context via the model node binding.

It is now your responsibility to check for new fields and adapt the UI layout accordingly. The code to do this must be executed from within method wdDoModifyView(), and can be implemented in the following way:

```
public static void wdDoModifyView(IPrivate{nᵥ} wdThis,
                                  IPrivate{nᵥ}.IContextNode
                                      wdContext,
                                  IWDView view,
                                  boolean firstTime) {
  //@@begin wdDoModifyView
  IWDNodeInfo nodeInfo =
    wdContext.nodeCurrentAddressData().getNodeInfo();
  IStructure structure = nodeInfo.getStructureType();

  // Is the context node based on a dictionary structure
  // and are we building the screen for the first time?
  if (structure != null && firstTime) {
    // Loop around all the attributes in the dictionary structure
    for (Iterator iterator = structure.fieldIterator();
      iterator.hasNext();) {
      IField field = (IField)iterator.next();

      // Have we found an append structure field yet?
      if (!appendFound)
        // Nope, check the current field
        appendFound = field.belongsToAppend();
      else
        // Yup, add all subsequent fields to the UI element
        // hierarchy
        addFieldToLayout(view, wdContext,
                    nodeInfo, field.getName());
    }
  }
  //@@end
}
```

Listing 10.19 wdDoModifyView() coding to check for additional field in a model node

Notice that the class names of the parameters to method `wdDoModify-View()` have been generalised!

The coding now starts to make use of the dictionary structure classes `IStructure` and `IField`. These classes can be found in package `com.sap.dictionary.runtime`. The processing is very straight forward here:

▶ Get a reference to the metadata of the context model node that may have changed.

▶ From the metadata object, get a reference to the dictionary structure that defines this model node.

▶ Check that the model node is defined on a dictionary structure and this is the first time the view has been processed.

▶ Loop around the iterator of fields supplied by the dictionary structure.

▶ Since we don't want to display the dummy field in the `.APPEND` structure, the coding should always skip the first field. This is achieved by switching on the flag `appendFound` after the first `.APPEND` field has been found. This allows all subsequent `.APPEND` fields to be processed and avoids the need for any explicit reference to field `WDY_DEMO_DUMMY`.

▶ If the current field belongs to an `.APPEND` structure, then call method `addFieldToLayout()` to include this field in the UI element hierarchy.

Figure 10.19 Static UI element hierarchy of SingleRecordView

Since method `addFieldToLayout()` is called from the static method `wdDo-ModifyView()`, it must be created between the `//@@begin` and `//@@end` comment markers.

Up till now, we have had no need to know about the structure of the static UI element hierarchy, but now that we are going to extend this hierarchy, some structural details need to be known. The static UI element hierarchy of `SingleRecordView` is shown in Figure 10.19. Compare this hierarchy with the rendered screen seen in Figure 10.12.

Since the static label/input field pairs live in the Group UI element `AddressGroup`, any additional label/input field pairs ought also to live in here.

```
//@@begin others
private static void addFieldToLayout(IWDView view,
                                     IPrivate{nᵥ}.IContextNode
                                        wdContext,
                                     IWDNodeInfo nodeInfo,
                                     String fieldName) {
  // New element for user input - we don't know what type it will
  // be yet
  IWDUIElement newElem = null;

  // New element identifier
  String newID = "elementFor" + fieldName;

  // Create a new label element
  IWDLabel newLabel = (IWDLabel)view.
                      createElement(IWDLabel.class,
                                    "labelFor" + fieldName);
  newLabel.setLabelFor(newID);
  newLabel.createLayoutData(IWDMatrixHeadData.class);

  // Get the metadata of the current field
  IWDAttributeInfo thisAttrib = nodeInfo.getAttribute(fieldName);

  // Get reference to group UI container
  IWDUIElementContainer container =
    (IWDUIElementContainer)view.getElement("AddressGroup");

  // Is this attribute based on a dictionary simple type?
  if (thisAttrib.getDataType().isSimpleType()) {
    // Yup. Get both the dictionary simple type and the built-in
    // type from which it is derived
    ISimpleType sType  = thisAttrib.getSimpleType();
```

```
String     biType = sType.getBuiltInType();

// Can the built-in type be represented by some type of input
// field?
if (biType.equalsIgnoreCase("string") ||
    biType.equalsIgnoreCase("date")   ||
    biType.equalsIgnoreCase("decimal")) {
  // Yup, can a list of possible inputs be derived for this
  // field? I.E. Does a simple value (SV) service exist for
  // this field, and will the SVService actually return
  // something?
  if ((sType.hasSVService()) &&
      (sType.getSVServices().getValues() != null)) {
    // Yup. Use a drop down to display possible input values
    IWDDropDownByKey newField = (IWDDropDownByKey)view.
              createElement(IWDDropDownByKey.class, newID);
    // Bind drop down key to context field having the
    // SVService
    newField.bindSelectedKey("CurrentAddressData." +
                          fieldName);
    newField.createLayoutData(IWDMatrixData.class);
    newElem = newField;
  }
  // No SVService exists (or can be obtained), so check
  // if this field is longer than 128 characters?
  else if (sType.getMaxExternalLength() > 128 ||
          sType.getMaxLength()          > 128) {
    // Yup, so display the value in a text edit UI element
    // with wrapping turned on
    IWDTextEdit newField = (IWDTextEdit)view.
                  createElement(IWDTextEdit.class, newID);
    newField.bindValue("CurrentAddressData." + fieldName);
    newField.setWrapping(WDTextWrapping.SOFT);
    newField.createLayoutData(IWDMatrixData.class);
    newElem = newField;
  }
  // No SVService exists (or can be obtained), and the field
  // is < 128 characters in length
  else {
    // Display the using an input field
    IWDInputField newField = (IWDInputField)view.
                  createElement(IWDInputField.class, newID);
    newField.bindValue("CurrentAddressData." + fieldName);
    newField.createLayoutData(IWDMatrixData.class);
    newElem = newField;
  }
}
```

```
// If the field type is boolean, then use a checkbox UI
// element
else if (biType.equals("boolean")) {
  IWDCheckBox newField = (IWDCheckBox)view.
                    createElement(IWDCheckBox.class, newID);
  newField.bindChecked("CurrentAddressData." + fieldName);
  newField.createLayoutData(IWDMatrixData.class);
  newElem = newField;
}

// As long as both the new label and the new element have
// been created,append them to the group UI container
if (newLabel != null &&
    newElem  != null) {
  container.addChild(newLabel);
  container.addChild(newElem);
}
  }
}
//@@end
```

Listing 10.20 Coding to incorporate new aRFC fields to an existing UI element hierarchy

The coding in Listing 10.20 above does not rigorously test all possible data types that could be returned for a given dictionary simple type. However, if you know that the aRFC interface will only add fields of the types shown in the coding, then the implementation above is sufficient.

Once you have changed the ABAP dictionary structure and activated your changes, then all the RFC modules that use structure WDY_DEMO_ADDRESS in their interface will be updated. At this point is will be necessary to restart your J2EE engine before the changes to the RFC module's interface can be used by your application.

Important: The J2EE engine contains a cache of all the model objects contained in all the deployed applications. This cache is optimised by technical system. This means that if several different Web Dynpro applications call RFC modules in the same SAP system, and they also share the same ABAP dictionary structures in their interfaces (as often happens with structure BAPIRET2), then only one copy of that dictionary structure will be held in the model cache.

Consequently, if that dictionary structure changes, then all applications that use that structure will be affected. In the current version of the J2EE engine shipped with SAP NetWeaver '04, there is no cross reference within the model cache to identify which applications use which cached objects. Without such a reverse lookup, it is not possible to know *a priori* which applications will be affected by flushing this cache. Therefore, until a reverse lookup mechanism is implemented, the entire J2EE engine must be bounced to flush the model object cache.

When the application is now restarted, the view layout will adapt to the new structure as shown in Figure 10.20.

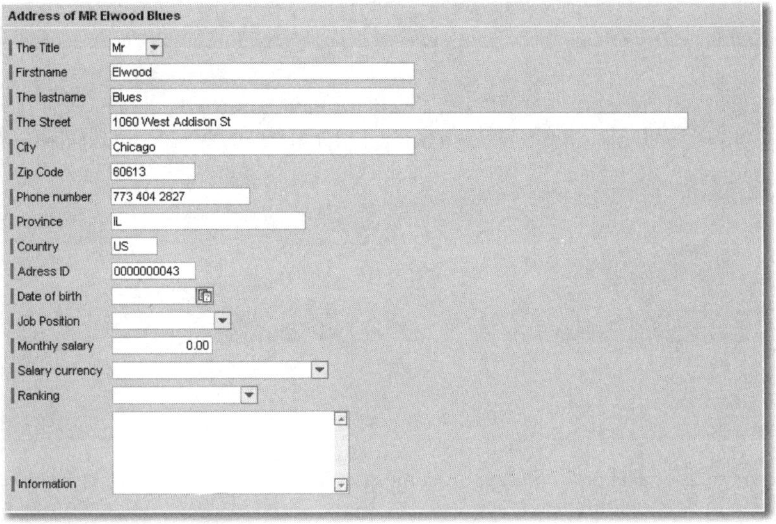

Figure 10.20 View SingleRecordView after it has adapted to the new RFC module interface

There are a couple of things to notice here:

The field WDY_DEMO_DUMMY does not appear (see Listing 10.19).

► If the data types of the new dictionary fields indicate that possible input values are available, then these are obtained and associated with the input field.

► Overall, view SingleRecordView has reacted intelligently to the new fields in the dictionary structure.

The Simple Value service automatically provides the possible information that could be entered into a particular field. Three fields on this screen have an associated Simple Value service:

Figure 10.21 Drop down lists whose values are supplied by the Simple Value Service

The Date Picker shown in Figure 10.22 appears automatically because the `InputField` UI element has been bound (dynamically) to a context field of type `Date`.

◄   September 2004   ►

Mo	Tu	We	Th	Fr	Sa	Su
30	31	1	2	3	4	5
6	7	8	9	10	11	12
13	14	15	16	17	18	19
20	21	22	23	24	25	26
27	28	29	30	1	2	3
4	5	6	7	8	9	10

Figure 10.22 A date picker will appear automatically when an InputField UI element is bound to context attribute of type Date

Since the `WDY_DEMO_APPEND-INFO` field is longer than 128 characters, it is displayed in a `TextEdit` UI element.

10.9 Connection management

In all the discussions of the previous section, one very important subject has not been mentioned – that of logging on to the SAP system. In order to invoke an RFC module in an SAP system, it is necessary for the invoking program to log on to the SAP system. The log on process for a program is identical to the log on process performed by an online user. Four pieces of information are always required:

- A user id
- A password
- The SAP client
- A logon language

There is a variety of techniques for supplying these values, but irrespective of the specific technique, without these four identifying values, no connection can be made with an SAP system.

For those readers not familiar with an SAP system, the user id and password will be familiar values, but you may not have encountered the need for a language; and you almost certainly will not know what a "client" is!

10.9.1 Language

Since SAP is a multi-lingual system, the logon process requires the two character ISO code for the language in which you would like to operate. The only languages available by default are English (EN) and German (DE). The text for any additional languages must be explicitly imported. The language import process is usually performed when the SAP system is installed.

10.9.2 Client

A "client" is the term used to describe a subdivision of an SAP system. These subdivisions, or clients, do not represent legal entities of your business, but rather administrative areas within which different data and configuration can be held.

Traditionally, the client value is any three digit number (with the exceptions of 000, 001, and 066[22]). But it is technically possible to identify a client using any three alphanumeric characters.

All data created by SAP business applications and almost all configuration settings are "client specific". This means that the information exists in only one client of the SAP system. If you were to logon on to a different client, you would find a totally different set of configuration and application data.[23]

---

22 Client 000 is the system client and is of fundamental importance to the normal running of your SAP system. Don't even *think* about deleting this client! Client 001 is only present in SAP Enterprise and R/3 systems, Client 066 is reserved for the SAP EarlyWatch health check service.
23 Technically, all client specific SAP data is stored in database tables that have the client value as the first field of the primary key.

There is also data in an SAP system that is client independent.[24] Certain areas of application configuration are client independent, but the most important types of data in this category are all ABAP source code, and the entire data dictionary.

This has the very important consequence that when a program or a dictionary structure is changed and then activated, *all users in all clients will be affected by this change*.

Caveat confector: Since ABAP programs are client independent, and the business data upon which they operate is client specific, it is entirely possible that when the same program is run by the same user logged on in different clients, that the program will produce totally different results.

Therefore, when setting up the JCo destinations in your J2EE engine, you must know exactly which client should be connected to.

10.9.3 How does a model object know which SAP system to connect to?

When a model object is created for the first time in the NWDS, in addition to the names of the RFC modules to be imported, two other pieces of information must be specified. These are the names of the JCo destinations in the J2EE engine that will be used for calling the RFC modules found in this model.

Important: You must always specify two JCo destinations for each model. The reason for this is that one will be used for obtaining metadata about the RFC module interfaces, and the other will be used for the actual invocation of the RFC module's functionality. In Figure 10.23, you can see the information specified for the `AddressModel` model object used in the previous section.

---

24 I.E., the database table in which this information is stored does not use the client value in its key.

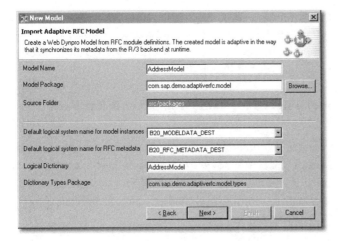

Figure 10.23 Information required for the definition of AddressModel model object

There are two important things to notice here:

▶ The model object lives in its own Java package. See Section 3.6.

▶ The logical system names for "model instances" and "RFC metadata" can be any names you like.

> **Important:** A logical system name should include some prefix to identify the type of data being consumed, not the name of the system being accessed. E.G. If a particular logical system is being used by an HR application that processes personnel data, then the logical system names should be called something like `HR_Personnel_Info_Data` and `HR_Personnel_Info_Metadata`.

The above example is used for coding that will not be transported anywhere, hence it does not matter that the system name (B20) is part of the logical system names. However, for real applications being developed under the control of the Java Development Infrastructure (JDI), you will not want to include the name of the R/3 system in the logical system name because once the coding has been transported from your development server to your test server, the logical system name will become inappropriate!

The logical system names specified for the model instances and the RFC metadata do not need to have been created at the time the model is imported, but they will need to have been created by the time you come to execute your application.

As their description implies, these names refer to logical systems, not physical SAP systems; but before we can set up these logical system names, some configuration must first be performed in the System Landscape Directory (SLD) of your J2EE engine.

Altering a model object's logical system after it has been created

Once you have created a model object, it would appear that the logical system names disappear into the bowels of the model declaration, never to be seen again. Fortunately, this is not true. If you wish to alter the name of a model's logical system name, then you can do the following:

1. An overview of all the logical systems being used by your Web Dynpro Project or DC can be obtained from the project properties screen. Right mouse click on the Web Dynpro Project or DC name, and select Properties. In the pop-up window, select Web Dynpro References from the list on the left, and then select the tab called JCO References. Here you will see all JCo logical systems referenced by your project or DC. See Figure 10.24.

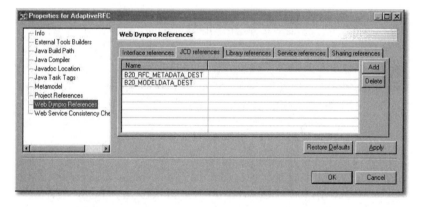

Figure 10.24 All JCo references used by a Web Dynpro project or DC

2. If you wish to change the references used by your model objects, don't try and change them in the screen above; instead, you will need to modify the model object definitions themselves.

3. To change the logical system for the RFC metadata, select the 🗐 Dictionaries node under your Web Dynpro project or DC, and then select the 🗐 Model node for the relevant model object. Now select the properties tab and you will see the name of the logical system as per Figure 10.25.

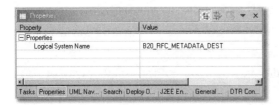

Figure 10.25 Model object property showing the logical system for RFC metadata

4. Then to change the logical system for model instances, open the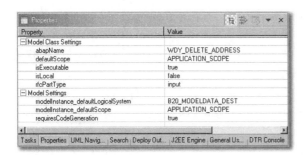
   Models node under your Web Dynpro project or DC, then the appro-
   priate ⚙ aRFC model object. Then double click on *any* of the subordinate model classes and again select the Properties tab. Now you will
   see two sets of properties: those that are specific to the individual
   model class you selected, and those that are specific to the model
   object in general. Under **Model Settings** you will see the name of the
   logical system.

Figure 10.26 Model object property showing the logical system for model instance
data

Prerequisites for creating a technical system

It is not the intention of this book to provide a detailed discussion of the
configuration and administration procedures required to make your J2EE
engine functional. These tasks are fully documented in the related SAP
documentation, and will only be dealt with here in overview. For the purposes of this overview, the following assumptions have been made:

▶ You will be connecting to a stand alone J2EE engine installed on your
   local development machine.

▶ The default HTTP port of 50000 has not been changed during installation.

▶ The J2EE engine has had the latest CIM data imported into it.

- ▶ You have a J2EE user id with administration authority.
- ▶ You have installed, or at least have access to, the latest version of the SAP client software SAPGUI.
- ▶ You have a valid SAP dialogue user with sufficient authority to perform a remote function call. For a productive environment, you will also need a valid SAP system user with the authority to perform a remote function call.[25]

Creating a technical system

The first task to perform is the creation of a technical system. The technical systems defined in your SLD form the base list of all external systems with which your J2EE engine can communicate.

- ▶ Connect to the System Landscape directory of your J2EE engine using the URL *http://localhost:50000/sld*.
- ▶ Enter your administrative user id and password.
- ▶ Use the Technical System Wizard to supply the necessary information to describe your SAP system. This includes the installation number of your SAP system, which can be obtained from the **System · Status** pop-up window in SAP GUI.

Once you have created the technical system, you will see a screen that is similar to Figure 10.27.

Here, two technical systems have been defined; B20 and DE7. Using the configuration in this particular SLD, when logical JCo destinations are created, only these two systems will be available for selection. In general, make sure that every external system with which you wish to communicate, has first been defined as a technical system!

Creating a JCo destination

Now that at least one technical system is available, the logical JCo destinations used in the Web Dynpro model object can be created.

Connect to the Web Dynpro Content Administrator using the URL *http://localhost:50000/webdynpro/welcome*, then press the **Maintain JCo Destinations** button. Figure 10.28 shows what this screen could look like.

---

25 SAP user ids come in various categories (Dialogue, Communication, System, Service, and Reference). For online use with SAP GUI, you must have a Dialogue user, but for programmatic access, a System user should be used instead.

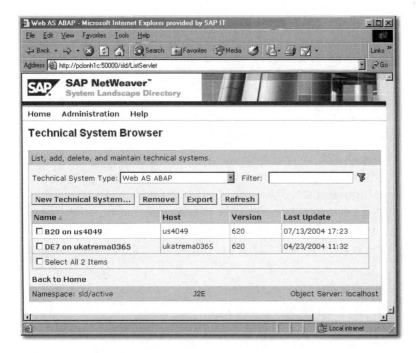

Figure 10.27 Technical System Browser

Figure 10.28 Maintain JCo destinations

All JCo destinations that have been deployed to the J2EE engine will appear in the table on the right of the screen. If the JCo destination has not been created yet, then there will be a red square next to it.

A JCo destination can either be created by specifying all the values explicitly, or the details can be copied from an existing JCo destination. The main points to remember are these:

▶ The client used by the JCo destination is specified on the first screen. For the model instance destination, always point to the client in which the business data lives. The RFC metadata destination will be requesting information from the ABAP data dictionary, therefore, the same client does not need to be specified since dictionary information is client independent. However, for simplicity it is advised to use the same client for each pair of JCo destinations.

▶ When the security information needs to be specified, your values will vary depending on the environment you are configuring. There are four options available, each with their relative merits:[26]

 ▶ User/Password
   Advantages: Quick and easy to setup. Good for a development environment setup.
   Disadvantages: No user audit trail, or user specific authorisation. All RFC modules are executed under the identity of this one user. This is good for testing, but not recommended for productive use.

 ▶ Ticket
   Advantages: User management can be handled by another SAP NetWeaver product such as Enterprise Portal.
   Disadvantages: Requires the use of another SAP NetWeaver compatible product that can generated SSO2 cookies.

 ▶ Client Certificate (X.509)
   Advantages: User management can be handled by any software layer that issues trusted X.509 certificates.
   Disadvantages: Extra J2EE setup required.

 ▶ User Mapping
   Advantages: User management can be handled by the SAP NetWeaver User Management Engine, which in turn can reference an LDAP server.
   Disadvantages: Extra J2EE setup required.

▶ In addition to this, communication between the J2EE engine and the SAP can be encrypted using the Secure Network Communication (SNC) Layer.

▶ The user id used for the RFC metadata destination can only be specified as a User/Password combination. This user should be created to be of type "System" within SAP. Users of type "System" are not permitted to logon using SAP GUI.

Once the JCo destinations have been set up, press the Test button to ensure that the connection details are correct.

---

26 These four options are only available for the model instance destination (I.E. the JCo destination that actually invokes the RFC module).

10.10   Relationship between JCO destinations and ABAP sessions

The documentation that follows is a brief overview of the standard SAP documentation that describes the procedures to be followed when writing RFC modules. Please refer to the standard SAP documentation for a complete discussion of the topic. The information contained here only covers the main points in summary form from a Web Dynpro point of view.

10.10.1   Logging on to an SAP system

When an external program wishes to invoke any functionality within an R/3 system, that program must first logon on to the R/3 system. Since R/3 is a client/server based application, not only must the external program supply valid user credentials, it must identify to which application server it wishes to connect. All this information is held within the JCo destination described above.

> **Important:** Once your external program has logged on to a particular application server, the SAP user session remains connected to that server until the logoff event takes place.

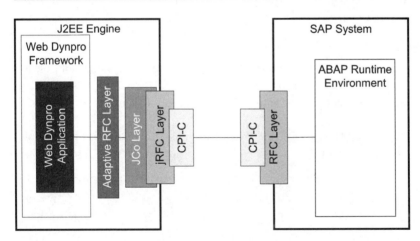

Figure 10.29 RFC connection between the J2EE engine and an SAP system

10.10.2   ABAP sessions

Once you have successfully logged on to an SAP system, you are allocated an area of memory within the application server called the "User Roll Area". The user roll area contains all the data related to your activity on that SAP system. This includes all the data used by all the programs you are currently executing.

The user roll area is subdivided into areas called ABAP sessions. Each ABAP session holds the current state of a logical unit of work (LUW) for a single program. Once an online user has logged on to SAP using the SAP GUI client software, they may create multiple sessions within their roll area by opening new SAP GUI windows. All the windows together belong to a single user (and therefore a single user roll area), but each SAP GUI window could be executing a different transaction. The current execution state of each transaction within each window is maintained in a distinct ABAP session.

Every time an LUW finishes, the ABAP session is considered closed and it is handed over to the database for completion. A new ABAP session is then started automatically, and the ABAP program continues processing.

Certain ABAP statements (such as COMMIT WORK) will cause the *explicit* completion of the current LUW. What is less well known is that there are certain ABAP statements that will cause an *implicit* completion of the current LUW. For instance, whenever the Open SQL statements UPDATE or MODIFY are performed, the current LUW must be terminated in order for the database update to take place. A new ABAP session (LUW) is then started automatically. This process is completely invisible to the ABAP programmer.

Why is this important?

When an RFC connection is established into an SAP system, not only is a user roll area created for that user, but an ABAP session is created. Then within this session, the required function module is executed.

Caveat confector: An RFC connection has a 1:1 relationship with the ABAP session within a user roll area, *not* just the user roll area!

The JCo layer receives a Global Unique Identifier (GUID) from the RFC layer that identifies not just the user roll area within the SAP system, but the ABAP session within the user roll area to which the RFC connection is attached[27]. Such a GUID could look like {414EF1BB-B843-566C-E100-00000A1550A8}. Every time there is an ABAP session change, you get a new GUID for your RFC connection.

---

27 For those readers familiar with CPI-C programming, the RFC GUID is synonymous with the CPI-C conversation id—both of which are visible in an RFC trace file.

From a database point of view, an ABAP session represents an atomic unit of processing. All database changes contained within a single ABAP session should be considered inseperable. These changes then form your unit of work to be committed or rolled back.

Writing custom ABAP function modules to behave as a transactional unit depends upon the ABAP programmer having a good understanding of these principles. Whilst this is a book about Web Dynpro for Java programming, you will find that certain concepts of ABAP software design must be understood in order for your Web Dynpro application to get the best results out of R/3.

This RFC GUID value is not currently available to the Web Dynpro developer because it cannot be manipulated. It is however visible in an RFC trace file.

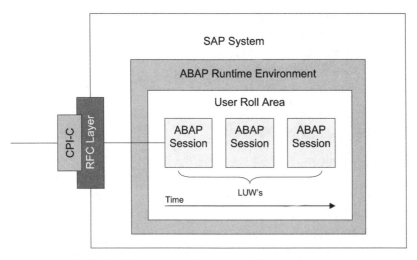

Figure 10.30 Multiple ABAP sessions within a user roll area

Important: The aRFC layer does not currently support SAP's transactional RFC (tRFC) interface.

10.10.3 The impact of an ABAP session change on an external program using the JCo layer

Consider the following situation. You wish to update a certain set of data within the SAP system, but because your Web Dynpro program is operating in a multi-user environment, you could jeopardise your data's referential integrity if you simply went ahead and performed an indiscriminate update. Therefore, you must first lock the data before displaying it for update on the user's screen. Once the update has completed, you then remove the lock.

Your update process now becomes a sequence of three RFC calls:

1. Call the RFC module to enqueue the necessary lock object.
2. Call the RFC module that performs the update.
3. Call the RFC module that dequeues the lock object

This seems nice and straight forward, but a massive assumption has been made here! In order for this sequence of steps to work, all three RFC modules *must* be executed within the same ABAP session.

The problem here is that a lock object is specific to an ABAP session, not an ABAP user! It can only be released by the same ABAP session that created it. Therefore, if the update RFC module issues any ABAP statement that causes a session change, then it will be impossible for the last RFC module to release the lock object. The ABAP session (and therefore the RFC GUID) will have changed. This effectively terminates your ability to release your own lock object.

In order for several RFC modules to be executed within the same ABAP session, two things are necessary:

1. Each module must be called using the same JCo connection. This is most easily achieved by ensuring that all the model objects are part of the same Web Dynpro model. This will ensure that they all share the same JCo destination, and therefore connect to the same user roll area.
2. The RFC module called to perform the update does not execute any ABAP statements that would cause an ABAP session change.

These two facts taken together mean that you must write your RFC enabled ABAP function modules very carefully! Indeed, this is a well known situation and is documented in the standard SAP help on RFC modules.

10.10.4 How do I perform ABAP database updates without causing a session change?

Again, this is a well known situation in ABAP and is well documented in the standard help pages; but in overview, the basic principles are as follows:

- The functionality to perform the actual database update should be encapsulated within a function module. In our example, we'll give this function module the simplistic name of ZUPDATE_DATABASE.[28] This function module *cannot* be called from outside the SAP system.

- The lock object is enqueued as before.

- The RFC module called by the Web Dynpro application receives the data to be updated, and performs any necessary pre-processing, then it calls function module ZUPDATE_DATABASE with the additional parameter of IN UPDATE TASK. (The execution of any function module called with the parameter of IN UPDATE TASK will be delayed until the end of the current LUW).

- Now that the execution of ZUPDATE_DATABASE is held in the update queue, and will only be executed when the ABAP session is terminated. The call to dequeue the lock object is now moved to ZUPDATE_DATABASE and will take place immediately after the database has been successfully updated.

- Finally, the LUW must be explicitly terminated by calling BAPI_TRANSACTION_COMMIT.

I have frequently found custom written ABAP function modules that contain direct database updates! The ABAP code (in itself) is perfectly correct, but what has not been realised is the effect that a direct database update has on the state of an RFC connection. Such function modules cannot be used as part of a transactional group.

It should now become clear why a Web Dynpro model was defined in a most particular way. See the Section 1.6.2.

10.10.5 Can I use any statements I like in an RFC module?

The short answer is no! The number of ABAP statements that cannot be used in an RFC module is small, but should you use them, then they will forcibly terminate an RFC connection. These statements are:

- LEAVE TO
- SUBMIT
- CALL FUNCTION ... DESTINATION ...

The type of RFC error that you will get from the use of these statements is documented in OSS note 174306.

---

28 Any customer written function module must start with the letter Z or Y.

10.11 Avoiding the Read-Write-Read problem

If custom ABAP function modules are written without a good understanding of ABAP session management,[29] then it is possible that the following problem can occur. This is related both to the time taken by the SAP system to complete a database update, and the way in which the custom RFC modules have been written.

Consider the steps in the following (simplistic) business scenario:

1. An RFC module is called to obtain some information from an SAP system. This data is presented to the Web Dynpro user in the form of an editable table. For the purposes of discussion, we shall give this RFC module the fictional name of ZREAD_DATA_FOR_WD.[30]

2. The user makes certain modifications to the data and presses the **Save changes** button.

3. The modified data is passed to the input side of the update RFC module, and the model object is executed. We shall give the update RFC module the fictional name of ZUPDATE_DATA_FOR_WD. This program has been coded in such a way that it performs an immediate database update (which, in this situation is OK).

4. As soon as ZUPDATE_DATA_FOR_WD returns control to the Web Dynpro application, ZREAD_DATA_FOR_WD is called a second time to reread the updated information.

5. Oops! The Web Dynpro application now displays the old, *unmodified* data.

The problem here caused by two factors:

1. The two RFC modules have not been written to function as a coordinated pair.

2. The time taken for an SAP system to complete a database update depends upon the workload it is currently under. In high load situations, there will be a slight delay between the completion of the LUW in ABAP and the *actual* update of the database table(s).

In our example, this delay could sometimes be greater than than interval between the call to ZUPDATE_DATA_FOR_WD and the subsequent call to ZREAD_DATA_FOR_WD.

---

29 As happens all too often!
30 The ABAP function module and function group names used in this particular example do not represent any functionality delivered by SAP. They are merely used as illustrations of what could be developed.

This is known as the Read-Write-Read problem and it can be avoided in the following manner. Firstly, it is important to state what assumptions have been made about this solution. These are:

▶ Data is supplied to Web Dynpro from an SAP system by calling the RFC module ZREAD_DATA_FOR_WD.

▶ Modified data from Web Dynpro is updated within the SAP system by calling the RFC module ZUPDATE_DATA_FOR_WD.

▶ Both of these function modules live in the same ABAP function group called ZWD_INTERFACE.

▶ Both of the executable model objects that represent these RFC modules live in the same adaptive RFC model.

▶ Both executable model objects connect to the SAP system with the same JCo destination (If both executable model objects live in the same aRFC Model, then this will be the default behaviour).

ZREAD_DATA_FOR_WD should be written such that it maintains a set of internal tables. These act as a cache for the data that could potentially be modified. The read process therefore amounts to the steps shown in Figure 10.31.

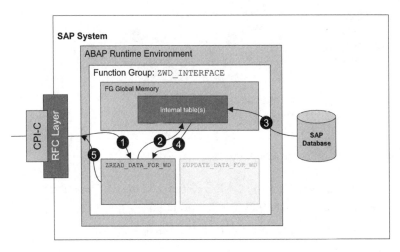

Figure 10.31 Avoiding the Read-Write-Read problem: Part 1

1. The RFC call is received by the R/3 system and the RFC module ZREAD_DATA_FOR_WD is called with the parameters required to identify the desired data.

2. The internal cache tables are checked to see if they already contain the required data. (Since these internal tables live in the function group's

global memory area, the data they contain will persist for the lifespan of the user roll area, not just the lifespan of the RFC module call).

3. If the internal cache tables do not hold the required information, then read the database, updating the internal cache tables. If the required information is found in the cache, then this step is omitted.

4. The required data is then taken from the internal tables and placed into the outbound side of the RFC module's interface.

5. Control is returned to the calling program.

Now when ZUPDATE_DATA_FOR_WD is called, the data being updated must, by definition, already exist in the function group's cache tables. This is a safe assumption to make because the RFC module ZUPDATE_DATA_FOR_WD will only ever be used in conjunction with ZREAD_DATA_FOR_WD. ZUPDATE_DATA_FOR_WD performs the steps shown in Figure 10.32.

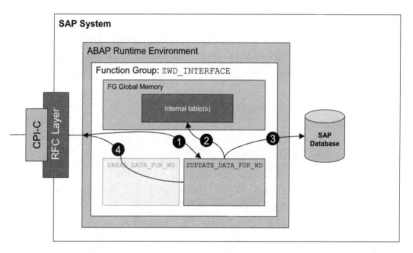

Figure 10.32 Avoiding the Read-Write-Read problem: Part 2

1. The RFC call is received by the R/3 system and the RFC module is called passing in all the data that is to be modified.

2. Update the appropriate rows in the internal cache. This is a synchronous update.

3. Update the database. This is an asynchronous update. Remember that the use of the ABAP statements MODIFY or UPDATE will implicitly cause the termination of the current ABAP session (I.E. the current LUW will be terminated).

4. Control is returned to the calling program

RFC module `ZREAD_DATA_FOR_WD` can now be called to reread the data irrespective of whether the database update has completed or not. The database will only be accessed for data that cannot be found in the internal cache tables. Such data cannot have been updated during the lifespan of this JCo connection; therefore, the database must contain the latest version.

10.12 Why can't I use two different JCo connections?

If two RFC modules need to function in coordination with each other, then this is best achieved by writing them such that they will always execute at least in the same user roll area, and probably also within the same ABAP session. This way, these RFC modules can easily share data with each; however, you must be careful not to include statements that inadvertently terminate the ABAP session.

Even after you have carefully written your RFC modules to function in this coordinated way, you can still negate all that work by calling each executable model object via a different JCo connection. Remember that one JCo connection equates to one user roll area within SAP; therefore, two different JCo connections equals two different user roll areas.

Under these circumstances, the data sharing solution documented above will not give the desired results. Data cannot be shared across separate user roll areas using the mechanism described above.

11 Web Dynpro phase model

The phase model is the name given to the various tasks that take place within the WDF to process a single request/response cycle. This cycle of processing phases starts and ends with a pair of client-dependent steps that translate the data to and from the client-specific format to the internal WDF format (the DataContainer). The bulk of the processing within the phase model acts on the client-independent information in the DataContainer.

The entire phase model is a stateless operation. That means that once the request/response cycle has completed, the object instances that provided the processing are not reused. The WDF will create a new set of phase model objects to handle each new application request. Once instantiated, the different phases of the cycle are processed sequentially without repetition. Depending on any error conditions that may occur, some phases may be omitted. This usually means that the steps in between the one reporting an error and the doPostProcessing step are skipped.

Irrespective of any error conditions that might arise during the request/response cycle, the step doPostProcessing is always called. This is the last point in time at which application developer code may be executed.

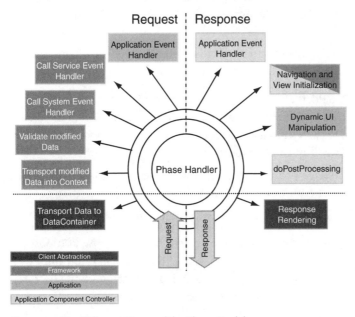

Figure 11.1 The Different Stages of the Phase Model

11.1 Transport data to DataContainer

This stage of the phase model transfers the data in the incoming request from the client-specific format received at the J2EE Engine into a standard client- and protocol-independent DataContainer for processing by the WDF.

11.2 Transport modified data into context

All data modified by the user is transported into the context in a type-safe manner. It is unusual for errors to occur in this step, but if they do, the WDF will terminate the entire application.

An example of an error that could occur in this step is "Mapping reference not found." This error is dealt with in Section 7.2.

11.3 Validate modified data

In this step of the phase model, general validation rules are applied to the data modified by the user. This is where value sets and typed data attributes are validated (converted to typed representation). If at least one validation routine fails, then processing jumps forward to `doPostProcessing`, omitting the intermediate phases.

Important: Validation errors will be presented to the user for correction only if a validating action triggered the server round trip.

Consider the following situation. You have three UI elements on the screen:

▶ An input field that is bound to a context attribute which in turn is defined by a dictionary simple type. Within the definition of the dictionary simple type, you have specified maximum and minimum inclusive values of say 999 and 0 respectively.

▶ A table UI element that displays some data, but the `onLeadSelect` event has *not* been associated with an action.

▶ A pushbutton that is associated with some action in the normal way.

Using only the UI elements on the screen, there are now two possible ways to initiate a server round trip. Either the user clicks on the pushbutton, in which case the server-side action associated with the button is performed, or the user changes the lead selection on the table UI element. Even though the table's `onLeadSelect` event has not been associated with a server-side action, a server round trip will take place.

If a value of 1000 is now entered into the input field (clearly violating the maximum inclusive constraint defined in the dictionary), whether the error is reported back to the user depends on how the server round trip is triggered.

If the user clicks the pushbutton (which has an associated server-side action), the validation check for the input field will fail, the message manager will report the error to the user, and the action event handler will *not* be processed. This is because the server round trip was triggered by a UI element associated with an action, i.e., a validating action has been triggered.

If, however, the table row selection is changed by clicking the mouse on a different row, a server round trip will be initiated, the validation check for the input field will still fail, but the message manager will *not* report the error back to the user; this is because the action that caused the round trip (in this case, an empty server round trip) is considered a non-validating action. Therefore, it does not matter whether there is junk on the screen—we're not interested in validating it anyway!

Events such as Web Dynpro logoff or browser shutdown are considered non-validating actions; these are actions that must be processed irrespective of whether the data on the screen is valid or not.

11.4   Call system event handler

System events are events that relate to the WDF itself, such as logoff. If such events are caught, the remaining steps of the phase model are not executed. Therefore, these system events are completely invisible to the application developer.

11.5   Call service event handler

The service event handler is an application-dependent step in which services like "ValueHelp Request" and "Load Data" are handled. If such service events are caught, then processing jumps forward to `doPostProcessing`, omitting the intermediate phases.

Service events are completely invisible to application developers. Nevertheless, if the service event requires the use of supply functions or similar functionality, these units of application code will be executed.

11.6   Application event handler

Now that the context contains valid data returned from the user interface, this is the first point in time at which application event handlers can be processed. This is where your onAction{n$_{act}$}() methods will be called.

If an application event is raised that requires navigation to another view (such as calling an outbound plug), then these navigation requests are stored in a navigation queue for processing by the navigation step.

If any error occurs during this step, processing jumps forward to the doPostProcessing phase, omitting the intermediate steps. Errors are now presented to the user for correction. Any events that have already been placed in the navigation queue are ignored, and the queue is flushed.

11.7   doBeforeNavigation

For large Web Dynpro applications, the consistency of user data often cannot be determined simply by examining the data in a single context, or even the data in all the controllers of a single component. The complexity of a Web Dynpro application could be such that in order to decide whether navigation should occur, it is necessary to check the validity of data in multiple contexts across multiple components.

The doBeforeNavigation phase provides the hook method in which you can perform these wide-ranging data validity checks. This phase corresponds directly to the wdDoBeforeNavigation() method found in a component controller.

11.8   Navigation and view initialization

The navigation events placed into the navigation queue are now processed. Each outbound plug in the navigation queue corresponds to an inbound plug on another view (unless the outbound plug is of type exit). The WDF processes each navigation event in the queue by calling the corresponding inbound plugs. If an inbound plug immediately invokes an outbound plug, the call to the outbound plug is stored in an internal queue for evaluation. All the calls to the corresponding inbound plugs (as defined by the navigational links) are then processed. This phase, therefore, also processes inbound plugs.

It is very important to understand that if a severe error occurs within an inbound plug, navigation *cannot* be suppressed. The inbound plug must run to completion, handling all errors gracefully, and the navigation will continue (as well as possible). The destination view of the inbound plug must then be able to report any errors that occurred during navigation. If you attempt to suppress or redirect navigation due to errors in an inbound plug, the WDF will abort your application with a stack trace.

11.9 Dynamic UI manipulation

All views that form part of the currently visible screen are referred to as the "view assembly". For all views in the view assembly, the `wdDoModify-View()` method is called during this phase.

Once processing reaches this phase, the view controller context should be considered stable. That is, all processing to prepare the data in the context for display should already have taken place.

There are certain types of processing that are not permitted in this phase:

▶ Do not attempt to call an outbound plug.

▶ Do not attempt to report error messages using the `MessageManager`.

Any attempt to perform either of these actions will cause the WDF to abort your application with a stack trace.

SAP *strongly* recommends that you do not write any data to the context during the execution of `wdDoModifyView()`.

11.10 doPostProcessing

This is the stage in which exception processing from supply functions can be performed. Since supply functions are called only when the data they provide is explicitly required, the exact step of the phase model in which they will execute cannot generally be predicted. Therefore, any exceptions raised by supply functions must be handled at the very last possible point in the phase model.

This phase corresponds directly to the method `wdDoPostProcessing()` found in a component controller.

SAP *strongly* recommends that you do not write any data to the context during the execution of `wdDoPostProcessing()`.

11.11 Response rendering

Application developers have no access to the processing contained within this step of the phase model. This is where the DataContainer is converted back into the client dependent format and sent back to the front end.

Caveat confector:

SAP strongly recommends that during the execution of the following methods, the respective contexts are accessed in a strictly read-only manner. The key point here is that, due to the dynamic nature of the processing performed by the WDF, situations could arise in which `wdDoModifyView()` and `wdDoPostProcessing()` are called without any previous event handler or navigation processing (for instance, pressing Refresh in the browser). Therefore, any updates made to the respective contexts during these method calls cannot be guaranteed to be free from unpredictable side effects.

By referring to the phase model diagram (see Figure 11.1), you will see that the stages Dynamic UI manipulation (method `wdDoModifyView()`) and doPostProcessing (method `wdDoPostProcessing()`) are the last points in time during which your own application code can execute. These methods have distinct roles which should not be confused or abused!

Each of these phase model stages (WDF hook methods) has a distinct role to perform:

▶ **wdDoModifyView()**
  By the time `wdDoModifyView()` is reached, all preparatory data processing in the context should have been completed. All this method should be concerned with is the manipulation of the UI element hierarchy using whatever information it finds in the context.

  `wdDoModifyView()` should take no part in defining the contents of context.

▶ **wdDoPostProcessing()**
  By the time `wdDoPostProcessing()` is reached, the only remaining tasks should be the handling of supply function exceptions.

  `wdDoPostProcessing()` should take no part in defining the contents of context.

12   Class and Interface Reference

The following reference section is not intended to be an exhaustive list of all available Web Dynrpo classes. Instead, it has been written to provide information on the most commonly used classes. Any classes used by Web Dynpro that are not listed here are documented in the standard help files and javadoc that accompanies the NWDS.

12.1   Controllers, their methods, and self reference

12.1.1   Controller constructors

You are not permitted to modify the constructor of any controller.

If a controller behaves as the root component in an application, it will be instantiated automatically by the WDF. If, however, the controller behaves as the child of some other component, the Lifespan parameter on the controller usage declaration determines how the child component is instantiated. If you specify a lifespan of Framework, the instance of the child component is created automatically by the WDF. If, however, you specify a lifespan of "Manual", an instance of the child controller will be created only when `wdThis.wdGet{`n_u`}Interface().createComponent()` is called.

Either way, you have no direct control over the contents of a controller's constructor.

A controller's constructor will always have the signature `{`n_{ctl}`}(IPrivate{`n_{ctl}`} wdThis)`.

The reference received in parameter `wdThis` becomes the controller's self-reference variable. `wdThis` should always be used in preference to the standard Java self reference `this`.

12.1.2   Standard hook methods

Each controller has its own set of standard hook methods. These methods are called automatically by the WDF during the execution of the phase model, and it is within these methods that you may implement your own code.

Apart from an interface view controller, all controllers have the standard hook methods `wdDoInit()` and `wdDoExit()`. Therefore, these methods will be documented only once.

▶ **void wdDoInit( )**

This method is always initially empty. The WDF executes this method automatically as soon as the controller is instantiated. It is executed only once during the lifecycle of the controller.

From an application point of view, you should regard this method as the place to perform all those tasks that are required only once at controller initialization.

▶ **void wdDoExit( )**

This method is always initially empty. The WDF executes this method automatically at the end of the controller's lifecycle.

All coding required only once at controller termination should be included in this method. For instance, you may need to perform an explicit log off from an R/3 system.

12.1.3 User-defined methods

If you want to create an instance method, declare the method name and its parameters in the **Methods** tab of the controller editor window.

If, however, you want to define a static method, you must manually define the method at the bottom of the source code editor, between the `//@@begin others` and `//@@end` comment tags.

An example of the need for a user-defined, static method would be if you wish to call your own method from within `wdDoModifyView()` in a view controller.

Important: Instance methods created through the NWDS may not be overloaded. This is because the Web Dynpro metamodel is designed to be independent of the implementation language. Since the Web Dynpro toolset has also been developed for Object Oriented ABAP, and this does not support method overloading, this feature has not been implemented in Web Dynpro for Java.

12.1.4 Self reference and shortcuts

Use of the standard Java self reference this

Within any Java class, it is customary to use the standard self reference this to make explicit programmatic reference to the current instance.

However, within your own Web Dynpro controllers, this should normally not be used. Instead, please use the alternative self reference called wdThis.

wdThis is a reference to the current controller's IPrivate{n_{ctl}} interface. This interface represents all the functionality implemented in the generated class Internal{n_{ctl}}.

If you use the standard Java self reference this, you will point only to the class {n_{ctl}}, thus bypassing all the generated functionality found in the internal class. This functionality includes logging, validation, and parameter mapping.

SAP reserves the right to change the behavior of the generated controller Internal{n_{ctl}} without warning. Therefore, for compatibility with future versions of Web Dynpro, you should always use wdThis to ensure that your controller has access to any new functionality SAP may add.

The only situation in which the use of the standard Java self reference this is appropriate is when you wish to make explicit reference to declarations made between the comment markers //@@begin others and //@@end. Any variables or methods declared here are invisible to the WDF.

Shortcut names

Within the constructor of any controller, you will find the following shortcut variables declared:

```
public {n_{ctl}}(IPrivate{n_{ctl}} wdThis) {
  this.wdThis = wdThis;
  this.wdContext = wdThis.wdGetContext();
  this.wdControllerAPI = wdThis.wdGetAPI();
  this.wdComponentAPI = wdThis.wdGetAPI().getComponent();
}
```

Listing 12.1 Shortcut Variables Declared in the Constructor of Any Controller

As previously mentioned, the variable wdThis should be used in preference to the standard Java self reference this.

`wdContext` is the reference to the context root node, from which all access to context starts.

`wdControllerAPI` is the reference to the API of the current controller—be it a custom controller or a view controller.

`wdComponentAPI` is the reference to the API of the component controller of the current controller. If this variable is used from within a component controller, `wdComponentAPI` and `wdControllerAPI` will point to the same object.

12.1.5   User modifications to generated code

SAP will not support any user attempts to modify, adjust, enhance, or otherwise alter any code that lies either outside any pair of `//@@begin` and `//@@end` comment tags, or is within a generated Java class.

Such modifications are very unlikely to survive the code regeneration process, but in the remote chance that they should end up being deployed to the J2EE server, SAP will offer no support for such code.

12.2   Controller classes

12.2.1   {n$_c$}—Component controller

Synopsis
A component controller is created automatically when a component is declared within the NWDS. The component controller is always of the same name as the component itself and is responsible for the overall management of the component.

Package

{pkg$_1$}.{pkg$_2$}.{pkg$_3$}...{pkg$_n$}

Properties
▶ **IPrivate{n$_c$} wdThis**
A reference to the private interface of the current component controller

▶ **IPrivate{n$_c$}.IContextNode wdContext**
A reference to the private interface of the component controller's context root node

Methods

▶ **void wdDoPostProcessing()**

This method is initially empty. It is automatically executed by the WDF. It provides you with a point in time in which you can ensure that every context node is valid after event handling has taken place, but before the view controllers perform their screen rendering.

By the time wdDoPostProcessing() is executed, it is usual for all supply function, relation role, and calculated attribute processing to have been completed.

Since components may embed other components, the method wdDoPostProcessing() will first be called for the root component controller, and then for all subordinate component controllers.

▶ **void wdDoBeforeNavigation()**

This method is initially empty. It is automatically executed by the WDF before the navigation stack is processed.

12.2.2 {n_c}Interface—Component interface controller

Synopsis

A component interface controller is created automatically when a component is declared within the NWDS. This controller manages all aspects of the component's public interface.

Package

$\{pkg_1\}.\{pkg_2\}.\{pkg_3\}...\{pkg_n\}$

Properties

▶ **IPrivate{n_c}Interface wdThis**

A reference to the private interface of the current component interface controller

▶ **IPrivate{n_c}Interface.IContextNode wdContext**

A reference to the private interface of the component interface controller's context

Methods

User-defined

12.2.3 {n_v}—View controller

Synopsis

A view controller is created automatically when a view is declared within the NWDS.

Package

$\{pkg_1\}.\{pkg_2\}.\{pkg_3\}...\{pkg_n\}$

Properties

▶ `IPrivate{n_v} wdThis`
A reference to the private interface of the current view controller

▶ `IPrivate{n_v}.IContextNode wdContext`
A reference to the private interface of the view controller's context

Methods

▶ `void wdDoModifyView()`
This standard hook method is initially empty. It is automatically executed immediately prior to screen rendering.

`wdDoModifyView()` is the only point during the request/response cycle at which you may perform dynamic alterations to the UI layout.

This method receives references to:

▶ Itself (`wdThis`)

▶ The current context (`wdContext`)

▶ The view's UI layout container (`view`)

▶ A boolean flag (`firstTime`) to indicate whether this is the first time this method has been called within the controller's lifecycle

A Web Dynpro view should be designed in such a way that by the time `wdDoModifyView()` is called, all manipulation of context data has been completed, leaving `wdDoModifyView()` simply with the task of assembling or modifying the UI layout.

The execution of `wdDoModifyView()` should be designed as a stateless activity.

12.2.4 Internal{n_{ctl}}, Internal{n_c}Interface—Generated controllers

These classes form the actual implementation of the declared controller {n_{ctl}}, and the coding they contain is generated automatically.

Class `Internal{nctl}` exists for all types of controllers, whereas `Internal{nc}Interface` exists only for component controllers—hence the use of the component controller identifier {n_c} rather than the generic controller identifier {n_{ctl}}.

> **Caveat confector:** Any attempt to change the coding found within these controllers will almost certainly render your application unusable by the WDF. It will also place it outside the SAP support agreement.

The following architecture is common to all three classes; therefore, to avoid duplication, only class `Internal{nctl}` is documented.

Architecture

In order for the WDF to be able to execute *any* user-defined controller, there must be an abstraction layer sitting between the user-defined code and the standard WDF.

This abstraction layer is known as the "delegating" layer. It is responsible for presenting your controllers to the WDF through a consistent interface, irrespective of any declarations you might have made at design time.

For any given controller {n_{ctl}}, there exists a generated controller called `Internal{nctl}`. However, `Internal{nctl}` implements the interface you declared at design time, and therefore cannot be executed directly by the WDF. The delegating layer acts as a wrapper around class `Internal{nctl}` and provides the consistent interface required by the WDF.

The delegating layer implements all controllers as appropriate instances of the different classes found in {pkg_1}...{pkg_n}`.progmodel.generation.Delegating*`. These classes have a static interface; therefore, irrespective of your design-time declarations, the WDF is able to execute any controller you care to create.

As their name implies, the classes in the delegating layer delegate their functionality to the generated classes belonging to {n_{ctl}}.

The WDF refers to the classes in the delegating layer as the "alter ego" of the generated classes belonging to $\{n_{ctl}\}$. In turn, the alter ego classes refer to the generated classes as their "delegates."

Synopsis

This class forms the generated implementation of the declared controller $\{n_{ctl}\}$.

All the standard hook methods found in class $\{n_{ctl}\}$ are replicated in class `Internal`$\{n_{ctl}\}$. When the WDF needs to call a standard hook method in class $\{n_{ctl}\}$, it does so by calling the same hook method in the alter ego class, which, in turn, delegates the call to `Internal`$\{n_{ctl}\}$.

Package

$\{pkg_1\}.\{pkg_2\}.\{pkg_3\}...\{pkg_n\}$`.wdp`

Interfaces implemented

▶ `IPrivate`$\{n_c\}$

▶ `IComponentDelegate`

Properties

▶ **`DelegatingComponent wdAlterEgo`**
A reference to the instance of the class in the delegating layer that wraps `Internal`$\{n_c\}$

▶ **$\{n_c\}$ `delegate`**
A reference from the delegating layer down to the generated controller class `Internal`$\{n_{ctl}\}$

▶ **`NodeInfo info{cn}`**
The static metadata for all nodes $\{cn\}$ in the context

▶ **`NodeInfo infoContext`**
The metadata of the context root node

▶ **`ContextNode contextNode`**
The context root node itself

Inner classes

▶ **`ContextNode extends Node`**
          `implements IContextNode`
This class contains the actual implementation of all context nodes

declared at design time. No hierarchical node relationships are defined in this class.

▶ `ContextElement extends NodeElement`
                 `implements IContextElement`
This class contains the actual implementation of the context node elements declared at design time.

▶ `{cn}Node extends Node implements I{cn}Node`
This class contains the actual implementation specific to context node `{cn}` declared at design time. All the child nodes `{chn}` of node `{cn}` are defined within this class.

▶ `{vn}Element extends NodeElement`
                 `implements I{vn}Element`
This class contains the actual implementation specific to an element of value node `{vn}` declared at design time.

▶ `{mn}Element extends ModelNodeElement`
                 `implements I{mn}Element`
This class contains the actual implementation specific to an element of model node `{mn}` declared at design time.

Methods
You are not permitted to access any of the methods in these classes.

12.3 Controller interfaces

12.3.1 IExternal{n_ctl}Interface—External public interface controller

Synopsis
This external public interface is created only for a component interface controller. You are not permitted to modify this class directly.

`IExternal{n_ctl}Interface` gives external components within the same application access to the public functionality of component $\{n_{ct1}\}$.

If you declare any methods within a component's interface controller, these methods are available through this interface.

> **Important:** An instance of this interface is created only if $\{n_{ct1}\}$ is embedded within another component through component usage.

Package

{pkg₁}.{pkg₂}.{pkg₃}…{pkgₙ}.wdp

Methods

▶ `IWDComponent wdGetAPI()`

Returns a reference to the generic API of the interface controller

12.3.2   IPublic{n_ctl}—Internal public interface controller

Synopsis

This internal public interface is created automatically when any controller {n_ctl} is declared. You are not allowed to modify this class directly.

`IPublic{n_ctl}` provides other controllers within the same component access to the public data and functionality of {n_ctl}.

All controllers, except for a view controller, implement this interface.

Package

{pkg₁}.{pkg₂}.{pkg₃}…{pkgₙ}.wdp

Inner interfaces

▶ `IContextNode extends IWDNode`

Generic interface to all context nodes in controller {n_ctl}

▶ `IContextElement extends IWDNodeElement`

Generic interface to all context node elements in controller {n_ctl}

Methods

▶ `IWDContext wdGetContext()`

Returns a reference to the controller's context

▶ `IWDComponent wdGetAPI()`

Returns a reference to the generic API of controller {n_ctl}

12.3.3   IPrivate{n_ctl}—Internal private interface controller

Synopsis

This internal private interface is created automatically when any controller {n_ctl} is declared. You are not allowed to modify this class directly.

IPrivate{n_{ct1}} provides controller {n_{ct1}} with access to its own functionality. It is this interface that becomes the Web Dynpro self reference wdThis.

IPrivate{n_{ct1}} is always an extension of IPublic{n_{ct1}}.

If any events for controller {n_{ct1}} are declared, the event handler methods are created within this private interface.

Package
{pkg_{sap}}.progmodel.wdp

Inner interfaces
▶ **IContextNode extends IWDNode**
  Generic interface to all context nodes in {n_{ct1}}

▶ **IContextElement extends IWDNodeElement**
  Generic interface to all context node elements in {n_{ct1}}

Methods
▶ **IWDContext wdGetContext( )**
  Returns a reference to the controller's context

▶ **IWDComponent wdGetAPI( )**
  Returns a reference to the generic API of controller {n_{ct1}}

12.3.4 IWDComponent—Generic interface for all component controllers

Synopsis
This interface extends IWDController and is implemented by all Web Dynpro components.

Package
{pkg_{sap}}.progmodel.api

Methods
▶ **IWDTextAccessor getTextAccessor( )**
  Returns the text accessor for this component. The text accessor provides access to language-specific (translatable) text in resource bundles.

▶ `IWDMessageManager getMessageManager()`
Returns a reference to this component's message manager. There is only ever one message manager per component.

A message manager is the interface through which all views in a component can report exceptions, warnings, and success messages to the client.

▶ `IWDValidationCheck getValidationCheck()`
This method returns the validation check interface for this component. The validation check is used to check for invalid context attributes and access external string representations.

▶ `IWDComponentInfo getComponentInfo()`
Returns the component metadata

▶ `IWDWindowManager getWindowManager()`
Returns the factory object to create windows. The window manager factory object provides the internal interface to the interface view of component $\{n_c\}$.

▶ `WDDeployableObjectPart getDeployableObjectPart()`
Returns the deployable object part of this component

▶ `void addEventHandler(IWDEventInfo event,`
`    IWDEventHandlerInfo eventHandler,`
`    IWDController controller)`
Connects the specified event handler to the specified event

▶ `void removeEventHandler(IWDEventInfo event,`
`    IWDEventHandlerInfo eventHandler,`
`    IWDController controller)`
Disconnects the specified event handler from the specified event

▶ `boolean isApplicationRoot()`
Returns true if this is the root component of the application

▶ `IWDApplication getApplication()`
Returns the application to which this component belongs

This method should be called only if `isApplicationRoot() == true`.

12.3.5 IWDComponentUsage—Generic component usage interface

Synopsis
All Web Dynpro embedded components implement this interface.

Package

`{pkgsap}.progmodel.api`

Methods

- **`void addEventHandler(IWDEventInfo event, IWDEventHandlerInfoeventHandler, IWDController controller)`**
  Causes parameter `eventHandler` to subscribe to parameter `event`. Within the scope of the current component usage, the event must be defined in the interface controller or configuration controller.

  Parameter `controller` must be part of the parent component of this component usage.

- **`void createComponent()`**
  Creates a component instance of the type defined by the component usage declared at design time.

  The method fails if the component usage is associated with a component interface definition.

  Before calling this method, ensure that `hasActiveComponent() == false && isReferencing() == false`.

- **`void createComponent(String componentName)`**
  Creates an instance of the component implementation specified by `componentName` for this component usage.

  Before calling this method, ensure that `hasActiveComponent() == false && isReferencing() == false`.

- **`void createComponent(String componentName, String deployableObjectName)`**
  Creates an instance of the component implementation specified by `componentName` for this component usage, and packages it into the deployable object specified by `deployableObjectName`.

  Before calling this method, ensure that `hasActiveComponent() == false && isReferencing() == false`.

- **`void createComponentUsageOfSameType(String name)`**
  Creates a component usage with the given name which has the same component interface type assigned as this component usage.

- **`void deleteComponent()`**
  Deletes the component instance associated with this component usage. If no instance exists, the method remains silent.

  Before calling this method, ensure that `isReferencing() == false`.

▶ `void enterReferencingMode(IWDComponentUsage component Usage)`

The lifecycle management of the current component usage is transferred to the component usage referenced by `componentUsage`. The component usage is now said to be in referencing mode.

Transferring lifecycle management from one component usage to another is supported only for component usages of the same type, and for "faceless" components (i.e., components that have no view controllers).

Before calling this method, ensure that `hasActiveComponent()` == `false || isReferencing()` == `true`.

▶ `IWDComponentUsageInfo getComponentUsageInfo()`

Returns the repository information of this component usage

▶ `boolean hasActiveComponent()`

Returns true if this component usage has an existing instance

▶ `IWDExternalControllerInterface getInterfaceController()`

Gets the interface controller of the component instance

The returned generic controller interface object should be cast as the specific component interface `IExternal{nc}Interface`.

Before calling this method, ensure that `hasActiveComponent()` == `true`.

▶ `void leaveReferencingMode()`

Restores the component usage's lifecycle management back to itself. If the component usage is not in referencing mode, then the method exits silently.

▶ `boolean isReferencing()`

Returns true if the lifecycle of this component usage is under the control of another component usage

▶ `boolean isReferenced()`

Returns true if this component usage is controlling the lifecycle of some other component usage

▶ `void removeEventHandler(IWDEventInfo event,`
   `IWDEventHandlerInfo eventHandler,`
   `IWDController controller)`

Disconnects the specified event handler from the specified event

12.3.6   IWDController—Generic interface for all controllers

Synopsis

All controllers created by the NWDS implement this interface. Unless explicitly stated, the methods listed for this interface are *not* available to parent components through the component usage interface.

Package

{pkg_{sap}}.progmodel.api

Methods

▶ `IWDAction getAction(String name)`
Returns the action object identified by the string `name` or `null`

▶ `IWDComponent getComponent()`
Returns the component object to which this controller belongs

▶ `IWDContext getContext()`
Returns a reference to the context of this controller

This method is visible through the component usage interface.

▶ `IWDControllerInfo getControllerInfo();`
Returns the metadata describing this controller

This method is visible through the component usage interface.

▶ `String getName()`
Returns the name of this controller

▶ `String getPackageName()`
Returns the package part of the qualified name of this controller

▶ `String getQualifiedName()`
Returns the qualified name of this controller

12.3.7   IWDView—Generic interface for a view layout

Synopsis

All view layouts within view controllers implement this interface. This interface extends `IWDViewController`.

Package

{pkg_{sap}}.progmodel.api

Methods

- **`IWDViewElement createElement(Class viewElementInterface, String id)`**
  Creates a new view element implementing the given interface and with the given name. The `id` parameter may be `null` if required.

- **`IWDViewElement getElement(String id)`**
  Returns the view element with the name `id` or `null` if it does not exist

- **`IWDViewElement getRootElement()`**
  Returns a reference to the root element of the view layout hierarchy

  This element is *always* called `RootUIElementContainer` and is *always* of type `IWDTransparentContainer`.

- **`void resetView()`**
  Resets the view's layout to the initial state declared at design time. That is, all dynamic modifications to the view layout are thrown away and the view layout returns to the state it was in when the view controller was initialized.

12.3.8 IWDViewController—Generic interface for all view controllers

Synopsis

All view controllers created by the NWDS implement this interface. This interface extends `IWDController`.

Package

{pkg$_{sap}$}.progmodel.api

Methods

- **`IWDAbstractViewInfo getViewInfo()`**
  Returns the repository information for this view

- **`void firePlug(IWDOutboundPlugInfo plug, Map parameters)`**
  Fires the given outbound plug with the given parameters and performs the navigation defined for that link

  Firing a plug of type "Exit" defined for the top-level component causes the application to terminate.

- **`void requestFocus(IWDAction action)`**
  Changes the keyboard input focus to the UI element having a primary event to which `action` is bound. If multiple UI elements events are

bound to the same action, then it is undefined which UI element will receive focus.

Secondary UI element event bindings are ignored during focus request evaluation. UI elements that are read-only or disabled are not considered at all.

▶ `void requestFocus(IWDNodeElement nodeElement,`
  `IWDAttributeInfo attribute)`
As per `requestFocus(IWDAction action)` except that the UI element is identified using the attribute with a specific context node element. This is how a specific cell in a table row can be given focus.

12.4   Application interfaces

12.4.1   IWDApplication—Generic interface for all applications

Synopsis
All applications created by the NWDS implement this interface.

Package
`{pkg`$_{sap}$`}.progmodel.api`

Methods
▶ `String getName()`
  Returns the name of the application

▶ `IWDApplicationInfo getApplicationInfo()`
  Returns the application metadata read from the runtime repository

▶ `WDDeployableObjectPart getDeployableObjectPart()`
  Returns the deployable object part of this application

12.5   Context interfaces

12.5.1   I{cn}Element—Node specific extension to IWDNodeElement

Synopsis
This interface is automatically created when a context node {cn} is declared at design time *and* the `TypedAccessRequired` property is set to `true`. It provides you with a typed interface to the elements of node collection {cn}.

This interface always extends the generic node interface `IWDNodeElement`.

Package

{pkg₁}.{pkg₂}.{pkg₃}…{pkgₙ}

Methods

▶ `I{chn}Node node{chn}()`
This method will exist only if child node {chn} is a non-singleton node.

▶ `I{chn}NodeElement current{chn}Element()`
Returns the element at the lead selection of child node {chn} or `null` if either the lead selection is not set, or the node collection is empty

▶ `I{chn}NodeElement get{chn}ElementAt(int index)`
Returns the element at position `index` of child node {chn} or `null` if no such index exists

▶ `{dt} get{ca}()`
Accessor method for attribute {ca}. Data type {dt} is defined at design time and may be of any available data type.

▶ `void set{ca}({dt} value)`
Mutator method for attribute {ca}. Data type {dt} is defined at design time and may be of any available data type.

12.5.2 I{cn}Node—Node specific extension to interface IWDNode

Synopsis

This interface is automatically created when a context node {cn} is declared at design time *and* the `TypedAccessRequired` property is set to `true`. It provides you with a typed interface to node {cn}.

This interface always extends the generic node interface `IWDNode`.

Package

{pkg₁}.{pkg₂}.{pkg₃}…{pkgₙ}

Methods

▶ `I{cn}Element create{cn}Element()`
Creates an element for context node {cn}

The element returned by this method is not yet a member of any node collection. Use `bind()` or `addElement()` to insert it into the appropriate node collection.

▶ `void bind(I{cn}Element element)`

Replaces the entire node collection with the single, node specific element. All data previously held in the node collection is lost.

If required, the entire node collection can be destroyed by calling `bind(null)` as long as this action does not violate node's cardinality.

▶ `void bind({mo} model)`

If {cn} is a model node, then {mo} represents a reference to the appropriate model object. The entire model node collection is replaced with the collection held within the `model` parameter. All data previously held in the node collection is lost.

If required, the entire node collection can be destroyed by calling `bind(null)` as long as this action does not violate {cn}'s cardinality.

▶ `I{cn}Element current{cn}Element()`

Returns the element at the lead selection or `null` if either the lead selection is not set or the node collection is empty

▶ `I{cn}Element get{cn}ElementAt()`

Returns the element at the given index or `null` if no element exists at that index

▶ `I{chn}Node node{chn}()`

Returns the child node {chn} belonging to the element at the lead selection of node {cn}. If the lead selection is not set, `null` is returned.

▶ `I{chn}Node node{chn}(int index)`

Returns the child node {chn} belonging to element `index` in node {cn}. If no such index exists, `null` is returned.

12.5.3 IContextElement—Controller specific extension to IWDNodeElement

Synopsis
This interface is automatically created as a controller specific extension to the generic context node interface `IWDNodeElement`.

Package
{pkg$_1$}.{pkg$_2$}.{pkg$_3$}...{pkg$_n$}

Methods
▶ `{dt} get{ca}()`

Generic accessor method for the *independent* context attribute {ca}

► void set{ca}({dt} value)

Generic mutator method for the *independent* context attribute {ca}. If the read-only flag is set for this attribute, this method will not be generated.

12.5.4 IContextNode—Controller specific extension to IWDNode

Synopsis

This interface is automatically created as a controller specific extension to the generic context node interface IWDNode.

Package

{pkg₁}.{pkg₂}.{pkg₃}…{pkgₙ}

Methods

► IWDContext wdGetAPI()

Provides access to the generic context API

► IContextElement createContextElement()

Creates a new generic element for this node

The element returned by this method is not yet bound to any node. Use bind() or addElement() to insert it into the appropriate node collection.

► void bind(IContextElement element)

Replaces the entire node collection with the single IContextElement parameter. All data previously held in the node collection is lost.

If required, the entire node collection can be destroyed by calling bind(null) as long as this action does not violate the node's cardinality.

► IContextElement currentContextElement()

Returns the generic element at the lead selection or null if either the lead selection is not set or the node collection is empty

► I{cn}Node node{cn}()

Returns the node {cn}

► I{cn}Element current{cn}Element()

Returns the element at the lead selection of node {cn}

12.5.5 IWDAttributeInfo—Interface for the metadata of a generic context attribute

Synopsis

The metadata of any context attribute {ca}, whether created statically or dynamically, will be described by an instance of this interface.

Package

{pkg_sap}.progmodel.api

Methods

▶ `String getName()`

Returns the name of the attribute. This name must be unique within the scope of the containing `IWDNodeInfo`, but may be reused across different instances of `IWDNodeInfo`.

▶ `IWDNodeInfo getNode()`

Returns the `IWDNodeInfo` object to which this attribute belongs

▶ `String getOriginName()`

Returns the name of the attribute to which the current attribute is mapped, either from the mapping origin value node, or the model object.

If the attribute is unmapped, `null` is returned.

▶ `IDataType getDataType()`

Returns the data type of the attribute

▶ `boolean hasSimpleType()`

Returns a boolean to indicate whether the attribute's data type is of type `ISimpleType`. You should always call this method as a safeguard before attempting to call `getSimpleType()`.

▶ `ISimpleType getSimpleType()`

Returns the `ISimpleType` associated with this attribute. If the data type of this attribute is not `ISimpleType`, then a `ContextException` is thrown.

▶ `ISimpleTypeModifiable getModifiableSimpleType()`

Returns a modifiable version of the `ISimpleType` data type of this attribute. This gives you the ability to modify the data type of an attribute dynamically. The modifiable type is cloned from the standard type upon first access and has two important features:

▶ The returned object is only ever used for this attribute.

▸ If subsequent calls are made to `getModifiableSimpleType()` for the same attribute, the same instance will always be returned as long as the attribute still exists.

A modifiable data type can be obtained only for a unmapped attribute. If you attempt to call `getModifiableSimpleType()` for a mapped attribute, then a `WDRuntimeException` will be thrown.

▶ **`IWDAttributeInfo getDataAttribute()`**
Returns the `IWDAttributeInfo` of this attribute's mapping origin or `null` if this attribute is unmapped

▶ **`boolean isReadOnly()`**
Checks whether this attribute is read-only for clients

Do not use this flag to attempt to determine whether this attribute is read-only for applications. Normally applications will always have write access to context attributes. However, the following conditions describe the circumstances under which applications will have only read access to context attributes:

▸ If a context attribute is mapped to a read-only model class property

▸ If the attribute is a calculated attribute and no mutator method has been defined

▶ **`Object getDefaultValue()`**
Returns the default value or `null` if one does not exist

12.5.6 IWDContext—Base interface for accessing context data in a controller

Synopsis
All data managed by a controller is stored within its context. This interface class provides a set of generic methods to access that data by exposing the root node, the metadata of the root node, and the data type information of context attributes.

The NWDS will generate typed sub-interfaces for all context nodes and attributes declared at design time.

Typed accessor methods will not exist for any context nodes or attributes created dynamically (that is, at runtime). Therefore, they can only be accessed using the generic context API.

Package
`{pkg`~sap~`}.progmodel.api`

Methods

▶ `String getName()`
Returns the name of this context. The context name is always the same as the name of the controller to which it belongs.

▶ `IWDNode getRootNode()`
Returns the root node of this context. Since the context root node is created at component creation time and always has a cardinality of `1..1`, it is guaranteed that the context root node will always exist, and that it will always contain exactly one element.

▶ `IWDNodeInfo getRootNodeInfo()`
Returns the static metadata describing the root node of this context

▶ `ISimpleType getTypeOf(String path)`
Returns the data type of the context attribute identified by the given dot-delimited path.

A `ContextException` is thrown if the path does not identify an attribute or the attribute's type is not `IWDSimpleType`.

▶ `ISimpleTypeModifiable getModifiableTypeOf(String path)`
Returns a modifiable data type of the context attribute identified by the given dot-delimited path. Subsequent calls to this method for the same value of `path` are guaranteed to return the same instance.

A `ContextException` is thrown if the path does not identify an attribute or the attribute's type is not `IWDSimpleType`.

▶ `void reset()`
Arbitrarily resets the context to its initial state. All node collections are reset to the minimum number of elements specified by their cardinality, and all dynamically added nodes and attributes are destroyed from the metadata.

Important: It is the responsibility of the application developer to ensure that all node and attribute mapping or binding dependencies are deactivated *before* this method is called.

Calling `reset()` when mapping or binding dependencies are still active will have unpredictable results and possibly lead to a fatal error in the WDF for your application.

▶ `void reset(boolean clear)`
Calling `reset(true)` is functionally equivalent to calling `reset()`.

Calling `reset(false)` causes all dynamically created nodes and attributes to be deleted, but any data held in static node elements is preserved.

Important: `IWDContext.reset(false)` behaves in a *subtractive* manner. For example, node {cn} has two attributes {ca1} and {ca2} defined at design time. At runtime, two new elements are created for {cn}, so the node collection now contains elements 0 and 1. Then the `IWDNodeInfo` object that describes {cn} is modified to include a new attribute {ca3}, and another element (2) is added to the node collection using the new metadata.

All three node elements now contain the attribute {ca3}, but only {ca3} in element 2 will contain a value. {ca3} in elements 0 and 1 will contain 0 or null or false (whichever is appropriate for {ca3}'s data type).

When `IWDContext.reset(false)` is called, {ca3} will be subtracted from the `IWDNodeInfo` describing {cn}. This means that all elements in {cn}'s node collection will still exist, *minus* the data held in {ca3}.

The same warning given for method `reset()` about mapped or bound nodes and attributes also applies to `reset(boolean clear)`.

▶ **void resetChangedByClient()**
Global reset of all `changedByClient` flags in all context node elements

12.5.7 IWDNode—Interface implemented by all context nodes

Synopsis
This interface class implements the functionality common to all context nodes. Nodes created dynamically can implement only this interface, whereas nodes created at design time (assuming the `TypedAccessRequired` property is set to `true`) extend this interface and supply the developer with a more convenient, typed sub-interface.

Package
{pkg$_{sap}$}.progmodel.api

Properties

▶ `int NO_SELECTION`

A constant value of -1 used to indicate that the node has no lead selection

▶ `int LEAD_SELECTION`

A placeholder that can be used when calling methods that take an element index as a parameter. It is used to indicate that you want the index of the lead selection without being concerned about its actual value.

Methods

▶ `IWDContext getContext()`

Returns a reference to the context to which this node belongs

▶ `void bind(Collection items)`

Replaces the current node collection with a new one.

If required, the entire node collection can be destroyed by calling `bind(null)`. This causes the node collection to be valid, but empty.

Do not call `bind(null)` for nodes that have a cardinality of `1..<something>`, as this would violate the constraint for the minimum number of elements and lead to a runtime error.

▶ `void invalidate()`

In the case of a value node, the element list is cleared and the supply function is called.

In the case of a model node, the data held in the context node is resynchronized with the data held in the model.

Calling `invalidate()` from within a supply function will cause a `ContextException` to be thrown.

▶ `boolean validate()`

Validates the node by performing the following sequence of checks:

▶ If the node is already valid, then do nothing and return false.

▶ If a supply function exists, then call it. The return value depends on the success or failure of the supply function.

▶ If the cardinality is `1..n`, then add an empty node element.

▶ If the node collection is null, then an empty collection is bound.

▶ `IWDNodeInfo getNodeInfo()`

Returns the metadata describing this node

▶ `IWDNodeElement getElementAt(int index)`
Returns the element at the given index

▶ `int size()`
Returns the number of elements in the node collection

▶ `boolean isEmpty()`
Returns whether or not the element list is empty

▶ `int getLeadSelection()`
Returns the index of the lead selection or the value of `NO_SELECTION` (-1) if the selection list is empty

▶ `void setLeadSelection(int index)`
Sets the lead selection to the given index value. If the value of `NO_SELECTION` (-1) is used, then the selection list is cleared.

A `ContextException` will be thrown if the caller tries to clear a selection list having a cardinality of `1..<something>`.

An `IllegalArgumentException` will be thrown if $0 \le$ `index` $<$ `size()`.

▶ `void clearSelection()`
Clears the node's selection list

▶ `boolean isSelected(int index)`
Returns whether or not the element at the given index is a member of the selection list

▶ `void setSelected(int index, boolean selected)`
The selection flag of element `index` is set to the value of the boolean parameter `selected`.

▶ `void setTreeSelection(IWDNodeElement element)`
Sets the lead selection values of the whole node's subtree such that the given element is selected

A `ContextException` is thrown if the element is not found in the node's subtree.

▶ `IWDNodeElement getCurrentElement()`
Returns the element at the lead selection or `null` if no element is selected

▶ `void addElement(IWDNodeElement element)`
Adds a new element to the node collection at position `size()`

A `ContextException` is thrown if the element being added does not match the node or if the node is a singleton and the parent node has no valid lead selection element.

► **boolean removeElement(IWDNodeElement element)**
Removes an element from the node collection. Returns `true` if the element removal was successful.

► **void moveElement(int from, int to)**
Moves an element to another position within the node collection

An `IllegalArgumentException` is thrown if either `from` or `to` is invalid.

► **void swapElements(int index1, int index2)**
Swaps the elements at positions `index1` and `index2`

An `IllegalArgumentException` is thrown if either `index1` or `index2` is invalid.

► **void moveFirst()**
If the node collection is non-empty, the lead selection is set to zero. Otherwise, the method returns silently.

► **void moveLast()**
If the node collection is non-empty, the lead selection is set to the element index given by `size()-1`. Otherwise, the method returns silently.

► **IWDNodeElement movePrevious()**
If such an element exists, the lead selection is set to the index given by `getLeadSelection()-1` and this element is returned.

If the node collection is empty, or the lead selection is zero, `movePrevious()` returns `null` and does not change the lead selection.

► **IWDNodeElement moveNext()**
If such an element exists, the lead selection is set to the index given by `getLeadSelection()+1` and this element is returned.

If the node collection is empty or the lead selection is set to `size()-1`, `movePrevious()` returns `null` and does not change the lead selection.

► **void moveTo(int index)**
Moves the lead selection to the specified element. This method is functionally equivalent to calling `setLeadSelection(int index)`.

An `IllegalArgumentException` is thrown if `size()-1 < index < 0`.

► **IWDNode getChildNode(String name, int index)**
Returns the child node identified by `name` belonging to the element at position `index`

If the child node is a singleton, then the only valid value for `index` is the one that corresponds to the parent node's lead selection.

Returns `null` if no node with that name exist.

There are two situations under which an `IllegalArgumentException` could be thrown:

- ▸ For non-singleton child nodes, if `size()-1 < index < 0`
- ▸ For a singleton child node, if `index` does not represent the lead selection. This exception can always be avoided by specifying `LEAD_SELECTION` as the value for `index`.

▶ **IWDNodeElement createElement()**
Returns a new node element of the type used by this **value** node. The element created by this method is not yet a member of the value node collection; consequently, a call to the element's `getNode()` method will return `null`.

A subsequent call either to `bind()` or `addElement()` is required to insert this element into the appropriate value node collection.

▶ **IWDNodeElement createElement(Object reference)**
Returns a new node element of the type used by this **model** node. The element created by this method is not yet a member of the model node collection; consequently, a call to the element's `getNode()` method will return `null`.

A subsequent call either to `bind()` or `addElement()` is required to insert this element into the appropriate model node collection.

The parameter `reference` refers to an instance of a model object from which the metadata for this node element can be derived.

▶ **void sortElements(Comparator comparator)**
Sorts the elements according to the value of `comparator`. The standard `Collections.sort(List)` is ultimately used to implement the sort and operates on each `IWDNodeElement` of the node collection. This has the added benefit of guaranteeing that the sort is stable. That is, equal elements will not be reordered.

Note that the calling `sort()` does not cause the collection to *remain* in sorted order. Further modifications to the collection (such as calls to `addElement()`) will probably render the collection unsorted again.

Typically, you will have to write your own class that implements `Comparator` in order to sort the elements in your node collection correctly.

▶ **void notifyAllMappedNodes(Object payload)**
Sends a notification and the `payload` to all nodes that are mapped (either directly or indirectly) to the current node.

An `IWDNodeNotificationListener` must be registered with the node's metadata before any processing can take place.

> **Important:** Due to Web Dynpro's lazy data access model, a mapping link between two context nodes is established only upon first access to the mapped node. Therefore, it is not possible to send a notification to any mapped node whose data has not yet been accessed.

12.5.8 IWDNodeElement—Interface implemented by all context node elements

Synopsis

This interface class implements the functionality common to all context node elements. Node elements created dynamically implement only this interface, but elements created at design time extend this interface and supply the developer with a more convenient, typed sub-interface.

Package

{pkg$_{sap}$}.progmodel.api

Methods

▶ `IWDNode node()`
Returns the node to which this element belongs. If the element has not yet been added to a node, `null` is returned.

▶ `int index()`
If the element has been added to a node, then the index of this element is returned; otherwise, –1 is returned.

▶ `void changed(String attributeName)`
Sets the changed flag for the attribute identified by `attributeName`.

This method is called automatically by all mutator methods in generated sub-interfaces of `IWDNodeElement` and by the method `setAttributeValue(String, Object)`. Consequently, it is very unlikely that you will ever need to call this method explicitly.

If `attributeName` is `null`, then all attributes are marked as changed.

The WDF consumes and then resets this flag when determining which element attributes have changed during the request/response cycle.

▶ `boolean isChanged()`
Returns a boolean value to indicate whether a node element has been changed during the request/response cycle

The WDF consumes and then resets this flag during screen rendering. This is the latest possible point during the phase model at which this flag can be consumed, and allows any changes made by event handlers or business logic within a model object to be detected.

For value nodes, `isChanged()` will return the result of a logical OR across all the change flags of the element's attributes.

For model nodes, `isChanged()` will behave in a way that is determined by the model's ability to track attribute changes. If the model object is able to track changes in its attributes, then the attribute change flags in the context element will reflect this, and `isChanged()` will behave in the same way as for the element of a value node.

Important: If the model object is unable to track changes in its attributes, then `isChanged()` will always return `true`. This functionality is outside the control of the context.

▶ **boolean isChangedByClient( )**
Returns `true` if the `changedByClient` flag has been set for this element. The WDF will set this flag when an update from the client arrives. It remains true until all change flags in the entire context are reset by a call to method `IWDContext.resetChangedByClient()`.

▶ **Object getAttributeValue(String attributeName)**
A generic accessor method that returns the value of `attributeName` as an `Object`. This method can be called for any attribute and is the only way of obtaining the value of a dynamically added attribute.

A `ContextException` is thrown if `attributeName` does not exist.

▶ **void setAttributeValue(String attributeName, Object value)**
A generic mutator method that sets the value of `attributeName` to be `value`. This method can be called for any attribute and is the only way of setting the value of a dynamically added attribute.

A `ContextException` is thrown if `attributeName` does not exist.

A `ClassCastException` is thrown if the class of `value` does not match the declared class for the attribute.

▶ **boolean hasModel( )**
Returns `true` if this element has a model object; otherwise, it returns `false`

▶ **Object model( )**
Returns the model object contained in this element

A `ContextException` will be thrown if the node element is not a model node element. To prevent this from happening, first check that `hasModel() == true`.

12.5.9 IWDNodeInfo — Interface for the metadata of a generic context node

Synopsis
The metadata for any context node {cn} is stored in an instance of this interface. Through this interface, new context nodes and attributes of any type can be created dynamically at runtime. However, you can delete dynamically created nodes and attributes only by resetting the entire context. See `IWDContext.reset()` and `IWDContext.reset(boolean clear)` for more details.

Package
{pkg~sap~}.progmodel.api

Methods
▶ `String getName()`
Returns the name of the {cn}

▶ `IWDContext getContext()`
Returns a reference to the context to which {cn} belongs

▶ `boolean isSingleton()`
Indicates whether or not {cn} is a singleton with respect to its parent node

▶ `boolean isMandatory()`
Indicates whether or not {cn}'s collection is guaranteed to have at least one element. This value forms the first part of the cardinality attribute.

▶ `boolean isMultiple()`
Indicates whether or not {cn}'s collection is allowed to have more than one element. This value forms the second part of the cardinality attribute.

▶ `boolean isMandatorySelection()`
Indicates whether or not {cn}'s selection is guaranteed to have at least one element. This value forms the first part of the selection cardinality attribute.

► **`boolean isMultipleSelection()`**
Indicates whether or not {cn}'s selection is allowed to have more than one element. This value forms the second part of the selection cardinality attribute.

► **`IDataType getDataType()`**
Returns the data type of {cn} or `null`

► **`IStructure getStructureType()`**
Returns the structured data type of {cn} or `null`

► **`IWDNodeInfo getParent()`**
Returns the metadata of {cn}'s parent node or `null` if {cn} is the root node

► **`IWDNodeInfo getChild(String id)`**
Returns the metadata for the child node {chn} specified by `id` or `null`

► **`IWDAttributeInfo getAttribute(String name)`**
Returns the metadata of the attribute specified by `name` or `null`

► **`Iterator iterateAttributes()`**
Returns an `Iterator` object for {cn}'s attributes

► **`Iterator iterateChildren()`**
Returns an `Iterator` object for {cn}'s child nodes

► **`String getPathDescription()`**
Returns the full dot-delimited path within the context to {cn}

► **`IWDNodeInfo addChild(String id,`**
  `Class elementClass,`
  `boolean singleton,`
  `boolean mandatory,`
  `boolean multiple,`
  `boolean mandatorySelection,`
  `boolean multipleSelection,`
  `String dataType,`
  `IWDNodeCollectionSupplier supplier,`
  `IWDNodeCollectionDisposer disposer)`
Dynamically declares the metadata for a new *unmapped* child node {chn} of node {cn}.addChild(). The name specified by parameter `id` must be unique within the scope of the controller's context; otherwise, a `ContextException` will be thrown.

{chn} will become a value node if parameter `elementClass` is `null`, or a model node if parameter `elementClass` is of type `ICMIModelClass`.

In theory, you can create a model node using an object of any class, but it will mean that standard methods such as getAttributeValue() and setAttributeValue() will have to be implemented using reflection. See the javadoc for ModelElement for more details.

Parameter dataType is either null (if you wish to add attributes manually) or the name of a dictionary data type, or an object of type IStructure.

Supply and disposer functions cannot be created dynamically since they refer to Java methods. If nodes that require such functions are to be created dynamically, then only existing supply and disposer functions can be referenced.

After a successful call to this method, an instance, or in the case of non-singleton nodes, instances, of the newly declared node can be retrieved with a call to (cn).getChildNode(String, int).

The returned object will contain attributes only if you specified a dictionary data type or an IStructure for the dataType parameter. If dataType was set to null, then attributes must be added manually by calling addAttribute(String, String).

▶ **IWDNodeInfo addMappedChild(String id,**
    Class elementClass,
    boolean singleton,
    boolean mandatorySelection,
    boolean multipleSelection,
    String mappedPath,
    boolean selectionMapped,
    boolean initializeLeadSelection)

This method is very similar to addChild(), except that the parameters mandatory, multiple, and dataType are inherited from the mapping origin node. The properties related to the selection are considered only if the node selection is unmapped.

If the mappedPath parameter is specified at the time addMappedChild() is called, then the node mapping is immutable until such time as the component lifecycle terminates or IWDContext.reset() is called. If you wish to alter the mapping origin dynamically, leave the mappedPath parameter null at node creation time, and make a subsequent call to either setMapping(IWDContext, String, boolean) or setMapping(IWD-NodeInfo, boolean).

Caveat confector: Do attempt to modify the mapping origin once the mapping reference has been traversed! Once the node collection of the mapping origin has been accessed, the node mapping should be considered fixed.

The `initializeLeadSelection` parameter will set the collection's lead selection to 0 if the collection is non-empty.

A `ContextConfigurationException` will be thrown if any of the properties are inconsistent (e.g., trying to create a non-singleton node directly under the context root node).

▶ **void setMapping(IWDNodeInfo mappedNode, boolean selectionMapped)**
Sets the mapping path of a mapped child node {chn} that has been previously declared by a call to {cn}.addMappedChild().

The metadata for {chn} is derived directly from the mapping origin `mappedNode`.

Calling this method is permitted only if the `mappingPath` parameter was set to `null` when {chn} was created.

A `ContextConfigurationException` will be thrown if any of the parameters are inconsistent or if the node already has a valid mapping path assigned.

▶ **void setMapping(IWDContext mappedContext, String mappedPath, boolean selectionMapped)**
Sets the mapping path of a mapped child node {chn} that has been previously declared by a call to {cn}.addMappedChild().

The metadata for {chn} is derived implicitly from the node identified by `mappedPath` within context `mappedContext`.

Calling this method is permitted only if the `mappingPath` parameter was set to `null` when {chn} was created.

A `ContextConfigurationException` will be thrown if any of the parameters are inconsistent or if the node already has a valid mapping path assigned.

▶ **IWDNodeInfo addRecursiveChild(IWDNodeInfo parent)**
Dynamically adds a recursive child node of the same type and *name* as `parent`. This action is not supported at design time by the NWDS due to metamodel restrictions, and can therefore only be performed dynamically.

- ▶ `IWDNodeInfo addRecursiveChild(String name,`
  `IWDNodeInfo parent)`
  Dynamically adds a recursive child node called `name` to node `parent`

- ▶ `IWDAttributeInfo addAttribute(String name, String dataType)`
  Creates an unmapped attribute `name` of data type `dataType` for a value node. The attribute name must be unique within the node.

  The naming convention for attribute data types is the full Java class name with prefix `java:` to indicate that the class belongs to standard Java, or `ddic:` to indicate that the class belongs to the Web Dynpro data dictionary.

  You may use any one of the standard dictionary data types, or you can define your own structured type. All standard Web Dynpro dictionary classes can be found in package `com.sap.dictionary`.

  Important: Attributes with data types prefixed by `java:` *cannot* be bound to UI elements. This is because only those data types defined within the Web Dynpro dictionary can be processed by the response renderer.

- ▶ `IWDAttributeInfo addAttribute(String name,`
  `IDataType dataType)`
  Exactly as `addAttribute(String, String)` above, but uses a reference to an `IDataType` object instead of specifying the data type as a string.

  `IDataType` can refer to a data type found within a model class.

- ▶ `IWDAttributeInfo addMappedAttribute(String name,`
  `String mappedName)`
  Adds a new mapped attribute to node element {cn}.

  You can map node attributes in three different ways, either at the node level, at the attribute level, or using a hybrid of the first two methods. See the javadoc for a full explanation.

  The fully qualified path name to any particular context attribute is specified using a dot-delimited syntax, and is in the general form:

  {n_u}.{ctx}.{cn}(.{cn}).{ca}

  If the attribute you are adding is mapped to another context attribute within the *same* component, the value for {n_u} in the above path will be empty. In this case, the dot that precedes the {ctx} placeholder *must be included!* If the preceding dot is omitted, `IWDNodeInfo` will assume that node-based mapping is required and will attempt to locate the attribute's mapping origin by first using the mapping path of the parent node.

▶ **ICMIModelClassInfo getModelClassInfo()**
Returns the metadata for an `ICMIGenericModelClass` or `null` for value nodes

▶ **void setModelClassInfo(ICMIModelClassInfo info)**
The model node will obtain its metadata from the object referenced by `info`. All the attributes defined in `info` are also automatically created by this method. Therefore, a call to `addAttributesFromModelClass-Info()` is unnecessary once this method has completed.

▶ **void addAttributesFromModelClassInfo()**
Automatically adds all attributes from the model's metadata. For this method to work, there must first have been a successful call to `set-ModelClassInfo(ICMIGenericModelClass)`.

▶ **void addAttributesFromDataNode()**
Automatically adds all attributes from the data node. This method can only be called for a node that uses node level mapping. This must first have been created by a call to `addMappedChild()`.

▶ **void setSupplyingRelationRole(String supplyingRelationRole)**
Sets the `supplyingRelationRole` attribute for an `ICMIGenericModel-Class`. The parent node must also be an `ICMIGenericModelClass`. The role is the one leading from the parent node's class to this one.

▶ **void setCollectionSupplier(IWDNodeCollectionSupplier supplier)**
Defines a new supply function for this node. To deactivate the use of the supply function, set `supplier` to `null`.

▶ **void setCollectionDisposer(IWDNodeCollectionDisposer disposer)**
Defines a new disposer function for this node. To deactivate the use of the disposer function, set `disposer` to `null`.

▶ **void addNotificationListener(IWDNodeNotificationListener listener)**
Defines a new notification listener for this node

▶ **void removeNotificationListener(IWDNodeNotificationListener listener)**
Removes the specified notification listener from this node

12.6   View layout interfaces

12.6.1   Generalized management of UI element properties

UI element implementation has been standardized such that, for any given UI element property $\{ui_p\}$, you will find one or more of the following methods:

▶ `void bind{uip}(String)`

▶ `void bind{uip}(IWD[Attribute|Node]Info)`

▶ `String bindingOf{uip}()`

▶ `{dtp} get{uip}()`

▶ `void set{uip}({dtp} value)`

Since all these methods differ only in the name of the property upon which they operate, they will be documented once in a generalized form.

Methods relating to context binding

▶ **void bind{uip}(String)**
Binds property $\{ui_p\}$ to the context node or attribute specified by the given context path string

▶ **void bind{uip}(IWD[Attribute|Node]Info)**
Binds property $\{ui_p\}$ to the context attribute or node specified by the given info object

▶ **String bindingOf{uip}()**
Returns the path name to the context node or attribute against which property $\{ui_p\}$ is bound

Accessor and mutator methods

The data type $\{dt_p\}$ of property $\{ui_p\}$ is specified at design time.

▶ **{dtp} get{uip}()**
Standard accessor method for property $\{ui_p\}$

▶ **void set{uip}({dtp})**
Standard mutator method for property $\{ui_p\}$

These five standard methods are implemented according to the following rules:

▶ If it is permitted for property $\{ui_p\}$ to have a binding, then:

▷ If $\{ui_p\}$ is read-only, only `get{uip}()` will be implemented.

▶ If {ui$_p$} is read-write, both get{ui$_p$}() and set{ui$_p$}() will be implemented.

▶ If it is mandatory that property {ui$_p$} has a binding, then:

  ▶ If {ui$_p$} must be bound to a context node, bind{ui$_p$}(String), bind{ui$_p$}(IWDNodeInfo), and bindingOf{ui$_p$}() will be implemented.

  ▶ If {ui$_p$} must be bound to a context attribute, then:

  ▶ If the context attribute belongs to a node of cardinality <something>..n, bind{ui$_p$}(String), bind{ui$_p$}(IWDAttributeInfo), and bindingOf{ui$_p$}() will be implemented.

▶ If it is optional for property {ui$_p$} to have a binding, then:

  ▶ If {ui$_p$} is a read-write property, all five standard methods will be implemented.

  ▶ If {ui$_p$} is a read only property, all standard methods will be implemented *except* the mutator method set{ui$_p$}({dt$_p$}).

12.6.2   Generalized management of UI element actions

Certain UI elements are capable of raising client-side events. These client-side events are transported to the WDF and automatically raised as server-side events known as "actions." For a given client-side event {ui$_{evt}$}, the following three standard methods are available:

▶ IWDAction get{ui$_{evt}$}()

▶ void set{ui$_{evt}$}(IWDAction)

▶ IWDParameterMapping mappingOf{ui$_{evt}$}()

Since all these methods differ only in the name of the event upon which they operate, they will be documented once in a generalized form.

Accessor and mutator methods

▶ **IWDAction get{ui$_{evt}$}()**
   Returns the server-side action object {act} assigned to the client-side event {ui$_{evt}$}

▶ **void set{ui$_{evt}$}(IWDAction)**
   Associates the server-side action object {act} with the client-side event {ui$_{evt}$}

Parameter mapping methods

▶ `IWDParameterMapping mappingOf{ui`_{evt}`}()`
Returns the parameter mapping object that links parameters of the client-side event to the parameters of the server-side `onAction{act}` event handler in the view controller

It can be assumed that if a UI element is capable of raising a client-side event, all three of the above methods will be implemented.

12.6.3 Appearance of UI elements

One of the basic Web Dynpro design philosophies is that server-side code should be completely decoupled, not only from any rendering capabilities possessed by the client layer, but also from the specific visual appearance of a rendered UI element. The SAP Product Design Centre (PDC) has defined an appearance for all rendered UI elements, but this appearance is completely independent from any coding written by a developer. This explains why the properties that control the appearance of a UI element are given abstract names and values.[1]

For instance, the `IWDLabel` UI element has a property called `design`. This property can be set to either `STANDARD` or `LIGHT`. These names are an abstraction of the two different appearances that the label could take on. But since the capability of the client software is unknown to the server, it would be incorrect to define presentation properties that assume the client is, for instance, a browser.

This principle is applied throughout the entire range of Web Dynpro UI elements.

Certain UI elements require properties that specify dimensional values such as `width` and `height`. In these cases, the UI elements do not have separate properties for the dimension's value and the dimension's units; rather, both values are defined within one property field. This requires that such properties are held as `String` values. For example, the width of a table could be 75 %, or the height of an image 200px.

It is a general convention that if the units are not specified, pixels are assumed.

---

1 The Portal Development Kit (PDK) can be used to edit the appearance of rendered UI elements without affecting any of the developed code.

12.6.4 The UI element source property

Several UI elements have a `source` property. This property may contain either:

▶ The name of a file deployed under the `src/mimes/Components/{n_v}` directory of the current project or

▶ A URL generated by the `WDURLGenerator` service

12.6.5 Naming of UI element properties

Each UI element has a variety of properties that are referenced both through method names and Java constants. The Java constants are provided to act as default values for a given property.

The name of property $\{ui_p\}$ is held in the standard Java manner – that is, in mixed case with the first letter of each word capitalized. The Java constant that holds the default value for property $\{ui_p\}$ is named in uppercase letters and starts with the string `DEFAULT_`. The property name is then split into individual uppercase words, separated by underscore characters.

For example, the UI element `IWDAbstractInputField` has a property called `PasswordField`. The Java constant holding the default value for this property is called `DEFAULT_PASSWORD_FIELD`.

This principle applies across all UI element properties.

12.6.6 IWDAbstractButton—Base interface for a push button

Synopsis
This interface extends `IWDAbstractCaption` and adds a `text` property.

It implements the standard property management methods.

Package
`{pkg_sap}.clientserver.uielib.standard.api`

Properties
▶ `String DEFAULT_TEXT = ""`
Default value of the property `text`

Event and event parameters

▶ `onAction`
This client-side event is raised when the user clicks the button.

This event has no parameters.

Methods

Only the standard property and action management methods are implemented.

12.6.7 IWDAbstractCaption—Base interface for a text caption

Synopsis

This interface extends `IWDUIElement` and defines a read-only text label with the additional feature of being able to place an image either before or after the text.

It implements the standard property management methods.

Package

$\{pkg_{sap}\}$`.clientserver.uielib.standard.api`

Properties

▶ `String DEFAULT_IMAGE_ALT = ""`
Default value of the property `imageAlt`

▶ `boolean DEFAULT_IMAGE_FIRST = true`
Default value of the property `imageFirst`. Determines the position of the image relative to the text.

▶ `String DEFAULT_IMAGE_SOURCE = ""`
The image source filename

Methods

Only the standard property management methods are implemented.

12.6.8 IWDAbstractDropDown—Base interface for a drop-down list

Synopsis

This interface extends `IWDUIElement`, adding the properties `state` and `width`.

It implements the standard property and action management methods.

Package

{pkg~sap~}.clientserver.uielib.standard.api

Properties

▶ **WDState DEFAULT_STATE = WDState.NORMAL**
Default value of property state. The values held in class WDSTATE are NORMAL and REQUIRED.

▶ **String DEFAULT_WIDTH = ""**
Default value of property width

Methods
Implements the standard property management methods.

12.6.9 IWDAbstractDropDownByIndex — Base interface for an index-based drop-down list

Synopsis
This interface extends IWDAbstractDropDown and represents a dropdown list that uses index-based context binding. This UI element provides a "one-from-many" selection implemented as a text field, a button, and a dropdown list. The default list item appears in the text field next to which is a down-arrow button. When the button is pushed, a dropdown list appears from which a selection can be made. The value in the text field is replaced by whatever value the user selects from the dropdown list.

The UI element that implements this interface must be bound to a context node {cn} of cardinality 0..n. In addition, {cn} must contain an attribute {ca} of type String. The dropdown list will then contain as many items as there are elements in {cn}, and the text of each dropdown list item will be the value of {ca} for the particular element of {cn}.

This UI element is ideal when you require the user to choose one item from a *dynamic* list.

Implements the standard property and action management methods.

Package

{pkg~sap~}.clientserver.uielib.standard.api

Properties

▶ `IWDAttributeInfo texts`

The context attribute {ca} from which the dropdown list item text will be derived

Event and event parameters

▶ `onSelect`

This client-side event is raised when the user selects an item from the `dropdown` list.

▶ **Parameters:** `int index`

The lead selection of {cn} corresponding to the selected item {ca}

Methods

Implements the standard property and action management methods

12.6.10 IWDAbstractDropDownByKey—Base interface for a key-based drop-down list

Synopsis

This interface extends `IWDAbstractDropDown` and represents a dropdown list that uses key-based context binding. This UI element provides a "one-from-many" selection implemented as a text field, a button, and a drop-down list. The default list item appears in the text field next to which is a down-arrow button. When the button is pushed, a dropdown list appears from which a selection can be made. The value in the text field is replaced by whatever value the user selects from the dropdown list.

The UI element that implements this interface must be bound to a context attribute {ca} that supplies a valueset (such as a String Enumeration). It is from this valueset that the text values displayed in the dropdown list and their corresponding keys are derived.

This UI element is ideal when you require the user to choose one item from a *static* list.

Implements the standard property and action management methods.

Package

`{pkg`~sap~`}.clientserver.uielib.standard.api`

Properties

▶ `String selectedKey`
The key value of the selected value set item

Event and event parameters

▶ `onSelect`
This client-side event is raised when the user selects an item from the `dropdown` list.

▶ **Parameters: `String key`**
The key of the selected valueset item

Methods

Implements the standard property and action management methods

12.6.11 IWDAbstractInputField—Base interface for an input field

Synopsis

This interface extends `IWDUIElement` and defines an abstraction of a single-line text-input field. It provides an API to manage the following properties:

▶ Length

▶ Read-only flag

▶ Input type (normal or password)

▶ Input status (optional or mandatory)

▶ Assignment of an action to the `onEnter` event

Implements the standard property and action management methods.

Package

`{pkgsap}.clientserver.uielib.standard.api`

Properties

▶ `int DEFAULT_LENGTH = 20`
Default value of the property `length`

Important: This property controls the length of the visible UI element on the client, *not* the length of the input data. In this respect, it functions in the same way as the `size` parameter of an HTML `<input>` tag, not the `maxlength` parameter.

If you wish to restrict the length of data entered into an input field, you must create a dictionary simple type of the required length, and then create a context attribute of this custom type. Finally, you should bind the `InputField` UI element to this context attribute.

▶ **boolean DEFAULT_READ_ONLY = false**
Default value of property `readOnly`

▶ **boolean DEFAULT_PASSWORD_FIELD = false**
Default value of property `passwordField`

▶ **WDState DEFAULT_STATE = WDState.NORMAL**
Default value of property `state`. The values held in class `WDState` are `NORMAL` and `REQUIRED`.

Important: If the `STATE` property is set to `REQUIRED`, a visual indicator (a red asterisk next to the field's label) is used to indicate that data entry is required in this UI element. It is still up to the application to check that the user has complied.

Event and event parameters

▶ **onAction**
This client-side event is raised if the user presses enter while focus is on this field.

This event has no parameters.

Methods
Only the standard property and action management methods are implemented.

12.6.12 IWDAbstractTreeNodeType—Base interface type for all tree nodes and items

Synopsis
This interface extends `IWDViewElement` and represents a single node of a tree.

Implements the standard property and action management methods.

Package
{pkg_{sap}}.clientserver.uielib.standard.api

Properties

▶ **WDTreeNodeDesign DEFAULT_DESIGN = WDTreeNodeDesign.STANDARD**
Default value of property design. The values held in class WDCellBackgroundDesign are STANDARD and EMPHASIZED.

▶ **String DEFAULT_ICON_ALT = ""**
Default value of property iconAlt and holds the Alt text for the icon for this tree node

▶ **String DEFAULT_ICON_SOURCE = ""**
Default value of property iconSource and holds the file name of the icon that appears next to this tree node

▶ **boolean DEFAULT_IGNORE_ACTION = false**
Default value of property ignoreAction

▶ **String DEFAULT_TEXT = ""**
Default value of property text and holds the label for this node of the tree

▶ **String DEFAULT_TOOLTIP = ""**
Default value of property tooltip and holds the tooltip text for this node of the tree

▶ **String dataSource**
The dataSource property holds the name of the context node from which the tree node will obtain its data. You must bind this property to a context node. It does not have an accessor or mutator method.

Event and event parameters

▶ **onAction**
This client-side event is raised every time a user clicks on the tree node.

▶ **Parameters: String path**
The path to the context element corresponding to the node that raised this event

Methods

▶ **IWDTree getTree()**
Returns the tree object to which this node belongs

12.6.13 IWDButton—Interface for a push button

Synopsis

This interface extends `IWDAbstractButton` and adds the properties `design`, `size`, and `width`.

Implements the standard property management methods.

Package

`{pkg`_{sap}`}.clientserver.uielib.standard.api`

Properties

▶ **WDButtonDesign DEFAULT_DESIGN = WDButtonDesign.STANDARD**
Default value of property design. The values held in class `WDButtonDe-sign` are `STANDARD`, `EMPHASIZED`, `PREVIOUS`, and `NEXT`.

▶ **String DEFAULT_SIZE = ""**
Default value of the property `size`

▶ **String DEFAULT_WIDTH = ""**
Default value of the property `width`

Methods

Only the standard property and action management methods are implemented.

12.6.14 IWDCaption—Base interface for a text caption

Synopsis

This interface extends `IWDAbstractCaption` and adds a text property to the base interface. This interface is used as a text placeholder in composite UI elements such as `IWDGroup`, `IWDTab`, `IWDTable`, `IWDTableColumn`, and `IWDTray`.

Implements the standard property management methods.

Package

`{pkg`_{sap}`}.clientserver.uielib.standard.api`

Properties

▶ **String DEFAULT_TEXT = ""**
Default value of the property `text`

Methods

Only the standard property management methods are implemented.

12.6.15 IWDCheckBox—Interface for a check box

Synopsis

This interface extends `IWDUIElement` and defines a `checkbox` representation of a boolean field, plus a label text.

Implements the standard property and action management methods.

Package

`{pkg`sap`}.clientserver.uielib.standard.api`

Properties

▶ `WDState DEFAULT_STATE = WDState.NORMAL`
Default value of property `state`. The values held in class `WDState` are `NORMAL` and `REQUIRED`. These correspond to optional and mandatory input fields respectively.

▶ `String DEFAULT_TEXT = ""`
Default value of the property `text`

▶ `boolean checked = false`
Default value of the property `checked`. This property must be bound to a context attribute!

Event and event parameters

▶ `onToggle`
This client-side event is raised when the user changes the state of the checkbox.

▶ Parameter: `boolean checked`
True = checked, false = unchecked.

Methods

Only the standard property and action management methods are implemented.

12.6.16 IWDCheckBoxGroup—Interface for a multiple checkbox selection group

Synopsis

This interface extends `IWDUIElement` and represents a multiple selection visualized by two or more checkboxes.

In order to supply each of the `checkboxes` with a label, the view context must provide a node {cn} whose cardinality is 0..n and whose selection is also 0..n. The node must have an attribute {ca} of type string containing the `checkbox` label text. The number of elements in {cn} at runtime then dictates the number of `checkboxes` that will appear in the `checkbox` group.

The node {cn} must allow multiple selection; otherwise, only one `checkbox` from the group could ever be selected!

The property `texts` must be bound to the context path of {cn}'s string attribute {ca}.

Implements the standard property and action management methods.

Package

{pkg_sap}.`clientserver.uielib.standard.api`

Properties

▶ **WDState DEFAULT_STATE = WDState.NORMAL**
  Default value of property `state`. The values held in class `WDState` are `NORMAL` and `REQUIRED`. These correspond to optional and mandatory input fields respectively.

▶ **String DEFAULT_WIDTH = ""**
  Default value of the property `width`

▶ **int DEFAULT_COL_COUNT = 1**
  Default value of the property `ColCount`

▶ **String texts[]**
  This property functions as if it were an array of `String`. This property must be bound to a context attribute {ca} of type `String`. At runtime, each occurrence of {ca} within {cn} will cause a grouped `checkbox` to be created. Each `checkbox` will be labeled with the value found in {ca}.

Event and event parameters

▶ `onToggle`
This client-side event is raised when the user changes the state of any `checkbox` within the group.

▶ Parameters:

  ▷ `boolean checked`: True = checked, false = unchecked.

  ▷ `int index`: Zero-based index indicating which element of {cn} was toggled

Methods

Only the standard property and action management methods are implemented. The property `texts` does not have accessor or mutator methods.

12.6.17 IWDDropDownByIndex — Interface for an index-based drop-down list

Synopsis

This interface extends `IWDAbstractDropDownByIndex` and adds the property `size`.

Implements the standard property and action management methods.

Package

{pkg~sap~}.`clientserver.uielib.standard.api`

Properties

▶ `WDDropDownListBoxSize DEFAULT_SIZE =`
`WDDropDownListBoxSize.STANDARD`
The default value for the `size` property. The values held in class `WDDropDownListBoxSize` are `STANDARD` and `SMALL`.

Methods

Implements the standard property and action management methods

12.6.18 IWDDropDownByKey — Interface for a key-based drop-down list

Synopsis

This interface extends `IWDAbstractDropDownByKey` and adds the property `size`.

Implements the standard property and action management methods.

Package

{pkg_sap}.clientserver.uielib.standard.api

Properties

▶ **WDDropDownListBoxSize DEFAULT_SIZE = WDDropDownListBoxSize. STANDARD**

The default value for the size property. The values held in class WDDropDownListBoxSize are STANDARD and SMALL.

Methods

Implements the standard property and action management methods

12.6.19 IWDFlowData—Interface for flow layout data

Synopsis

This interface extends IWDLayoutData and provides the methods to manage the appearance of UI elements within a flow layout managed container.

Package

{pkg_sap}.clientserver.uielib.standard.api

Properties

▶ **String DEFAULT_DEFAULT_PADDING_BOTTOM = ""**

Default value of property defaultPaddingBottom

▶ **String DEFAULT_DEFAULT_PADDING_LEFT = ""**

Default value of property defaultPaddingLeft

▶ **String DEFAULT_DEFAULT_PADDING_RIGHT = ""**

Default value of property defaultPaddingRight

▶ **String DEFAULT_DEFAULT_PADDING_TOP = ""**

Default value of property defaultPaddingTop

Methods

Implements the standard property management methods. These properties may not be bound to context attributes.

12.6.20 IWDFlowLayout—Interface for the flow layout manager

Synopsis
This interface extends `IWDLayout` and implements a layout manager in which the child elements flow across the screen from left to right. If there is insufficient space across the screen, the elements are automatically divided into rows.

Implements the standard property management methods.

Package
`{pkg`_{sap}`}.clientserver.uielib.standard.api`

Properties
▶ `String DEFAULT_DEFAULT_PADDING_BOTTOM = ""`
  Default value of property `defaultPaddingBottom`

▶ `String DEFAULT_DEFAULT_PADDING_LEFT = ""`
  Default value of property `defaultPaddingLeft`

▶ `String DEFAULT_DEFAULT_PADDING_RIGHT = ""`
  Default value of property `defaultPaddingRight`

▶ `String DEFAULT_DEFAULT_PADDING_TOP = ""`
  Default value of property `defaultPaddingTop`

▶ `boolean DEFAULT_WRAPPING = true`
  Default value of property `wrapping`

Methods
Implements the standard property management methods. These properties may not be bound to context attributes.

12.6.21 IWDGridData—Interface for grid layout data

Synopsis
This interface extends `IWDLayoutData` and provides the methods to manage the appearance of UI elements within a grid layout managed container.

Package
`{pkg`_{sap}`}.clientserver.uielib.standard.api`

Properties

▶ **WDCellBackgroundDesign**
   DEFAULT_CELL_BACKGROUND_DESIGN
   = WDCellBackgroundDesign.TRANSPARENT
   Default value of property cellBackgroundDesign. The values held in class WDCellBackgroundDesign are TRANSPARENT, FILL1, FILL2, FILL3, PLAIN, HEADER, and BORDER.

▶ **int DEFAULT_COL_SPAN = 1**
   Default value of property colSpan

▶ **WDCellHAlign DEFAULT_H_ALIGN = WDCellHAlign.LEFT**
   Default value of property hAlign. The values held in class WDCell-HAlign are CENTER, CHAR, JUSTIFY, LEFT, RIGHT.

▶ **WDCellVAlign DEFAULT_V_ALIGN = WDCellVAlign.BASELINE**
   Default value of property vAlign. The values held in class WDCellVAlign are BASELINE, TOP, MIDDLE, and BOTTOM.

▶ **String DEFAULT_HEIGHT = ""**
   Default value of property height

▶ **String DEFAULT_WIDTH = ""**
   Default value of property width

▶ **String DEFAULT_PADDING_BOTTOM = ""**
   Default value of property paddingBottom

▶ **String DEFAULT_PADDING_LEFT = ""**
   Default value of property paddingLeft

▶ **String DEFAULT_PADDING_RIGHT = ""**
   Default value of property paddingRight

▶ **String DEFAULT_PADDING_TOP = ""**
   Default value of property paddingTop

Methods

Implements the standard property management methods.

The cellBackgroundDesign property is the only property in this interface that may be bound to a context attribute.

12.6.22 IWDGridLayout—Interface for the grid layout manager

Synopsis

This interface extends `IWDLayout` and implements a layout manager in which the child elements flow from left to right across a grid of some fixed number of columns. The number of columns is determined by the `colCount` property.

Implements the standard property management methods.

Package

`{pkg`_{sap}`}.clientserver.uielib.standard.api`

Properties

▶ `int DEFAULT_CELL_PADDING = 0`
Default value of property `cellPadding`

▶ `int DEFAULT_CELL_SPACING = 0`
Default value of property `cellSpacing`

▶ `int DEFAULT_COL_COUNT = 1`
Default value of property `colCount`

▶ `boolean DEFAULT_STRETCHED_HORIZONTALLY = true`
Default value of property `stretchedHorizontally`

▶ `boolean DEFAULT_STRETCHED_VERTICALLY = true`
Default value of property `stretchedVertically`

Methods

Implements the standard property management methods. These properties may not be bound to context attributes.

12.6.23 IWDIFrame—Base interface for an HTML IFrame

Synopsis

This interface extends `IWDUIElement` and manages additional properties such as its height, width, source, border, and scrolling mode.

Implements the standard property management methods.

Package

`{pkg`_{sap}`}.clientserver.uielib.standard.api`

Properties

▶ **String DEFAULT_HEIGHT = "300"**
Default value of the property height is set to 300.

▶ **String DEFAULT_WIDTH = "300"**
Default value of the property width is set to 300.

▶ **boolean DEFAULT_BORDER = false**
Boolean value to control whether the IFrame has a border around it.

▶ **String DEFAULT_SOURCE = ""**
The source from which this IFrame will obtain its content.

▶ **WDScrollingMode DEFAULT_SCROLLING_MODE = WDScrollingMode.Auto**
Default value of property ScrollingMode. The values held in class WDScrollingMode are strings that correspond to the Cascading Style Sheet (CSS) scroll mode values of AUTO, BOTH, and NONE.

Methods

Only the standard property management methods are implemented.

12.6.24 IWDImage—Interface for an image

Synopsis

This interface extends IWDUIElement and IWDTableCellEditor.

Implements the standard property management methods.

Package

(pkg$_{sap}$).clientserver.uielib.standard.api

Properties

▶ **String DEFAULT_ALT = ""**
Default value of property alt

▶ **int DEFAULT_BORDER = 0**
Default value of property border

▶ **String DEFAULT_WIDTH = ""**
Default value of property width

▶ **String DEFAULT_HEIGHT = ""**
Default value of property height

▶ **String DEFAULT_SOURCE = ""**
The source for this image

Methods

Only the standard property management methods are implemented.

12.6.25 IWDInputField—Interface for an input field

Synopsis

This interface extends `IWDAbstractInputField` adding the `size` property.

Implements the standard property management methods.

Package

{pkg_{sap}}.clientserver.uielib.standard.api

Properties

▶ `WDInputFieldSize DEFAULT_SIZE = WDInputFieldSize.STANDARD`
Default value of property `size`. This is a symbolic representation of the field size and currently accepts only the values of `STANDARD` and `SMALL`, the latter being half the size of the former.

Methods

Only the standard property management methods are implemented.

12.6.26 IWDLabel—Interface for a text label

Synopsis

This interface extends `IWDUIElement` and defines a simple read-only text label.

Implements the standard property management methods.

Package

{pkg_{sap}}.clientserver.uielib.standard.api

Properties

▶ `String DEFAULT_TEXT = ""`
Default value of property `text`

▶ `String DEFAULT_WIDTH = ""`
Default value of property `width`

- ▶ **String DEFAULT_LABEL_FOR = ""**
  Default value for the property labelFor. If set, the labelFor property associates this UI element with the named input field.

- ▶ **String DEFAULT_SOURCE = ""**
  The source from which this IFrame will obtain its content

- ▶ **WDLabelDesign DEFAULT_DESIGN = WDLabelDesign.STANDARD**
  Default value of property design. The values held in class WDLabelDesign are STANDARD and LIGHT; the only difference is that if you set the design to LIGHT, the vertical bar to the left of the label (known as the "notch") is removed.

- ▶ **boolean DEFAULT_WRAPPING = false**
  Default value of property wrapping

Methods
Only the standard property management methods are implemented.

12.6.27 IWDLayout—Base interface for all layout managers

Synopsis
This interface extends IWDViewElement and provides access to the UI element container.

All other view layout managers implement this interface.

Package
{pkg_{sap}}.progmodel.api

Methods
- ▶ **IWDUIElementContainer getUIElementContainer()**
  Returns the UI element container within which all the view UI elements live

12.6.28 IWDLayoutData—Base interface for all layout data

Synopsis
This interface extends IWDViewElement.

Most UI elements require some sort of layout data so that they can be correctly rendered by their layout manager. This interface provides a method to return the UI element to which this layout data belongs.

All other layout data classes implement this interface.

Package

{pkg_{sap}}.progmodel.api

Methods

▶ `IWDUIElement getUIElement()`
Returns the UI element to which this layout data belongs

12.6.29 IWDLink—Base interface for a generic hypertext link

Synopsis

This interface extends `IWDAbstractCaption` and adds a `text` property.

Implements the standard property management methods.

Package

{pkg_{sap}}.clientserver.uielib.standard.api

Properties

▶ `String DEFAULT_IMAGE_HEIGHT = ""`
Default value of property `imageHeight`

▶ `String DEFAULT_IMAGE_WIDTH = true`
Default value of property `imageWidth`

▶ `WDLinkSize DEFAULT_SIZE = WDLinkSize.STANDARD`
Default value of property `size`. This is a symbolic representation of the field size, and currently accepts only the values of `STANDARD` and `SMALL`.

▶ `String DEFAULT_TEXT = ""`
Default value of property `text`

▶ `boolean DEFAULT_WRAPPING = false`
Default value of property `wrapping`

Methods

Only the standard property management methods are implemented.

12.6.30 IWDLinkToAction—Interface for a hypertext link to a Web Dynpro action

Synopsis

This interface extends `IWDLink` and adds a `WDLinkType` property called `type`.

Implements the standard property and action management methods.

Package

`{pkg`_{sap}`}.clientserver.uielib.standard.api`

Properties

▶ `WDLinkType DEFAULT_TYPE = WDLinkType.FUNCTION`
Default value of property `type`. The values held within `WDLinkType` are `NAVIGATION`, `FUNCTION`, `REPORTING`, and `RESULT`.

Event and event parameters

▶ `onAction`
This client-side event is raised when the user clicks on this hypertext link.

This event has no parameters.

Methods

Only the standard property and action management methods are implemented.

12.6.31 IWDLinkToURL—Interface for a hypertext link to a URL

Synopsis

This interface extends `IWDLink` and adds a `WDLinkType` property called `type`, and the two string properties `reference` and `target`.

Implements the standard property management methods.

Package

`{pkg`_{sap}`}.clientserver.uielib.standard.api`

Properties

▶ **WDLinkType DEFAULT_TYPE = WDLinkType.NAVIGATION**
Default value of property type. The values held within WDLinkType are
NAVIGATION, FUNCTION, REPORTING, and RESULT.

▶ **String DEFAULT_TARGET = "_blank"**
Default value of property target. This corresponds to the target
parameter of the HTML anchor tag. The default value of _blank causes
the link target to appear in a new browser window.

▶ **String DEFAULT_REFERENCE = ""**
Default value of property reference. This corresponds to the href
parameter of the HTML anchor tag.

Methods

Only the standard property management methods are implemented.

12.6.32 IWDMatrixData—Interface for matrix layout data

Synopsis

This interface extends IWDLayout and provides the methods to adjust the
appearance of a UI element within a matrix layout managed container.

Implements the standard property management methods.

Package

(pkg_{sap}).clientserver.uielib.standard.api

Properties

▶ **WDCellBackgroundDesign DEFAULT_CELL_BACKGROUND_DESIGN =**
WDCellBackgroundDesign.TRANSPARENT
Default value of property cellBackgroundDesign. The values held in
class WDCellBackgroundDesign are TRANSPARENT, FILL1, FILL2, FILL3,
PLAIN, HEADER, and BORDER.

▶ **WDLayoutCellDesign DEFAULT_CELL_DESIGN =**
WDLayoutCellDesign.R_PAD
Default value of property cellDesign. The values held in class WDLay-
outCellDesign are R_PAD, L_PAD, LR_PAD, LR_NO_PAD, and PADLESS.

▶ **int DEFAULT_COL_SPAN = 1**
Default value of property colSpan

▶ **WDCellHAlign DEFAULT_H_ALIGN = WDCellHAlign.LEFT**
Default value of property `hAlign`. The values held in class `WDCell-HAlign` are `CENTER, CHAR, JUSTIFY, LEFT, RIGHT`.

▶ **String DEFAULT_HEIGHT = ""**
Default value of property `height`

▶ **WDCellVAlign DEFAULT_V_ALIGN = WDCellVAlign.BASELINE**
Default value of property `vAlign`. The values held in class `WDCellVAlign` are `BASELINE, TOP, MIDDLE,` and `BOTTOM`.

▶ **WDCellVAlign DEFAULT_V_GUTTER = WDLayoutCellSeparator.NONE**
Default value of property `vGutter`. The values held in class `WDLayout-CellSeparator` are `NONE, MEDIUM, MEDIUMWITHRULE, LARGE,` and `LARGE-WITHRULE`.

▶ **String DEFAULT_WIDTH = ""**
Default value of property `width`

Methods
Only the standard property management methods are implemented.

12.6.33 IWDMatrixHeadData—Interface for matrix layout head data

Synopsis
This interface extends `IWDMatrixData`. In future, this interface will provide the methods to adjust the appearance of a UI element at the start of a row within a matrix layout managed container.

At the moment, this interface serves only to identify that a particular UI element starts a new row in a matrix layout managed container.

Package
{pkg$_{sap}$}`.clientserver.uielib.standard.api`

Properties
None

Methods
None

12.6.34 IWDMatrixLayout—Interface for the matrix layout manager

Synopsis

This interface extends `IWDLayout` and implements a layout manager in which the child elements flow from left to right across a grid of an unknown number of columns.

Implements the standard property management methods.

Package

`{pkg_sap}.clientserver.uielib.standard.api`

Properties

▶ `boolean DEFAULT_STRETCHED_HORIZONTALLY = true`
Default value of the property `stretchedHorizontally`. Determines whether the elements managed by this container are stretched to their container's size.

▶ `boolean DEFAULT_STRETCHED_VERTICALLY = true`
Default value of the property `stretchedVertically`. Determines whether the elements managed by this container are stretched to their container's size.

Methods

Only the standard property management methods are implemented.

12.6.35 IWDRadioButton—Interface for a radio button

Synopsis

This interface extends `IWDUIElement` and represents a standard two-state radio button UI element.

Each radio button has a property called `keyToSelect` that holds the value that will be placed into the view context if this radio button is selected. The property `selectedKey` must be bound to a context attribute {ca} of type `string`.

If, when the view is first displayed, {ca} contains the value found in `key-ToSelect`, then the radio button will automatically be selected. Conversely, if the user selects this particular radio button, then the value found in `KeyToSelect` is transferred to the `selectedKey` property, and thus the view context is updated.

All radio buttons in the same group must have their `selectedKey` properties bound to the same context attribute; otherwise, they won't function as a group.

The property `texts` must be bound to the context path of the string attribute {ca}.

Implements the standard property and action management methods.

Package
{pkg~sap~}.`clientserver.uielib.standard.api`

Properties
▶ **WDState DEFAULT_STATE = WDState.NORMAL**
Default value of property `state`. The values held in class `WDState` are `NORMAL` and `REQUIRED`. These correspond to optional and mandatory input fields respectively.

▶ **String DEFAULT_KEY_TO_SELECT = ""**
Default value of property `keyToSelect`. This property holds the value of this radio button.

▶ **int DEFAULT_TEXT = ""**
Default value of property `text`.`String SelectedKey`

The property into which the value of `keyToSelect` is transferred if this radio button is selected. This property must be bound to a context attribute of type `string`.

Event and event parameters
▶ **onSelect**
This client-side event is raised when the user selects this radio button.

▶ **Parameter: String key**
The `keyToSelect` value of the selected radio button

Methods
Only the standard property and action management methods are implemented.

12.6.36 IWDTab—Interface for an individual tab page

Synopsis
This interface extends `IWDViewElement` and represents a single tab page within a tab strip. A tab consists of a header area, a content area, and an optional toolbar.

Implements the standard property and action management methods.

Package
(pkg$_{sap}$).`clientserver.uielib.standard.api`

Properties
▶ boolean `DEFAULT_ENABLED` = `true`
  Default value of property `enabled`

▶ boolean `DEFAULT_HAS_CONTENT_PADDING` = `true`
  Default value of property `hasContentPadding`

▶ boolean `DEFAULT_VISIBLE` = `true`
  Default value of property `visible`

Methods
▶ `IWDUIELement getContent()`
  Returns the content of this tab page as an `IWDUIElement` object

▶ `void setContent()`
  Sets the `IWDUIElement` object to be the content of this tab page

▶ `void destroyContent()`
  Destroys the content of this tab page. All UI element object IDs become available for reuse.

▶ `IWDCaption getHeader()`
  Returns the caption object in the header of this tab page

▶ `void setHeader()`
  Sets the caption object in the header of this tab page

▶ `void destroyHeader()`
  Destroys the caption object in the header of this tab page. The ID of the `IWDCaption` object becomes available for reuse.

▶ `IWDToolBar getToolBar()`
  Returns the toolbar object in the header of this tab page

▶ void setToolBar()
Sets the toolbar object in the header of this tab page

▶ void destroyToolBar()
Destroys the toolbar object in the header of this tab page. The ID of the IWDToolBar object becomes available for reuse.

▶ IWDTabStrip getTabStrip()
Returns a reference to the tab strip object to which this tab page belongs

12.6.37 IWDTabStrip—Interface for an aggregation of tab pages

Synopsis
This interface extends IWDUIElement and represents an aggregation of IWDTab objects. Only one tab is visible at any one time, and each may be selected by clicking on its caption.

Important: When a tab strip is instantiated, all the views contained within the child IWDTab containers are instantiated – even though only one view will be visible at any one time.

Implements the standard property and action management methods.

Package
{pkg$_{sap}$}.clientserver.uielib.standard.api

Properties
▶ String DEFAULT_ACCESSIBILITY_DESCRIPTION = ""
Default value of property accessibilityDescription

▶ String DEFAULT_HEIGHT = ""
Default value of property height

▶ String DEFAULT_SELECTED_TAB = ""
Default value of property selectedTab

▶ String DEFAULT_WIDTH = ""
Default value of property width

Event and event parameters
▶ onSelect
This client-side event is raised when the user clicks on a tab caption

▶ Parameter: `String tab`
The name of the tab page object on which the user clicked

Methods

▶ `void addTab(IWDTab aTab)`
Appends tab page `aTab` to the end of the tab aggregation

▶ `void addTab(IWDTab aTab, int index)`
Inserts tab page `aTab` at position `index` within the tab aggregation

▶ `IWDTab[] getTabs()`
Returns the tab page aggregation as an array of `IWDTab` objects

▶ `int numberOfTabs()`
Returns the current size of the tab aggregation

▶ `boolean hasTabs()`
Check whether the tab aggregation contains any members

▶ `Iterator iterateTabs()`
Returns an iterator over the current tab aggregation

▶ `IWDTab removeTab(int index)`
Non-destructive removal of the tab object at position `index` from the tab aggregation

▶ `IWDTab removeTab(String id)`
Non-destructive removal of tab object `id` from the tab aggregation

▶ `void removeAllTabs()`
Non-destructive removal of all entries from the tab aggregation. The tabs removed by this method are still children of the current `IWDView` object and can be accessed by calling `IWDView.getElement(String)`.

▶ `void destroyAllTabs()`
All instances of child `IWDTab` objects are destroyed and their IDs become available for reuse

12.6.38 IWDTable—Interface for a table

Synopsis
This interface extends `IWDUIElement` and represents a two-dimensional data set arranged in rows and columns.

An `IWDTable` object is a composite UI element made up of an aggregation of `IWDTableColumn` objects. In turn, each table column object is a composite UI element made up of a table cell editor, a caption, a tool tip, and an image.

An `IWDTable` object must obtain its data from a context node {cn} that has a cardinality of <something>..n. The node {cn} that supplies data to the `IWDTable` object will be used in the following manner:

▶ Each attribute within {cn} is a candidate for becoming a distinct table column.

▶ Each element within {cn}'s node collection becomes a row.

▶ The lead selection of {cn} indicates which table row is currently selected. If no table row is currently selected, this corresponds to a lead selection of -1. When a user clicks on a table row, the lead selection of {cn} is set to that row. If the mouse click occurred over an editable table cell, then the cursor is placed into that cell.

▶ However, if you set the lead selection programmatically, the corresponding table row will be displayed in a selected state, but no edit cursor will appear in that row. This is an extra programming step requiring the use of method `requestFocus()` on the appropriate table cell editor object.

▶ The number of rows that can be selected in the table is given by the selection cardinality of {cn}.

▶ Each table column must be bound to at least one attribute of node {cn}.

Important: The columns of a table should only ever be bound to the attributes of a single context node. Do *not* try to display attributes from different context nodes in the same table UI element.

Implements the standard property and action management methods.

Package
{pkg_{sap}}.clientserver.uielib.standard.api

Properties
▶ **WDTableDesign DEFAULT_DESIGN = WDTableDesign.STANDARD**
Default value of property `design`. The values held in class `WDTable-Design` are ALTERNATING, STANDARD, and TRANSPARENT.

▶ **int DEFAULT_FIRST_VISIBLE_ROW = 0**
Default value of property `firstVisibleRow`. The values held in class `WDState` are NORMAL and REQUIRED. These correspond to optional and mandatory input fields respectively.

▶ boolean DEFAULT_FOOTER_VISIBLE = true
Default value of property footerVisible

▶ boolean DEFAULT_READ_ONLY = false
Default value of property readOnly

▶ WDTableSelectionMode DEFAULT_SELECTION_MODE = WDTableSelectionMode.AUTO
Default value of property selectionMode. The values held in class WDTableSelectionMode are AUTO, SINGLE, MULTI, and NONE.

This property does not implement either of the standard bind{uip}() methods or the bindingOf{uip}().

▶ int DEFAULT_VISIBLE_ROW_COUNT = 5
Default value of property visibleRowCount

▶ String dataSource
The context node from which the table data is derived.

This property has no accessor or mutator methods and must be bound to a context node of cardinality of ⟨something⟩..n.

▶ String width
The width of the table

Event and event parameters

▶ onFilter
This client-side event is raised when the user presses the filter button.

This event has no parameters.

▶ onLeadSelect
This client-side event is raised when the user changes the lead selection of the table.

▶ Parameters:

   ▶ String col
The column name in which the user clicked

   ▶ int row
Index of the row in which the user clicked

Methods

▶ void addColumn(IWDTableColumn aTableColumn)
Adds the specified table column at the end of the column list

▶ **void addColumn(IWDTableColumn aTableColumn, int index)**
Adds the specified table column at the specified index of the column list

▶ **IWDTableColumn[] getColumns()**
Returns the current column list as an array of table columns

▶ **int numberOfColumns()**
Returns the number of columns in the table's column list

▶ **boolean hasColumns()**
Returns true if the table's column list is not empty

▶ **Iterator iterateColumns()**
Returns an iterator over the list of columns

▶ **IWDTableColumn removeColumn(int index)**
Non-destructive removal of the column at position index of the column list

▶ **IWDTableColumn removeColumn(String id)**
Non-destructive removal of the column with the name id from the column list. The column removed by this method is still a child of the current IWDView object and can be accessed by calling IWDView.getElement(String).

▶ **void removeAllColumns()**
Non-destructive removal of all entries from the column list. The columns removed by this method are still children of the current IWDView object and can be accessed by calling IWDView.getElement(String).

▶ **void destroyAllColumns()**
All instances of child IWDTableColumn objects are destroyed and their IDs become available for reuse.

▶ **IWDCaption getHeader()**
Gets the instance of the IWDCaption object used as the table header

▶ **void setHeader(IWDCaption header)**
Sets the instance of the IWDCaption object to be used in the table header

▶ **void destroyHeader()**
Destroys the instance of the IWDCaption object used as the table header. Once this method has completed, the name used to identify the header caption is available for reuse.

▶ **IWDToolBar getToolBar()**
Gets the instance of the IWDToolBar object associated with this table

▶ **void setToolBar(IWDToolBar toolBar)**
Sets the instance of the IWDToolBar object to be associated with this table

▶ **void destroyToolBar()**
Destroys the instance of the IWDToolBar object associated with this table. Once this method has completed, the name used to identify the toolbar is available for reuse.

12.6.39 IWDTableColumn—Interface for a table column

Synopsis
This interface extends IWDViewElement and represents a single table column. A table column is composed of a column header (implemented by an IWDCaption), a table cell editor (implemented by an IWDTableCell-Editor), a tool tip, and an image.

Without the specification of a table cell editor, it is not possible even to display the contents of the cells in that column.

The behavior of a table cell editor may be controlled by binding its properties to appropriate context attributes in the following way:

▶ If you wish every table cell editor in every row of the table to behave in the same way, then bind the table cell editor properties to context attributes that are independent of the context node {cn} from which the table data is being obtained.

▶ If you wish to customize the properties of each table cell editor in each row, then the table cell editor properties must be bound to attributes from the same context node {cn} as the table column.

▶ A table column may have only one UI element as its table cell editor.

Implements the standard property and action management methods.

Package
{pkg$_{sap}$}.clientserver.uielib.standard.api

Properties
▶ **WDCellBackgroundDesign DEFAULT_DESIGN =**
WDCellBackgroundDesign.TRANSPARENT
Default value of property design. The values held in class WDCellBack-

groundDesign are TRANSPARENT, FILL1, FILL2, FILL3, PLAIN, HEADER, and BORDER.

▶ **String DEFAULT_FILTER_VALUE = ""**
Default value of property filterValue

▶ **WDTableColumnHAlign DEFAULT_H_ALIGN = WDTableColumnHAlign.AUTO**
Default value of property hAlign. The values held in WDTableColumn-HAlign are AUTO, CENTER, LEFT, and RIGHT.

▶ **boolean DEFAULT_RESIZABLE = true**
Default value of property resizable

▶ **String DEFAULT_WIDTH = ""**
Default value of property width

▶ **WDVisibility DEFAULT_VISIBLE = WDVisibility.VISIBLE**
Default value of property visible. The values held in class WDVisibility are BLANK, NONE, and VISIBLE.

Event and event parameters

▶ **onAction**
This client-side event is raised when the user clicks on the header of the table column.

▶ **Parameter: String col**
The name of the column that has focus

Methods

▶ **IWDCaption getHeader()**
Gets the instance of the IWDCaption object used as the table header

▶ **void setHeader(IWDCaption header)**
Sets the instance of the IWDCaption object to be used in the table header

▶ **void destroyHeader()**
Destroys the instance of the IWDCaption object used as the table header. Once this method has completed, the name used to identify the header caption is available for reuse.

▶ **IWDTableCellEditor getTableCellEditor()**
Gets the instance of the IWDTableCellEditor object used by the table column

- ▶ **void setTableCellEditor(IWDTableCellEditor tableCellEditor)**
  Sets the instance of the `IWDTableCellEditor` object to be used by the table column

- ▶ **void destroyTableCellEditor()**
  Destroys the instance of the `IWDTableCellEditor` object used by this table column. Once this method has completed, the name used to identify the table cell editor is available for reuse.

12.6.40 IWDTextEdit—Interface for a multi-line text editor

Synopsis
This interface extends `IWDUIElement` and represents a multi-line text editor.

The size of the displayed text area is controlled by the properties `cols` and `rows`. These properties default to 40 and 5 respectively.

Implements the standard property management methods.

Package
$\{pkg_{sap}\}$`.clientserver.uielib.standard.api`

Properties
- ▶ **WDState DEFAULT_STATE = WDState.NORMAL**
  Default value of property `state`. The values held in class `WDState` are `NORMAL` and `REQUIRED`. These correspond to optional and mandatory input fields respectively.

- ▶ **WDtextWrapping DEFAULT_WRAPPING = WDTextWrapping.SOFT**
  Default value of property `wrapping`. The values held in class `WDText-Wrapping` are `OFF`, `HARD`, and `SOFT`.

- ▶ **int DEFAULT_COLS = 40**
  Default value of property `cols`

- ▶ **int DEFAULT_ROWS = 5**
  Default value of property `rows`

- ▶ **boolean DEFAULT_READ_ONLY = false**
  Default value of property `readOnly`

- ▶ **String DEFAULT_HEIGHT = ""**
  Default value of property `height`

▶ `String DEFAULT_WIDTH = ""`
Default value of property `width`

Methods
Only the standard property management methods are implemented.

12.6.41 IWDTextView—Interface for a read-only text display

Synopsis
This interface extends `IWDUIElement` and represents a read-only text display area.

The layout of the text display area can be set to correspond to an HTML `<div>`, `<span>`, or `<p>`.

Implements the standard property management methods.

Package
`{pkg`_{`sap`}`}.clientserver.uielib.standard.api`

Properties
▶ `WDTextViewDesign DEFAULT_DESIGN = WDTextViewDesign.STANDARD`
Default value of property `design`. The values held in class `WDTextViewDesign` are `EMPHASIZED`, `HEADER1`, `HEADER2`, `HEADER3`, `HEADER4`, `LABEL`, `LABEL_SMALL`, `LEGEND`, `REFERENCE`, `STANDARD`, and `MONOSPACE`.

▶ `boolean DEFAULT_WRAPPING = false`
Default value of property `wrapping`

▶ `WDTextViewLayout DEFAULT_LAYOUT = WDTextViewLayout.NATIVE`
Default value of the property `layout`. The values held in class `WDTextViewLayout` are `BLOCK`, `NATIVE`, and `PARAGRAPH`, and correspond to the HTML tags `<div>`, `<span>`, and `<p>` respectively.

▶ `String DEFAULT_TEXT = ""`
Default value of property `text`

Methods
Only the standard property management methods are implemented.

12.6.42 IWDTree—Interface for the root node of a tree

Synopsis

This interface extends `IWDUIElement` and displays data that has previously been arranged in a hierarchical manner.

Implements the standard property management methods.

Package

`{pkg}.clientserver.uielib.standard.api`

Properties

▶ `String DEFAULT_DEFAULT_ITEM_ICON_ALT = ""`
Default value of property `defaultItemIconAlt`. It holds the `Alt` text for the default icon that appears next to each tree item.

▶ `String DEFAULT_DEFAULT_ITEM_ICON_SOURCE = ""`
Default value of property `defaultItemIconSource`. It holds the file name of the default icon that appears next to a tree item.

▶ `String DEFAULT_DEFAULT_NODE_ICON_ALT = ""`
Default value of property `defaultNodeIconAlt`. It holds the `Alt` text for the default icon that appears next to each tree node.

▶ `String DEFAULT_DEFAULT_NODE_ICON_SOURCE = ""`
Default value of property `defaultNodeIconSource`. It holds the file name of the default icon that appears next to a tree node.

▶ `String DEFAULT_MIN_HEIGHT = ""`
Default value of property `minHeight`

▶ `String DEFAULT_ROOT_TEXT = ""`
Default value of property `rootText`. It holds the label text for the root node of the tree.

▶ `boolean DEFAULT_ROOT_VISIBLE = true`
Default value of property `rootVisible`. It controls whether the root node is visible or not.

▶ `String DEFAULT_TITLE = ""`
Default value of property `title`

▶ `WDVisibility DEFAULT_TITLE_VISIBLE = WDVisibility.VISIBLE`
Default value of property `titleVisible`. The values held in class `WDVisibility` are `BLANK`, `NONE` and `VISIBLE`.

▶ `String DEFAULT_WIDTH = ""`
Default value of property `width`

▶ `String dataSource`
The `dataSource` property holds the name of the context node from which the tree will obtain its data.

This property does not have any accessor or mutator methods and must be bound to a context node of cardinality `<something>..n`.

Methods

▶ `void addNodeType(IWDAbstractTreeNodeType aAbstractTreeNodeType)`
Adds the given `TreeNodeType` to the end of the node list

▶ `void addNodeType(IWDAbstractTreeNodeType aAbstractTreeNodeType, int index);`
Adds the given `TreeNodeType` to the node list at position `index`

▶ `IWDAbstractTreeNodeType[] getNodeTypes()`
Returns the node list as an array of tree node types. The only difference between a tree node and a tree item is that the node is permitted to have children, whereas the item is not. For ease of programming, all entities in a tree can be considered `IWDTreeNodeTypes` where the items will appear as nodes with zero children.

▶ `int numberOfNodeTypes()`
Returns the number of nodes in the tree

▶ `boolean hasNodeTypes()`
Returns true if the node list is not empty

▶ `Iterator iterateNodeTypes()`
Returns an iterator over the node list. All elements of the iterator can be cast as `IWDTreeNodeType` objects, irrespective of whether they are nodes or items. Items can be considered nodes with zero children.

▶ `IWDAbstractTreeNodeType removeNodeType(int index)`
Non-destructive removal of the node list entry at the given index

▶ `IWDAbstractTreeNodeType removeNodeType(String id)`
Non-destructive removal of the node list entry with the given name

▶ `void removeAllNodeTypes()`
Non-destructive removal of all entries in the node list. Once the entries have been removed from the tree's node list, they can still be accessed by name by calling `IWDView.getElement(String)`.

▶ `void destroyAllNodeTypes()`
All child node type instances are destroyed and the element IDs become available for reuse.

12.6.43 IWDTreeItemType—Interface for a tree item

Synopsis
This interface extends `IWDAbstractTreeNodeType`, but adds no further functionality. It will allow future versions of Web Dynpro the ability to expand the functionality of a tree item. Since this class currently adds no new functionality, all tree items should be implemented as tree nodes with zero children.

Package
{pkg_{sap}}`.clientserver.uielib.standard.api`

Properties
None

Methods
None

12.6.44 IWDTreeNodeType—Interface for a tree node

Synopsis
This interface extends `IWDAbstractTreeNodeType`, adding the two further properties of `expanded` and `hasChildren`. It represents a tree node that can have both nodes and items as children.

Implements the standard property and action management methods.

Package
{pkg_{sap}}`.clientserver.uielib.standard.api`

Properties
▶ `boolean DEFAULT_EXPANDED = false`
Default value of property `expanded`

▶ `boolean DEFAULT_HAS_CHILDREN = true`
Default value of property `hasChildren`. Since this is a tree node, it is assumed to have children.

Event and event parameters

▶ `onLoadChildren`

This client-side event is raised only when the user expands a tree node *for the first time*.

This event differs from the `IWDAbstractTreeNodeType` event `onAction` in that it is only fired if the context node it represents contains zero elements. This will typically be the situation when the node is expanded for the first time.

The purpose of this event is to give the opportunity to calculate tree node children on demand.

▶ Parameter: `String path`

The path to the context element corresponding to the node that raised this event

Methods

▶ `IWDTree getTree()`

Returns the tree object to which this node belongs

12.6.45 IWDUIElement—Base interface for UI elements

Synopsis

This interface extends `IWDViewElement` and manages the additional properties that define whether the UI element is enabled. It also manages the tool tip and visibility properties and provides access to the layout data.

All UI elements implement this interface.

Implements the standard property management methods.

Package

`{pkg`~sap~`}.progmodel.api`

Properties

▶ `boolean DEFAULT_ENABLED`

Default value of property `enabled` is true. It determines whether the UI element is enabled on the client. Only an enabled UI element can respond to user input and generate events.

▶ `String DEFAULT_TOOLTIP = ""`

Default value of property `tooltip`

► **WDVisibility DEFAULT_VISIBLE = WDVisibility.VISIBLE**
Default value of property `visible`. The values held in class `WDVisibi-lity` are strings that correspond to the CSS visibility values of `BLANK`, `NONE`, and `VISIBLE`.

Methods

► **IWDLayoutData getLayoutData()**
Returns the layout data for this UI element, typically for use by the UI element's parent layout manager.

► **IWDUIElementContainer getContainer()**
Returns the UI container within which the current UI element is defined. All UI elements with which a user can interact must have some container element as their parent.

► **IWDLayoutData createLayoutData(Class layoutDataInterface)**
Both creates a layout data object of the type specified by `layout-DataInterface`, and assigns it to the UI element

12.6.46 IWDUIElementContainer—Base interface for a container UI element

Synopsis

All Web Dynpro view layouts are constructed as UI trees. This interface represents a generic container that may contain any number of UI elements as children.

This interface extends `IWDUIElement` and manages additional properties such as `height` and `width`, and provides an API to manage its children.

All UI element containers must have a layout manager. When creating UI containers through the NWDS, the layout manager will default to "Flow Layout."

Implements the standard property management methods.

Package

{pkg~sap~}.progmodel.api

Properties

► **String DEFAULT_HEIGHT = ""**
Default value of property `height`

▶ `String DEFAULT_WIDTH = ""`
Default value of property `width`

Methods

▶ `void addChild(IWDUIElement aUIElement)`
Appends the given child to the end of the container's element list

▶ `void addChild(IWDUIElement aUIElement, int index)`
Adds the given child at the specified index within the container's element list

▶ `IWDUIElement[] getChildren()`
Returns the container's element list

▶ `int numberOfChildren()`
Returns the number of children in the container's element list

▶ `boolean hasChildren()`
Returns `true` if the element list has one or more children

▶ `Iterator iterateChildren()`
Returns an iterator over the element list

▶ `IWDUIElement removeChild(int index)`
The non-destructive removal of the element at position `index` in the container's element list

▶ `IWDUIElement removeChild(String id)`
The non-destructive removal of the element of name `id` from the container's element list

▶ `void removeAllChildren()`
The non-destructive removal of all elements from the container's element list. Once the elements have been removed from the container's element list, they can still be accessed by name by calling `IWD-View.getElement(String)`.

▶ `void destroyAllChildren()`
All child element instances are destroyed and the element IDs become available for reuse.

▶ `IWDLayout getLayout()`
Gets the layout instance for this container

▶ `IWDLayout createLayout(Class layoutInterface)`
Creates and sets a layout of the given type. For example, `IWDGrid-Layout.class`.

Since a layout is specific to a given UI element container, calling `createLayout()` both creates the layout object *and* assigns it to the container. The `IWDLayout` object returned by this method must be cast so that it is of the same type as parameter `layoutDataInterface`. Once the `IWDLayout` object has been created and assigned, the appearance of the container can be manipulated by calling its specific methods.

12.6.47 IWDViewElement — Base interface of all UI elements

Synopsis

This interface represents the lowest level of commonality that exists across all UI elements in a view. The resulting elements based on this interface do not necessarily correspond to visible elements on the client (for example, `IWDFlowData`). This interface knows only that the element has a name, belongs to a view, and can request to have focus.

All view UI elements implement this interface.

Package

`{pkg_{sap}}.progmodel.api`

Properties

None

Methods

▶ `String getId()`
Returns the name of this UI element

▶ `String getView()`
Returns a reference to the `IWDView` parent object

▶ `String requestFocus()`
Requests that, if applicable, the client's input focus be placed on this view element. If multiple UI elements all request focus within the same request/response cycle, it is unspecified which request will win. See `IWDViewController.requestFocus()` for more details.

If multiple occurrences of this view element live in a table row, the first occurrence in the current row will receive focus.

A   ABAP coding

The following ABAP function modules are used in the coding example in the chapter on the adaptive RFC layer.

```
FUNCTION WDY_GET_LIST_ADDRESS.
*"----------------------------------------------------------------
*"*"Local Interface:
*"  TABLES
*"      ADDRESS_LIST STRUCTURE  WDY_DEMO_ADDRESS
*"----------------------------------------------------------------
data:
  wa       type WDY_DEMO_ADDRESS,
  all_ids type standard table of WDY_DEMO_ADDRESS-id,
  id       type WDY_DEMO_ADDRESS-id.
field-symbols <fsaddr>.

  clear address_list.

  select addr_key from WDY_DEMO_CUSTOM
    into id
   where name = 'ID'.
    append id to all_ids.
  endselect.

  loop at all_ids into id.
    CALL FUNCTION 'WDY_GET_SINGLE_ADDRESS'
        EXPORTING ID      = id
        IMPORTING ADDRESS = wa.
    append wa to address_list.
  endloop.

  sort address_list ascending by last_name first_name id.
ENDFUNCTION.
```

Listing A.1 ABAP function module WDY_GET_LIST_ADDRESS returns a list of addresses

```
FUNCTION WDY_GET_SINGLE_ADDRESS.
*"----------------------------------------------------------------
*"*"Local Interface:
*"  IMPORTING
*"      VALUE(ID) TYPE  WDY_DEMO_ID
*"  EXPORTING
*"      VALUE(ADDRESS) TYPE  WDY_DEMO_ADDRESS
*"----------------------------------------------------------------
```

```
data WA type WDY_DEMO_CUSTOM.

  CALL FUNCTION 'WDY_DEMO_FILL_REC_FROM_CUST'
      EXPORTING ID      = id
        CHANGING ADDRESS = address.
ENDFUNCTION.
```

Listing A.2 ABAP function module WDY_GET_SINGLE_ADDRESS returns a single address identified by an Address Id

```
FUNCTION WDY_DEMO_FILL_REC_FROM_CUST.
*"----------------------------------------------------------------
*"*"Local Interface:
*"  IMPORTING
*"     REFERENCE(ID) TYPE  WDY_DEMO_ADDRESS-ID
*"  CHANGING
*"     REFERENCE(ADDRESS) TYPE  WDY_DEMO_ADDRESS
*"----------------------------------------------------------------
data wa type WDY_DEMO_CUSTOM.
field-symbols <fs>.

  select * from WDY_DEMO_CUSTOM
    into wa
   where ADDR_KEY = id.
    assign component wa-name of structure address to <fs>.

    if sy-subrc eq 0.
      <fs> = wa-value.
    endif.
  endselect.
ENDFUNCTION.
```

Listing A.3 ABAP function module WDY_DEMO_FILL_REC_FROM_CUST populates the address parameter with the relevant details

```
FUNCTION WDY_DELETE_ADDRESS.
*"----------------------------------------------------------------
*"*"Local Interface:
*"  IMPORTING
*"     VALUE(ID) TYPE  WDY_DEMO_ADDRESS-ID
*"----------------------------------------------------------------
  delete from WDY_DEMO_CUSTOM where addr_key = id.
ENDFUNCTION.
```

Listing A.4 ABAP function module WDY_DELETE_ADDRESS deletes an address identified by an Address Id

```
FUNCTION WDY_NEW_ADDRESS.
*"----------------------------------------------------------------
*"*"Local Interface:
*"  IMPORTING
*"     VALUE(ADDRESS) TYPE  WDY_DEMO_ADDRESS
*"----------------------------------------------------------------
data:
  highestID type I value 0,
  currentID type I,
  wa        type WDY_DEMO_ADDRESS,
  id        type WDY_DEMO_CUSTOM-VALUE.

  currentID = address-id.

  if currentID eq 0.
    select addr_key from WDY_DEMO_CUSTOM
      into id
     where name = 'ID'.
      currentID = id.

      if currentID gt highestID.
        highestID = currentID.
      endif.
    endselect.

    currentID = highestID + 1.
  endif.

  address-id = currentID.

  CALL FUNCTION 'WDY_DEMO_FILL_CUST_FROM_REC'
      EXPORTING ADDRESS = address.
ENDFUNCTION.
```

Listing A.5 ABAP function module WDY_NEW_ADDRESS creates a new address

```
FUNCTION WDY_DEMO_FILL_CUST_FROM_REC.
*"----------------------------------------------------------------
*"*"Local Interface:
*"  IMPORTING
*"     REFERENCE(ADDRESS) TYPE  WDY_DEMO_ADDRESS
*"----------------------------------------------------------------
data
  wa        type WDY_DEMO_CUSTOM,
  values    type standard table of WDY_DEMO_CUSTOM,
  dfies_tab type standard table of DFIES,
```

```
    dfies_wa  type dfies,
    length    type I.
field-symbols <fs>.

    CALL FUNCTION 'DDIF_FIELDINFO_GET'
        EXPORTING TABNAME   = 'WDY_DEMO_ADDRESS'
           TABLES DFIES_TAB = dfies_tab.

    loop at dfies_tab into dfies_wa.
      assign component dfies_wa-fieldname
          of structure address to <fs>.

      if not <fs> is initial.
        wa-value = <fs>.
        wa-name = dfies_wa-fieldname.
        wa-addr_key = address-id.
        append wa to values.
      endif.
    endloop.

    describe table values lines length.

    if length > 0.
      CALL FUNCTION 'WDY_DELETE_ADDRESS'
          EXPORTING ID = address-id.
      insert WDY_DEMO_CUSTOM from table values.
    endif.
ENDFUNCTION.
```

Listing A.6 ABAP function module WDY_DEMO_FILL_CUST_FROM_REC interrogates the data dictionary and populates the address parameter according to its current definition

B Dictionary structures

The following ABAP dictionary structures are used by the function modules listed above.

Component	Component Type	Data Type	Length	Decimal Places	Short Text
ID	WDY_DEMO_ID	NUMC	10	0	Address ID
LAST_NAME	WDY_DEMO_NAME	CHAR	50	0	Last name
FIRST_NAME	WDY_DEMO_FIRST-NAME	CHAR	50	0	First name
TITLE	WDY_DEMO_TITLE	CHAR	5	0	Title
STREET	WDY_DEMO_STREET	CHAR	30	0	Street
CITY	WDY_DEMO_CITY	CHAR	50	0	City
POSTCODE	WDY_DEMO_ZIP	CHAR	10	0	Zip code
COUNTRY	WDY_DEMO_COUNTRY	CHAR	3	0	Country
PHONE	WDY_DEMO_PHONE	CHAR	20	0	Phone number
STATE	WDY_DEMO_STATE	CHAR	30	0	State
.APPEND	WDY_DEMO_APPEND		0	0	Append for customization

Table B.1 Dictionary Structure WDY_DEMO_ADDRESS

Component	Component Type	Data Type	Length	Decimal Places	Short Text
WDY_DEMO_DUMMY	CHAR1	CHAR	1	0	Single-character flag
BIRTHDAY	WDY_DEMO_BIRTHDAY	DATS	8	0	Date of birth
JOBPOSITION	WDY_DEMO_POSITION	CHAR	15	0	Position
SALARY	WDY_DEMO_SALARY	CURR	10	2	Salary
SAL_CUR	WDY_DEMO_CURR	CUKY	5	0	Currency of salary

Table B.2 Dictionary Structure WDY_DEMO_APPEND after New Fields Have Been Added

Component	Component Type	Data Type	Length	Decimal Places	Short Text
RANKING	WDY_DEMO_RANKING	CHAR	10	0	Ranking
INFO	WDY_DEMO_ADDINFO	CHAR	256	0	Additional information

Table B.2 Dictionary Structure WDY_DEMO_APPEND after New Fields Have Been Added (cont.)

Field	Key	Initial Value	Data Element	Data Type	Length	Decimal Places	Short Text
ADDR_KEY	✓	✓	WDY_DEMO_ID	NUMC	10	0	Address ID
NAME	✓	✓	CHAR30	CHAR	30	0	Short text
VALUE				STRING	0	0	

Table B.3 Transparent Table WDY_DEMO_CUSTOM

C   The Author

Chris Whealy first started working on SAP R/2 systems in 1993 making assembler and ABAP modifications to the RV and RF modules. With the launch of SAP R/3 version 2.0, he started working in the Basis area performing installations, upgrades and system administration. This work went hand in hand with his on going ABAP work.

Joining SAP UK in May 1995, Chris has always had an interest in custom interfaces into and out of the R/3 system, so in 1996 when the internet boom started to take hold, he began to focus on browser based interfaces to R/3 using SAP's Internet Transaction Server. Chris has worked with SAP's web based technology as it has grown and matured, and in late 2002 turned his attention to Web Dynpro. Chris spent a significant proportion of 2003 working closely with the Web Dynpro development team in Walldorf both learning the new technology and documenting its inner workings.

In October 2003, Chris was able to put his knowledge into practice when he started work as the lead technical consultant for a large Web Dynpro based project at the UK subsidiary of a major international Tax and Audit firm.

Index

Learn Java the easy way: from the ABAP point of view!

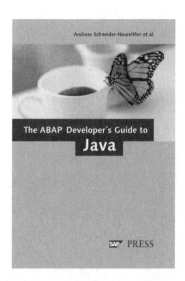

500 pp., approx. US$ 69.95
ISBN 1-59229-027-2, Dec 2004

The ABAP Developer's Guide to
Java
www.sap-press.com

A. Schneider-Neureither (Ed.)

The ABAP Developer's Guide to Java

Leverage your ABAP skills to climb up the Java learning curve

This all-new reference book is an indispensable guide for readers who need a rapid and in-depth introduction to Java. Detailed insights help you leverage ABAP development skills you've already honed, for a smooth transition to Java. The authors highlight each fundamental aspect pertaining to the development of business applications in both languages, and the differences as well as similarities are analyzed in detail. This must-have resource helps any serious developer learn exclusive techniques to master development tools and objects, application design, and application layers. Learn about Beans, OpenSQL for Java, JDBC, Security, and much more.